GREAT CAMPAIGNS

THE ANTIETAM CAMPAIGN

GREAT CAMPAIGNS

THE ANTIETAM CAMPAIGN

August–September 1862

Revised and Expanded Edition

John Cannan

COMBINED BOOKS
Pennsylvania

PUBLISHER'S NOTE

The headquarters of Combined Publishing are located midway between Valley Forge and the Germantown battlefield, on the outskirts of Philadelphia. From its beginnings, our company has been steeped in the oldest traditions of American military history and publishing. Our historic surroundings help maintain our focus on military history and our books strive to uphold the standards of style, quality and durability first established by the earliest bookmakers of Germantown and Philadelphia so many years ago. Our famous monk-and-console logo reflects our commitment to the modern and yet historic enterprise of publishing.

We call ourselves Combined Publishing because we have always felt that our goals could only be achieved through a "combined" effort by authors, publishers and readers. We have always tried to maintain maximum communication between these three key players in the reading experience.

We are always interested in hearing from prospective authors about new books in our field. We also like to hear from our readers and invite you to contact us at our offices in Pennsylvania with any questions, comments or suggestions, or if you are having difficulty finding our books at your local bookseller.

For information, address:
Combined Publishing   E-mail: combined@dca.net
1024 Fayette Street   Web: www.dca.net/combinedbooks
P.O. Box 307   Orders: 1-800-4-1860-65
Conshohocken, PA 19428

Library of Congress Cataloging-in-Publication Data
Cannan, John, 1967-
    The Antietam campaign : August-September 1862 / John Cannan.— Rev. ed.
    ISBN 0-938289-36-5(hbk)
    ISBN 0-938289-91-8(pbk)
    1. Maryland Campaign, 1862. 2. Antietam, Battle of, Md., 1862.   I. Title.
E474.61.C36   1994   94-10348
973.7'336—dc20   CIP

Paperback Edition   1 2 3 4 5
First published in the U.S.A. in 1990 and revised and expanded in 1994 by Combined Publishing and distributed internationally by Greenhill Books, Lionel Levanthal, Ltd., Park House, 1 Russell Gardens, London NW11 9NN

Printed in the United States of America.
Maps by Paul Dangel.

To My Family: Mom, Pop, Edward, Jane, Gwynedd, Catherine, David, Celia, Clare, Teresa, Fran, Alice, Paul, and Marc.

Contents

Contents

Maps

Sidebars

Acknowledgments

There are so many people who, knowingly or unknowingly, assisted me in the creation of this my first effort at a book and of course I would like to thank them all. Much thanks go to Robert Pigeon and Albert Nofi who gave me the chance in the first place. For assistance in preparing the research and writing, gratitude must be extended to the friendly people at the Falvey Library, Philadelphia Free Library, Civil War Library and Museum, Boston Public Library, Dartmouth College Library, University of Georgia Library, University of Maryland Library, Library of Congress, and IMS Department/Villanova University. Also thanks to Dr. Joseph Casino whose immense wisdom helped me deal with some of the many difficulties of trying to describe a battle and for getting me interested in the Civil War in the first place. And my gratitude to Gavin Spiers for being there for so many years, putting me up in Washington, and for driving me around most of Maryland. I am indebted to Bill Byrne whose advice, auspices as a good friend, and incredible patience about overdue library books contributed immensely to this volume. Other people who have helped with the many aspects of this work in their own special ways are: Carol Breedlove, Park Ranger David Fox, Erik Schmidt, Troy Lowry, Jim Weeks, Sam La, Gary Cywinski, Luisa Cywinski, Charles Desnoyers, Dave Chen, Charles Johnson, Joe Muscella, Fred Marcantonio, Team Bookstore (Rick Markham, Kevin McDonnell, Rod Jaballis, Jim Burnett, Joe Sigey), Jeff Middleton, Arthur Yao, Mike Hicks, and, of course, Alexandra, Edmund, Dan and John Owen.

Preface to the Series

Jonathan Swift termed war "that mad game the world so loves to play." He had a point. Universally condemned, it has nevertheless been almost as universally practiced. For good or ill, war has played a significant role in the shaping of history. Indeed, there is hardly a human institution which has not in some fashion been influenced and molded by war, even as it helped shape and mold war in turn. Yet the study of war has been as remarkably neglected as its practice commonplace. With a few outstanding exceptions, the history of wars and of military operations has until quite recently been largely the province of the inspired patriot or the regimental polemist. Only in our times have serious, detailed and objective accounts come to be considered the norm in the treatment of military history and related matters.

Yet there still remains a gap in the literature, for there are two types of military history. One type is written from a very serious, highly technical, professional perspective and presupposes that the reader is deeply familiar with the background, technology and general situation. The other is perhaps less dry, but merely lightly reviews the events with the intention of informing and entertaining the layperson. The qualitative gap between the last two is vast. Moreover, there are professionals in both the military and academia whose credentials are limited to particular moments in the long, sad history of war, and there are interested persons who have more than a passing understanding of the field; and then there is the concerned citizen, interested in understanding the military phenomena in an age of unusual violence and unprecedented armaments. It is to bridge the gap between the two types of military history, and to reach the professional and the serious amateur and the concerned citizen alike, that this series, GREAT CAMPAIGNS, is designed. Each volume in GREAT CAMPAIGNS is thus not merely an account of a particular military operation, but it is a unique reference to the theory and practice of war in the period in question.

The GREAT CAMPAIGNS series is a distinctive contribution to the study of war and of military history, which will remain of value for many years to come.

CHAPTER I

Lee Takes a Gamble

*T*he nature of the Civil War in Virginia, and the course of the entire conflict, was changed markedly on the evening of 31 May 1862 when Major General Joseph E. Johnston, commander of the Confederate army defending Richmond, was wounded near the front during the battle of Seven Pines. Johnston was promptly replaced by General Robert E. Lee, a Virginian who had been serving as military advisor to President Jefferson Davis. Though Lee's prewar credentials were impressive (he had fought well in Mexico and served as superintendent at West Point from 1852-1855), Lee had so far done nothing of distinction in the war against Lincoln's troops—he had conducted an unsuccessful campaign in western Virginia that culminated in defeat at the battle of Cheat Mountain in September 1861, and had spent the ensuing winter overseeing coastal defenses in South Carolina and Georgia. For this reason few Southern leaders anticipated the aggressiveness and skill Lee would use to drive George McClellan's army back in the Seven Days Battles of 25 June-1 July. Not content with this victory, Lee pushed north towards Washington and defeated John Pope's army at Second Bull Run on 29-30 August. In only three months as commander, Lee had saved the Confederate capital and literally transferred the seat of operations from the James River to the banks of the Potomac.

Ironically, Lee's success at Second Bull Run left him in quite a quandary about what to do next. Pope's defeated army managed to escape to the defenses of Washington, whose guns and forts were too strong to attack in a frontal assault. To make matters

General Robert E. Lee made a serious mistake when he decided to stay and fight at Sharpsburg. He had little to gain from a victory, and risked being driven into the Potomac River.

worse, the Union capital already possessed a large garrison, which was being reinforced daily by troops from McClellan's army that had so recently threatened Richmond. Clearly, Lee would gain no advantage by waiting near Fairfax while the enemy reorganized his superior forces. A logical step might have been to fall back to Centreville and the defenses which had been constructed when the Confederate army encamped there during the winter of 1861-62. This position, however, did not prove attractive because almost all the provisions and forage in the area had been stripped away in the previous year. In addition, all the firewood near the old Centreville camps had been used up the previous winter. Centreville simply was not an attractive base of operations, especially in view of its closeness to the enemy's greatly augmented force in Washington.

Since Lee was not able to attack the enemy or stay where he was, his remaining options were to withdraw to the south or west. The safest move would have been to move south to the line of the Rappahannock. This position, which had been held by Johnston before McClellan started the Peninsula campaign, effectively shielded Richmond and would offer Lee the opportunity to react to Lincoln's next move against Richmond. However, such a move would allow the North time to recover from their recent defeats and would surrender all the initiative and impetus Lee had acquired through his hard fought victories. The same logic argued against a withdrawal to Warrenton. Setting up camp there (as Lee would do for the winter of 1863-64) would place Lee's command on the right flank of any Union force advancing towards Richmond, and would offer opportunities similar to those Lee exploited in the opening stages of the recently completed Second Bull Run campaign.

Lee was attracted much more by the possibilities presented by a move to the west. Right after the battle of Chantilly he directed his command to move into Loudoun County, whose resources had not been depleted nearly as much as those of Fairfax County. He would rest his men there while pondering his next move—the recapture of the Shenandoah Valley, a counterattack against any Union troops advancing southward out of the Washington defenses, or an invasion of Maryland.

The possible invasion of Maryland seemed attractive to Lee for a number of reasons, military, political and psychological. He outlined his thoughts in a revealing letter to President Davis that was penned at Dranesville on 3 September: "The present seems to be the most propitious time of the war for the Confederate army to enter Maryland. The two grand armies of the United States that have been operating in Virginia, though now united, are much weakened and demoralized. Their new levies of which I understand 60,000 men have already been posted in Washington, are not yet organized, and will take some time to prepare for the field. If it is ever desired to give material aid to Maryland and afford her an opportunity of throwing off the oppression to which she is now subject, this would seem the most favorable."

Indeed, many Southerners had been pushing for some time for an invasion of Northern soil that would turn the course of the war and bring aid to the oppressed citizens of Maryland. There had been anti-Federal riots in Baltimore in April 1861, and the state might indeed have seceded had Lincoln not ordered the imprisonment of 31 secessionist leaders in September. The presence of a large Confederate force north of the Potomac might encourage loyal Marylanders to overthrow their government and establish a pro-Confederate administration, thereby isolating and embarrassing Lincoln's capital in Washington. In addition, a military victory on Maryland's soil might enable Lee to capture Washington by advancing on its less fortified northern side.

A Confederate victory in Maryland, or even just the simple presence of Southern troops north of the Potomac, might also be sufficient to ruin foreign intervention or even an alliance that would surely turn the course of the war. Everyone was well aware that the French Alliance of 1778 had marked the turning point in the War of Independence. The interest of France and England in the course of the war was also well known in Richmond (see sidebar on Intervention).

Lee and President Davis also hoped that a Confederate success in Maryland would give support to the anti-war factions in the North. Both were well aware that many Northerners objected to the United Act of 1862 (which gave Lincoln the power to Federalize state militias), and to Lincoln's suppression of civil rights, particularly in Maryland. Any further Confederate victories, especially if they could be achieved north of the Potomac, would surely have a profound effect on the upcoming Congressional elections to be held in the North in November.

Nor could the public outcry for an invasion of Maryland be ignored. The South's appetite for a campaign in Maryland had been stirred up by Jackson's successes in the Shenandoah Valley in May and June, and numerous newspapers continued to clamor for such an invasion. Other editors argued that the South could not afford to surrender the initiative Lee had gained. The Charleston *Mercury* stated their case succinctly in the following

James Ryder Randall was an English professor at Poydras College in Louisiana when he wrote "My Maryland" in 1861.

editorial published on 6 September: "Our victorious troops in Virginia, reduced though they be in numbers, and shattered in organization, must be led promptly into Maryland, before the enemy can rally the masses of recruits whom he is rapidly and steadily gathering together. When the government of the North shall have fled into Pennsylvania, when the public buildings in Washington shall have been razed to the ground, so as to forbid the hope of their ever again becoming the nest of Yankee despotism, then at last, may we expect to see the hope of success vanish from the northern mind, and reap the fruit of our bloody and long continued trials."

Lee certainly had political considerations in mind when he wrote to Davis on 4 September that he "was more fully persuaded of the benefit that will result from an expedition into Maryland, and I shall proceed to make the movement at once, unless you should signify your disapprobation at once." However, his primary goals were strategic, as Colonel Bradley T. Johnson clearly pointed out in a postwar article. Johnson was a native of Maryland, and was interviewed at length by both Jackson and Lee on 4 September concerning the topography of the Potomac from Leesburg to Harpers Ferry, the nature of the resources in western Maryland, and the political climate there. Johnson was certain that "the first Maryland campaign was undertaken by General Lee solely and entirely as part of a defensive operation for the protection of Virginia. It was an offensive-defensive operation, having as its objective neither the invasion of Pennsylvania nor the redemption of Maryland, but only the relief of the Confederacy, as far as the means at his command would admit.... I believe I know that the Maryland campaign was not undertaken by General Lee under any delusive hope that his presence there would produce a revolution in Maryland, and such a rising would give a large force of reinforcements to him."

Lee does not appear to have had any specific aims when he entered Maryland, other than to gather supplies and be on the alert to take advantage of any strategic or other errors the enemy might make. He probably hoped that Lincoln would hold back a relatively large force for the immediate defense of Washington, as he had been doing all year, thereby reducing the size of any field army Lee would have to face. In addition, Lee was aware that any army sent against him would contain a large proportion of inexperienced troops and a great number of tired veterans dispirited by their recent defeats. He also must have expected to meet a new and untried Federal army commander, since it was highly unlikely that Lincoln would allow either Pope or McClellan to take the field again.

Lee does not appear to have been concerned for the safety of Richmond "as long as the army of the enemy are engaged on this frontier." On 3 September he urged President Davis to see to the improvement of the capital's defensive works, and was confident that the steamer *Richmond* would be able to keep enemy vessels from advancing too far up the James River. If the enemy did elect to march on Richmond or not follow him to the north side of the Potomac, this would "not result in much evil," since he could simply return to Virginia or march quickly to Richmond's relief if necessary. Lee, however, did have a concern for the enemy's numerical superiority, and suggested to Davis in the same letter that most of General Braxton Bragg's army at Chattanooga be brought east if Bragg were to "find it impractical to operate to advantage on his present frontier." This suggestion makes it clear that Lee was not aware of Bragg's week-old invasion of Kentucky; it is therefore clear that the Maryland invasion was not planned as part of a twofold threat to the north, as some historians of the campaign claim.

Lee was well aware that his intended movement was "attended with much risk," and he was particularly concerned about shortages in munitions and transport. He had a severe shortage of animals, and his men were "poorly provided with clothes, and in thousands of instances are destitute of shoes." His troops might be able to resupply their clothing and other personal needs in the untouched counties of western Maryland, particularly the rich city of Frederick, but the transportation of supplies, especially munitions, provided a special problem. The army's base of operations would have to be set up at Staunton, located on the Virginia Central Railroad in the upper Shenandoah Valley about 90 miles south of the Potomac. The farther north the invasion went, the longer and more vulnerable the army's supply lines would become.

As has already been mentioned, Lee was also greatly concerned about the diminished size of his army, especially in view of the large Union force he might expect to face. During the Seven Days Battles he had experienced the pleasure of commanding almost 90,000 men, the largest single field army the South would see during the entire war. The heavy fighting and hard campaigning of the past ten weeks had cost the army severely in both numbers and leadership. There had been over 20,000 casualties before Richmond and another 10,000 at Second Bull Run. These and other losses, plus the detachment of some units to guard Richmond, left him with at most 40,000 men right after Second Bull Run. Fortunately a number of reinforcements reached the army soon after Bull Run—D.H. Hill's and McClaws' veteran divisions, Walker's smaller division of only two brigades, Hampton's cavalry brigade, and Pendleton's Reserve artillery. These units raised Lee's strength to about 53,000 men, less than half the total number of available Union strength.

Lee's battle-tested army consisted of two balanced wings, a structure that had worked well at Second Bull Run. Longstreet's wing (1st Corps) now consisted of 21 brigades after being reinforced by McClaws' and Walker's divisions, and Jackson's wing (2nd Corps) had 19 brigades after being joined by D.H. Hill's division.

Each of the two corps had its own individual strengths and weaknesses. Longstreet's command at Second Bull Run had consisted of four small divisions of three brigades each and a fifth (Hood's) of only two. For greater command efficiency the four three brigade divisions were concentrated into two. Because Cadmus Wilcox was ill, his three brigades were attached to Richard H. Anderson's command; Anderson was a solid commander who would rise to the command of the first corps in 1864. It was also deemed best to reunite the two halves of Longstreet's old division, which had been divided into two half divisions under David R. Jones and James Kemper for the Second Bull Run campaign. Jones was a good fighter in 1862, but his name is not very familiar because he died of heart trouble in January 1863. Lafayette McLaws was a solid fighter and the return of his four veteran brigades was a welcome reinforcement.

Thus Longstreet had 16 brigades centralized in three good divisions. His other five brigades were much more spread out. Veteran John B. Hood still led a mini division of two brigades that was actually too small for his ability. Hood was one of the South's best fighters, as he had shown at Gaines' Mill, and would show again on many a future field (see sidebar). John G. Walker and his two North Carolina brigades was a last minute addition to the corps. He was an adequate commander who would perform better after he was transferred west following the end of the Antietam campaign.

The status of Longstreet's final brigade, a good South Carolina unit under the command of feisty Brigadier General Nathan G. "Shanks" Evans, is difficult to explain. Evans had joined the army during the march north to Manassas, and during the battle led a provisional division consisting of his own unit and the two brigades led by Hood (whom he out ranked). The two officers had a confrontation late on 30 August over some ambulances that Hood had captured. Evans directed Hood to turn them over to him as senior officer, but Hood refused. Evans then had Hood

Major General A.P. Hill was an aggressive and able division commander who saved Lee's army by his last minute counterattack at Antietam.

arrested for insubordination, and Longstreet sent him to Culpeper to await trial. When Lee heard of the affair, he directed Hood to be returned to his command, though without command authority. This awkward situation dragged on until the eve of Antietam, when Lee permitted Hood to resume command of his men. Because of the bad blood between Hood and Evans, Longstreet sent Hood and his two brigades to another part of the field, which pleased Hood greatly.

Evans in his Antietam battle report claims to have commanded a four brigade division that included not only his own and Hood's brigades, but also G.T. Anderson's Georgia brigade. Anderson, however, was clearly a part of D.R. Jones' command. Apparently Anderson was placed temporarily under Evan's command during the early part of the battle. During the stress of the engagement, Anderson was rushed to the left, and Evans was left with only his own brigade in his position on the army's right center. Because of this command confusion, most orders of battle for the engagement list Evans' command as an independent brigade, with a note that Evans for a time commanded a provisional division.

Jackson's corps was more compactly organized than Longstreet's, but had more severe command and internal difficulties.

His three principal divisions (Ewell's, A.P. Hill's, and Winder's) contained fourteen brigades in the same assignments that they had held since before Second Bull Run. A fourth division of five brigades, under D.H. Hill, had missed Second Bull Run, but had fought well under Jackson in the Seven Days. D.H. Hill (sometimes called "the other Hill" to avoid confusion with A.P. Hill) was a fierce fighter and was Jackson's former brother-in-law. He would be at his tactical best during the coming campaign (see sidebar).

Due to its heavy losses in the Second Bull Run campaign, Jackson's command suffered a severe officer shortage at all levels. Only 6 of his 14 brigades that had fought in the recently completed campaign were led by brigadier generals, and all three of his veteran divisions had new commanders.

A.P. Hill's "Light Division" had the best and most experienced commanders in the Corps. Hill, who would rise to command the newly created Third Corps after Chancellorsville, was an aggressive fighter who had performed well since the Seven Days. All of his six brigade commanders were veterans, five being brigadiers. The division's only command problem at the beginning of the campaign was the fact that A.P. Hill was under arrest, at the orders of no one other than old "Stonewall" himself. It seems that Jackson had ordered Hill to march out early on 4 September, and all Hill's men failed to do so in a timely fashion. Jackson was annoyed by this and became still more angered when Hill made no effort to keep his column closed up and prevent straggling. At noon that day the two generals had a confrontation during which Hill took offense and surrendered his sword to his commander. Jackson then arrested Hill for "neglect of duty" and assigned the Light Division to its senior brigadier, Lawrence O. Branch.

Jackson's arrest of Hill seems all the more strange in view of the fact that both of his other two veteran divisions were being led by relatively inexperienced brigadiers. Stonewall's loyal lieutenant Richard S. Ewell had been badly wounded at Groveton on 28 August, where he lost a leg, and was replaced by A.R. Lawton. Jackson's old division had lost two commanders during the recent campaign—Charles Winder had been killed at Cedar Mountain on 9 August, and William B. Taliaferro was also wounded at Groveton. Command for the moment devolved on the division's only remaining brigadier, William S. Starke, since Starke's senior officer, John R. Jones, had already been incapacitated at the battle. All four brigades of Jackson's once crack division were led by colonels, and there was a corresponding shortage in regimental officers. Most of the division's regiments were being commanded by lieutenant colonels and majors, and three regiments of the old Stonewall Brigade were being led by captains.

Yankee and Rebel

In viewing the prints of Louis Kurz and Alexander Allison one is attracted by the romantic notion of war envisioned in the drawing. Soldiers in pristine uniforms pose in heroic stances as they engage in an almost bloodless conflict. It is a child's version of war, devoid of the grim realities of bloody strife, the terror of combat, the senseless death and cruel destruction. One wonders if veterans looked at these prints with grim amusement or hateful disgust at the misrepresentation of the way Kurz and Allison portrayed their exploits. Perhaps no better proof of the fallacies prevalent in these overly romantic paintings can be found than in the dress and equipage of both sides.

The ideal Union soldier was as he appears in the Kurz and Allison prints. The Yankee usually wore a dark blue jacket, with upturned collar, light blue pants, blue kepi with black visor, and unwieldy shoes called "gunboats" which must have been sheer murder to walk any long distance in. Dressed somewhat differently than their counterparts in the infantry, cavalry and artillery personnel wore shorter jackets and boots instead of shoes. Uniforms were usually trimmed with color to distinguish which branch of the service a soldier belonged to: red meaning artillery and yellow, cavalry.

Originally, as units were hastily organized across the North, soldiers arrived in camp with a variety of uniforms. In one instance, the *79th New York*, comprised mainly of Americans of Scottish ancestry, wore kilts to display their heritage. They abandoned such dress when low-minded individuals taunted them. Some units even wore Confederate gray which tended to cause confusion on the battlefield. Perhaps the most fantastic uniforms belonged to the Zouaves who copied the dress of French troops engaged in North Africa. The attire usually consisted of bright red pantaloons, short blue jackets with braids, and fezzes instead of the usual kepi.

For the most part, uniforms were made out of wool that made marching in the intense heat of the Southern summer unbearable. Resulting heat exhaustion was common during the treks of the army; in many of the reports from the Battle of Cedar Mountain, officers tell of several soldiers falling dead from sunstroke. In the winter, long overcoats were available to protect soldiers from the elements.

Soldiers did not often find their military clothes comfortable in the heat or cold, as a good fit was rare. Yankees often made a series of trades with comrades to acquire outfits of proper size. Worse still, early in the war, when contracts were hastily awarded to companies to provide clothing for the masses of troops entering the army, seedy individuals provided shoddy goods which quickly fell apart after limited wear or after a rain storm, leaving soldiers nearly naked.

At any rate, long campaigning reduced even well made uniforms to tatters. After the battle of Antietam, a reporter wrote after a call on the *30th New York*, "The most notable feature that I remember of this visit was the lack of clothing of the rank and file. I don't think that one man

24

in the regiment had a full suit of clothes and many had scarcely sufficient to save them from the complaints of indecent exposure." Things were not much better in the *88th Pennsylvania* as the regimental historian noted while encamped on the fields near Sharpsburg a month after the battle, "The men were badly off for clothing and shoes, many being in rags and almost barefoot, and consequently suffering much these cool October nights."

Perhaps the most prized possession of the Yankee, like any soldier, was his primary instrument of death, the rifle. Many unfortunate soldiers got stuck with smoothbores and poor European rifles; the *118th Pennsylvania* suffered severely when it was attacked by Confederate troops at Shepherdstown on 20 September, while armed with defective Belgian muskets. The more fortunate found themselves with British .57 calibre Enfield Rifles or .58 calibre Springfield rifles. The Springfield was usually the weapon of choice as it was somewhat lighter and easier to bear on a long march.

As for the rest of his load, the Federal infantryman usually carried a haversack, cap box, cartridge box, rubber or woolen blanket, bayonet with scabbard, canteen, and knapsack. All of a fighting man's possessions, which could include underwear, socks, knick-knacks from home, brush and soap, were placed in the knapsack. Usually, the total weight carried was some 50 pounds. Sometimes, however, to lighten their loads, soldiers rolled up their things in a blanket, tied both ends together and carried it over their shoulders.

Considering the state of the Con-

federate infantryman, he must have envied his Federal counterpart. Had the Southern government been able to provide proper dress for all of its soldiers, Johnny Reb's uniform should have consisted of a double-breasted gray coat, trousers of either light blue or gray, and a kepi. As the government lacked the proper facilities to clothe its troops, at first soldiers were required to furnish their own uniforms. In some cases the state would provide proper attire or companies would put together a collection from among members and even citizens to purchase what they needed. Of course, this led to a diverse variety of uniforms; the Louisiana Tigers were a Zouave outfit from New Orleans and wore red tasseled caps, short brown jackets with red trim and baggy white trousers with blue or red, white, and blue stripes. As the war progressed, the Confederacy tried to standardize the uniforms of its soldiers, with little success.

By 1862 the government was issuing standard gray uniforms, sometimes with foreign contractors manufacturing the dress. But the South was still unable to provide for a significant number of its men. Thus, more often then not, a soldier's ability to get an outfit depended on his own ingenuity. Usually, a major source of supply was captured Federal stores. Jackson's men were notorious for supplying their needs from Federal sources, including Manassas and Harpers Ferry during the Antietam Campaign. In some cases, even the dead were deprived of their shirts, coats, and trousers to serve the needs of the living. Belt buckles obtained from Federals were likewise turned upside down to mark the allegiance of the wearer. At Antietam, the Confederates unintentionally used captured Federal uniforms to some advantage. A.P. Hill's men confused the Yankees on the Federal left, and so were able to get closer before being fired on. As the Federal blockade tightened and reduced the South's access to gray cloth, uniforms were usually dyed in an infusion of nutshells, resulting in a yellowish brown color called butternut.

Two important commodities to the Confederates were hats and shoes. During campaigns, some form of headgear was absolutely necessary for protection from both rain and sun. Most Rebels preferred the brimmed slouch hat which came in many sizes and varieties. In one instance at Hagerstown, some of Lee's troops bought a merchant's total supply of beaver hats which gave the soldiers who wore them a certain resemblance to Daniel Boone. The supply of shoes was a desperate problem for the Confederates. Lacking them, many soldiers were forced to fall out of the ranks due to cut and scraped feet. The problem was especially endemic during the Antietam campaign and a major cause of the disastrous plague of straggling which hampered Lee's effective strength. Of course, the lore of the Civil War records General Harry Heth's quest for shoes during the Confederate campaign in Pennsylvania that led him to the town of Gettysburg on 1 July 1863, thus inaugurating the fateful three-day battle there.

The Southerners also lacked the ability to provide their troops with the proper arms needed to wage war. Most troops used the common .69 calibre musket which fired buck and ball with an effective range of 100 yards and permitted its owners to get two to three shots off in a minute. Armed with Springfields and Enfields firing accurately at about ten times that distance, Yankees were often in a good position to deal heavy blows to their adversaries while receiving few casualties in return. The commander of the 3rd North Carolina suffered severely from such fire at Antietam, even though his own troops had used their buck and ball muskets with such good effect that some of them were asked, "What were your men armed with? We never saw so many men wounded in one battle."

Rebel soldiers also lacked knapsacks to carry their equipage. As a result many men had to lug their belongings in a rolled up blanket. Because tin canteens were scarce, jugs, bottles, and small wooden containers were often employed to carry desperately needed water on the march and into battle. They carried their food in haversacks and ammunition in cartridge boxes attached to the belt.

The appearance of the Confederates in the Kurz and Allison prints is fanciful to say the least. An actual representation of their appearance during the Antietam campaign is given by Private Alexander Hunter of the 17th Virginia in his description of some of the veterans of Longstreet's command:

> What a set of ragamuffins they looked! It seemed as if every cornfield in Maryland had been robbed of its scarecrows....None had any underclothing. My costume

26

consisted of a ragged pair of trousers, a stained, dirty jacket; an old slouch hat, the brim pinned up with a thorn; a begrimed blanket over my shoulder, a grease-smeared cotton haversack full of apples and corn, a cartridge box full and a musket. I was barefooted and had a stone bruise on each foot. Some of my comrades were a little better dressed, some were worse. I was in average, but there was no one there who would not have been "run in" by the police had he appeared on the streets of any populous city, and would have been fined the next day for undue exposure.

Ambrose Powell Hill (1825-1865)

Ambrose Hill was born into the Virginia aristocracy and embarked on a military career after graduating from West Point in 1847, a respectable third in his class. He saw action in Mexico and the Third Seminole War. Later he was a competitor of George B. McClellan for the affections of the lovely Ellen "Nelly" Marcy, daughter of an eminent army officer. He won Ellen's assent to marriage, but her parents intervened when they heard rumors of a venereal disease Hill had contracted during a fling at West Point. His intended bride then married McClellan.

At the start of the Civil War Hill became colonel of the 13th Virginia and soon received command of a brigade. His skill and aggressiveness at the battle of Williamsburg won him the rank of major general. Supposedly, Hill's ferocity in combat, especially against the *Army of the Potomac*, was motivated by the grudge he maintained against McClellan over Ellen Marcy. While his troops were engaged against Little Mac's Yankees, one war weary Confederate was heard to exclaim, "For God's sake, Nelly—why didn't you marry him." During the Seven Days, Second Manassas, Antietam, Fredericksburg, and Chancellorsville, Hill consistently displayed his fighting prowess, playing an instrumental part in Confederate victories as a division commander. Before Gettysburg, Hill took command of the III Corps of the Army of the Northern Virginia as a lieutenant general. Unfortunately, the Virginian's abilities seemed to decline with his increased responsibilities. At Gettysburg, Hill's performance was lackluster at best, then at Bristoe Station he lost 1,300 men in an ill-advised assault.

Hill fought well in the Wilderness and at Petersburg, but had to go on extended sick leave twice. He was killed in action on 2 April 1865, just a week before Lee's surrender. Some of his troops believed that he deliberately sought death rather than witness the loss of the war.

Maryland, My Maryland

Perhaps the most symbolic battle cry of the Southern soldiers during the Antietam campaign was the anthem "Maryland, My Maryland," written by a 22-year-old denizen of the Free State, James Ryder Randall. While he was teaching in Louisiana, Randall read an account of the riot by Confederate sympathizers against the *6th Massachusetts* in Baltimore on 19 April 1861. Inspired by the incident and his hatred for the Yankees, he immediately put his words to verse, so creating an epic work displaying his yearning to see his native state free from Federal dominance. It had what one writer called "the fire and dash of Southern temperament through an impassioned crescendo." Southern bands played the song gaily as they crossed the Potomac at the beginning of the 1862 Maryland invasion. However, the song later fell out of favor after the army's poor reception by the primarily pro-Union elements of western Maryland.

The despot's heel is on thy shore,
Maryland!
His torch is at thy temple door.
Maryland!
Avenge the patriotic gore
That flecked the streets of Baltimore,
And be the battle-queen of yore,
Maryland, my Maryland!

Hark to an exiled son's appeal,
Maryland!
My Mother State, to thee I kneel,
Maryland!
For life and death, for woe and weal,
Thy peerless chivalry reveal,
And gird thy beauteous limbs with steel,
Maryland, my Maryland!

Thou wilt not cower in the dust,
Maryland!
Thy beaming sword shall never rust,
Maryland!
Remember Carroll's sacred trust,
Remember Howard's warlike thrust,
All thy slumberers with the just,
Maryland, my Maryland!

Come! 'tis the red dawn of day,
Maryland!
Come with thy panoplied array,
Maryland!
With Ringgold's spirit for the fray,
With Watson's blood at Monterey,
With fearless Lowe and dashing May,
Maryland, my Maryland!

Come! for thy shield is bright and strong,
Maryland!
Come! for thy dalliance does thee wrong,
Maryland!
Come to thine own heroic throng,
Stalking with Liberty along,
And chant thy dauntless slogan-song,
Maryland, my Maryland!

Dear Mother, burst thy tyrant's chain,
Maryland!
Virginia should not call in vain,
Maryland!
She meets her sisters on the plain,—
"Sic semper!" 'tis the proud refrain
That baffles minions back amain,
Maryland, my Maryland!

I see the blush upon thy cheek,
Maryland!
For thou wast never bravely meek,
Maryland!
But lo! there surges forth a shriek
From hill to hill, from creek to creek,—
Potomac calls to Chesapeake,
Maryland, my Maryland!

Thou wilt not yield the Vandal toll,
Maryland!
Thou wilt not crook to his control,
Maryland!
Better the fire upon thee roll,
Better the blade, the shot, the ball,
Than crucifixion of my soul,
Maryland, my Maryland!

I hear the distant thunder-hum
Maryland!
The old Line's bugle, fife, and drum,
Maryland!
She is not dead, nor deaf, nor dumb;
Huzzah! She spurns the Northern scum!
She breathes! She burns! She'll come! She'll come!
Maryland, my Maryland!

CHAPTER II

McClellan Again

*J*ohn Pope's defeated *Army of Virginia* was not a pretty sight as the dispirited Yankees trudged back towards Washington in the rain and mud after their defeat in the two-day battle of Second Bull Run on 29-30 August 1862. Their retreat was not as hectic as the riot that had followed Irvin McDowell's disaster at First Bull Run a little over 13 months earlier, but they still resembled a disorganized mob more than a regular army. Colonel Regis DeTrobriand of the *55th New York*, which had missed the battle and was being held in reserve at Fairfax Court House, described the dispirited troops as they straggled past his position: "...everything was in terrible confusion. By the light of the fires kindled all around in the streets, in the yards, in the fields, one could see the confused mass of wagons, ambulances, caissons around which thousands of men invaded houses, filled up barns, broke down the fences, dug up gardens, cooked their suppers, smoked or slept in the rain. These men belonged to a different corps. They were either sick or wounded; but, favored by the disorder inseparable from a defeat; they had left their regiments at Centreville, to mingle with the train escorts, or had come away, each by himself, hurried on by the fear of new combat; stragglers and marauders, a contemptible multitude, whose sole desire was to flee from danger."

Fortunately for the Yankees, Lee called off his pursuit on 2 September after fighting a sharp inconclusive action at Chantilly the night before. The mass of troops moved on towards Alexandria in their depleted regiments, isolated squads and stragglers;

Major General George B. McClellan with his wife, Ellen Marcy McClellan, who was once courted by Confederate General A.P. Hill. During the campaign he missed several opportunities to smash Lee's army.

it made no sense to anyone to try and find their commands until they reached the safety of Washington's outer defenses. All the troops were totally worn out from marching and fighting or both, and everyone needed rations. One soldier from the *11th Pennsylvania* noted that: "The men had marched and counter-marched, fought and skirmished unceasingly for ten days. Their rations had been insufficient; their sleep broken and scanty. The cavalry men reported that the saddles had not been removed from the backs of their horses since the opening of the campaign, and the condition of the animals assigned to the artillery and wagons was no better. The Army might justly be described as used up."

Everyone at the War Office was justifiably gloomy when confirmation arrived of Pope's defeat. The only remaining question was how severe the disaster really was. Pope had clearly lost control of his army, and Lincoln and Halleck had a

McClellan visited the front lines only once during the battle of Antietam, between 1400 and 1500. He is shown here astride his horse "Daniel Webster," which usually outdistanced the rest of his staff.

true concern for the safety of the capital. This led them to meet with Major General George McClellan on the morning of 1 September and urge him to take command of the capital's defenses. McClellan had been a "general without army" since he had arrived in Alexandria from the Peninsula on 27 August. His orders were to forward the troops of the *Army of the Potomac* to Pope as expeditiously as possible. The President and Halleck conferred with him frequently that week, but he saw no prospect of being allowed to return to the field. Due to his intense dislike of Pope, McClellan purposely did not push his own troops forward as quickly as he could have, and so contributed materially to his rival's demise. Though he did not relish the prospect of trying to rally Pope's defeated command within the defenses of the capital, he reluctantly accepted the assignment. He gravely feared that he might be only a caretaker until the administration appointed a new commander for the army. He wrote his wife Ellen that if "when the whole army returns here (if it ever does) I am not placed in command of all I will either insist upon a long leave of absence or resign."

When Pope's dispatches became increasingly desperate, McClellan was recalled a second time by Lincoln and Halleck. It seems that Pope was now complaining of unsoldierly and dangerous conduct of many of the officers of the *Army of the Potomac*. The President and his advisor requested McClellan to use his influence to persuade Porter and his other friends to help correct "this state of things." McClellan understood the stern tone in Lincoln's voice and readily assented.

Lincoln was thoroughly exhausted and did not know what to do next. He stopped in to see Quartermaster General Montgomery Meigs, who wrote later that Lincoln "drew himself way down into a big chair, and, with a mingled groan and sigh exclaimed, 'Chase says we can't raise any more money; Pope is licked and McClellan has the diarrhea. What shall I do? The bottom is out of the tub!'"

The President then went to visit with Halleck and try to determine what to do next. He did not trust Pope any longer, and the most qualified successor, Major General Ambrose E. Burnside, was not interested in the post because of a strange combination of diffidence in his own ability and loyalty to McClellan. The only way to save the situation seemed to be to give McClellan command of both Pope's *Army of Virginia* and the *Army of the Potomac*. He certainly knew McClellan's strengths and weaknesses all too well. The general could be stubborn, slow, and overly cautious, but he was also a skilled organizer and inspired the respect and admiration of his men. It was the latter talent that the North needed most now. As Lincoln told Secretary of the Navy Gideon Welles a few days later, "I must have McClellan to reorganize this army and bring it out of chaos."

McClellan was totally surprised on the morning of 2 September when Lincoln and Stanton appeared at his door unannounced while he was having breakfast and entrusted him with command of the two combined armies. Lincoln, though, did not intend for McClellan to take the field; the orders he drafted later in the day were carefully worded to read, "Major General McClellan will have command of the fortifications of Washington, and all the troops for the defense of the Capital."

Later in the morning Lincoln met with his cabinet to announce his decision. Most of them were as surprised as McClellan had been at breakfast. Secretary of War Edwin Stanton was most astonished of all. He had been a bitter foe of McClellan and hoped to be rid of him once and for all on that very day—he had prepared a memorandum for the President signed by most members of the Cabinet stating "our deliberate opinion that, at this time, it is not safe to entrust to Major General McClellan the command of any army of the United States." Stanton now had no choice but to keep the missive, undelivered, in his pocket. Secretary of the Treasury Salmon P. Chase was almost as distressed as Stanton and screamed that reappointing McClellan was the same as giving up the capital to the enemy. Lincoln responded that "the decision was his and he would be responsible for it to the country." To one of his personal secretaries the President later confided, "We must use what tools we have. There is no man in the entire army who can man these fortifications and lick these troops into shape half as well as he...unquestionably he has acted badly towards Pope. That is unpardonable, but he is just too useful just now to sacrifice."

McCellan's initial reaction to his new command was one of concerned excitement. Later in the day he wrote his wife that the President "expressed the opinion that the troubles now impending could be overcome better by me than anyone else. Pope is ordered to fall back on Washington and as he reenters everything is to come under my command again! A terrible and thankless task—yet I will do my best with God's blessing to perform it." Within a few days, though, his pride began to get the better of him, and he began to seriously consider demanding that Lincoln fire both Stanton and Halleck if the President really wanted him to resume command. He was talked out of such a notion by none other than Ambrose E. Burnside, who rightly pointed out that such a strong demand might lead the nation to turn against him and would surely cause the President to withdraw his support.

McClellan energetically assumed his new duties, and rode out to meet and encourage his exhausted troops. Soon there was hardly a soldier in the army who did not know that "Little Mac" was back in command. The effect of the news was instantaneous. All of a sudden, the Federals forgot their defeat, weariness, and hunger and exploded into triumphant hurrahs; multitudes of caps were thrown into the air. One soldier described the scene as shouts of "General McClellan is here" went up through the entire army during the evening:

> The enlisted men caught the sound and those who were awake aroused their sleeping neighbor. Eyes were rubbed and those tired fellows, as the news was passed down the columns, jumped to their feet and sent up such a hurrah as the *Army of the Potomac* had never heard before. Shout after shout went out into the stillness on the night and as it was taken up along the road and repeated by regiment, brigade, division and corps, we could hear the roar dying away in the night.

McClellan worked a minor miracle in the next few days as he restored the army's morale and organization, and, equally significant, its pride and sense of purpose. He knew the *Army of the Potomac* and its men well, for it was he who had revived its troops in similar circumstances after McDowell's defeat at First Bull Run the previous summer. His rapid success and control of what had been perceived as a totally desperate situation also helped silence his enemies, who wanted him to be dismissed or disgraced for his role in delaying reinforcements to Pope the week before.

The cornerstone of McClellan's program was the preservation and augmentation of the *Army of the Potomac*. Pope's *Army of Virginia* was discontinued, and to all intents and purposes ceased to exist when Pope was fired on 2 September. Its three infantry corps operated under McClellan's direct orders for the next ten days until they were formally renumbered and absorbed into the *Army of the Potomac*. Pope's *III Corps*, which had been McClellan's *I Corps* before the Peninsula campaign began, was returned to its "true" designation as *I Corps, Army of the Potomac*. This meant that Pope's *I Corps* needed a new identity, so McClellan relabeled it the *XI Corps*. For a similar reason Pope's *II Corps* had to be renumbered. It had been McClellan's *V Corps* before the Peninsula campaign, but a new *V Corps* had been created in May, so that designation was no longer available. For this reason McClellan relabeled it *XII Corps, Army of the Potomac*.

In the course of dismantling Pope's army, McClellan found it necessary to change its command structure also. He did not care at all for Irvin McDowell, commander of Pope's *I Corps*, and was aware that most of the country now blamed him for the loss of two battles at Bull Run. For these reasons McClellan sacked McDowell on 5 September and replaced him the next day with "Fighting Joe" Hooker, lately a division commander in *III Corps*. He wrote his wife that he hoped Hooker would "soon bring them out of the kinks and make them fight if anyone can." The troops were first rate fighters as future battles would reveal, and, in McClellan's estimation, were "in bad condition as to discipline and everything else" due to their association with Pope and McDowell.

McClellan also found it necessary to replace the commander of Pope's *II Corps*. These troops had been misused in the Shenandoah Valley and later by Major General Nathaniel P. Banks, a political general from Massachusetts. McClellan found it difficult to sack Banks because of his connections in Washington, so he cleverly removed him by elevating Banks to command of the defenses of Washington. Banks was replaced as corps commander by an elderly West Pointer, Joseph K. Mansfield, who had been commanding a division of the *VII Corps*.

It should be mentioned that McClellan did not much care for Pope's other corps commander, German born Franz Sigel, either. Sigel's troops had been soundly defeated several times by "Stonewall" Jackson and deserved better leadership, a benefit they would not receive until six months later when O.O. Howard was put in charge before Chancellorsville. McClellan, though, found it awkward to replace Sigel because of his political connections and significant role as leader of the country's German-American element ("I goes to fight mit Sigel" was a popular recruiting song). McClellan chose to deal with the situation by leaving Sigel in command but keeping his troops back in the rear of the army.

McClellan also used his newly regained powers to win reinstatement for three of his friends and supporters who had been relieved from duty pending hearing on charges Pope had filed for alleged misconduct at Second Bull Run. After much discussion he persuaded Stanton and Halleck to reinstate Major General Fitz John Porter (commander of the *V Corps*), William Franklin (commander of the *VI Corps*), and Brigadier General Charles Griffin (brigade commander in the *V Corps*) for service "in the present crisis." (Of the three, only Porter was eventually brought to trial; he was cashiered in January 1863 but was exonerated in 1878-1886.)

In another move to increase the army's efficiency and effectiveness, McClellan strengthened and expanded the units that he would have to rely on in order to meet Lee's next threat. Major General Edwin Sumner's *II Corps*, which had not been engaged at Second Bull Run, was assigned a new third division on 10 September to augment the corps' two veteran divisions that had fought so well in the Peninsula. (The new division, under the command of Brigadier General W.H. French, consisted of a mixture of fresh units, garrison troops, and veterans of the Valley campaign, a melange that would prove awkward at Antietam). William Franklin's *VI Corps* was also fresh and consisted only of two divisions. McClellan augmented its strength by putting Darius Couch's veteran division of the *IV Corps* under Franklin's command. (The rest of the *IV Corps* had been left on the Peninsula near Fort Monroe; its commander, Erasmus Keyes, had proven to be the weakest of McClellan's original corps commander appointments that spring.) For some reason Couch's division carried its *IV Corps* designation through the Antietam campaign and was not redesignated as *Third Division, VI Corps* until 26 September.

At this time McClellan also reinforced the *IX Corps*, commanded by his friend and supporter Ambrose E. Burnside. Burnside was assigned a veteran unit from the West Virginia theater called the *Kanawha Division*, so named after the river that ran through Charleston and the center of the state. The addition of this division gave Burnside a total of four, the most in any corps in the army.

Lastly, there was quite a large number of newly raised regiments in Washington awaiting assignment when McClellan took over. Instead of forming them into new brigades and divisions, McClellan wisely scattered them about in his veteran brigades, especially those that were understrength from recent heavy campaigning.

The Fighting Man's Friend

Probably no other Federal general in the war commanded more respect and admiration from his men than did George Brinton McClellan. In organizing and leading the *Army of the Potomac*, he had the knack for inspiring troops even after leading them to defeat in the Peninsula and wasting their lives at Antietam. One singular instance between McClellan and one of his soldiers displays the general's uncanny aptitude for winning the devotion of his troops.

After the Battle of South Mountain, a corporal of the *Iron Brigade* was bringing prisoners to the rear to turn them over to the proper authorities. Directed to a house where McClellan had set up his headquarters, the soldier was searching for someone to take his captives when he stumbled into a room where an officer was seated, writing at a desk. When the man looked up, the stunned Federal found himself in the presence of none other than George Brinton McClellan. No doubt irritated by the sudden intrusion, the general demanded, "What do you want?" Taken aback, the corporal could only reply, "I have some prisoners, General, I am ordered to turn them over to you." "Who are you and where do you come from?" asked McClellan gruffly to which the corporal gave his name and command. "Ah, you belong to *Gibbon's brigade*. You had some heavy fighting," McClellan remarked, his irritation over the interruption gradually slipping away. "Yes, sir, but I think we gave them as good as they sent." "Indeed you did," McClellan said, "You made a splendid fight." The corporal found the time to relax a tad, at least enough to boldly venture, "Well, General, that's the way we boys calculate to fight under a general like you." Greatly impressed and enlivened by the statement, McClellan rose from his seat to shake the soldier's hand, saying proudly, "My man, if I can get that kind of feeling amongst the men of this army, I can whip Lee with no trouble at all!"

That night the corporal returned to his command with a story that quickly spread through the ranks; McClellan had shaken the hand of an enlisted man and complimented him on a fight.

William B. Franklin (1823-1903)

A Pennsylvanian by birth, William B. Franklin distinguished himself by graduating first in his class at West Point in 1843, outperforming classmate Ulysses S. Grant. From the Academy, Franklin achieved an illustrious military career: he helped survey the Great Lakes, participated in the search for a southern pass through the Rockies with the Corps of Topographical Engineers, served with distinction in the Mexican American War, and even supervised the construction of the dome of the capitol building in Washington, D.C.. He held the rank of brigadier general of volunteers when the Civil War broke out, and commanded a brigade of Massachusetts troops at First Bull Run. When the *Army of the Potomac* was organized, Franklin worked his way into the clique of the unit's commander, George B. McClellan and received command of the *VI Corps*.

Franklin displayed a singular lack of imagination in engaging the small Confederate force at Crampton's Gap during the Antietam Campaign. Though he managed to seize the pass, he halted before a reorganized enemy line which was dwarfed by his command. He regained his fighting nerve at Antietam only to be held back by Sumner who had wasted his *II Corps* on the Confederates earlier in the day. Taking command of a grand division in Burnside's reorganized *Army of the Potomac*, Franklin was among those blamed by that general for his crippling loss at Fredericksburg. Franklin was exculpated from this accusation by a court of inquiry, and returned to corps command in the *Department of the Gulf* during Nathaniel Banks' ill fated Red River Campaign. He was struck down by a wound in battle, and did not return to the field.

After resigning his commission, the former soldier returned to a successful career in engineering.

The Question of Foreign Intervention

Europe's two principal powers, England and France, watched with concern the outbreak of Civil War in America in 1860. Each nation traded heavily with both the North and the South, and so they were rightly concerned about the economic effects that would arise at home as a result of the situation in America. In addition, France, and England to a much greater extent, both depended heavily on Southern cotton to keep their textile mills running at full steam. The Northern blockade declared by Lincoln on 17 April 1861 threatened to close down many of Europe's mills and cause extensive economic dislocation and possible political unrest.

This tense situation almost erupted into war at the end of 1861 when Captain Charles Wilkes intercepted the British mail steamer *Trent* on 8 November and forcibly removed two of its passengers—James M. Mason, the Confederacy's ambassador to England, and John Slidell, the South's ambassador to France. England particularly complained of this violation of her maritime neutrality and began preparing for a possible war; the situation was much the reverse of what caused the United States to declare war in 1812.

Even though Wilkes had acted completely on his own accord, he placed President Lincoln and his able Secretary of State, William Seward, in a most awkward position. Wilkes' boldness had made him a national folk hero, and an immense popular outcry would arise if the two ambassadors were released. On the other hand, a refusal to free Mason and Slidell might provoke a war with England and/or France. Such a war was clearly undesirable to the administration, even though there were some parties in the North who openly welcomed an excuse to try to conquer Canada a third time.

When England issued an ultimatum that Mason and Slidell be released, Secretary Seward successfully worked out a scenario that might defuse the situation. Instead of disavowing Wilkes' action, he announced that the United States had not acted illegally in any way. Even so, President Lincoln would set the two ambassadors free. In addition, the Federal government thanked England for its concern for the maritime rights of the neutrals, an issue which had long been of the utmost importance to America. His scheme worked—England was appeased by the release of the ambassadors, and the American people were partly assuaged by Seward's reaffirmation of the rights of neutrals.

Despite the defusing of the *Trent* crisis, there were still leading parties in England who favored the South for economic and other reasons. Chief among them were British Prime Minister Viscount Palmerston and Chancellor of the Exchequer William Gladstone. In July Palmerston had almost succeeded at organizing a tripartite mediation by England, France, and Russia; the coalition fell apart when Russia backed out at the last minute. France then began deferring to England, since she feared that an independent Confederacy might interfere with Emperor Louis Napoleon's designs in Mexico.

Palmerston continued lobbying for English mediation, and on 6 August proposed to Queen Victoria that England offer an armistice in October. Lee's success at Second Bull Run won the attention of Lord Russell, head of the Foreign Office, who had not previously been interested in supporting the South. Likewise Henri Mercier, the French ambassador to the United States, wrote home on 2 September that Lee's victories made the moment attractive for offering mediation.

Thus conditions in September 1862 were as ripe as they could be for European mediation to end the war. In fact, on 17 September—the very day of the battle of Antietam— Lord Russell agreed with Palmerston that England should offer mediation "with a view to the recognition of the Confederates." If that failed, Russell felt that "we ought ourselves to recognize the Southern States as an independent State."

Lee's repulse from Maryland effectively put an end to England's interest in bringing about mediation to the conflict. There was a strong party in Britain that never approved of the Confederacy because of the South's "peculiar institution" of slavery; Britain had outlawed slavery in her own possessions several decades earlier. When Lincoln issued the Emancipation Proclamation and made abolition one of the North's avowed war aims, it became increasingly awkward for England to support the South.

In addition, English mill owners came to the surprising realization that they did not need Southern cotton in order to survive. They had a few months' supply stockpiled when the war began, and before it ran out they managed to locate a source of superior grade cotton in India. As a result, Britain no longer had an economic need to support the South's war effort. Ironically, the Confederacy had severely harmed its own war effort when President Davis ordered an embargo on Southern cotton in 1861. Davis had hoped to starve the English mills of cotton and so force Britain to intervene in the war, but he failed for the reasons just cited. The move hurt the Confederacy because they were voluntarily holding their cotton back at a time when Lincoln's blockade was not yet effective. Had they persevered in exporting all the cotton they could in 1861, they would have received in exchange a large amount of munitions and other supplies that would have greatly aided their war effort.

CHAPTER III

The Die Is Cast

As has been already explained in Chapter I, General Lee began shifting his troops westward into Loudoun County immediately after the fight at Chantilly in order to take advantage of the better forage and provisions available there. The more he pondered the invasion of Maryland, the more he liked the idea. He was at Dranesville on 3 September when he wrote to President Davis that he was considering a crossing of the Potomac, and was at Leesburg the next day when he informed the President that he would carry out the invasion unless Davis had immediate and strong opposition.

The next major decision facing Lee was whether to enter Maryland east of the Blue Ridge Mountains, or west. A movement to the west of the mountains would give much greater protection to the army, and would enable him to move directly on the city of Hagerstown, situated at the entrance of the rich Cumberland Valley of Maryland and Pennsylvania. Such a move would also give him a secure supply line through the lower Shenandoah Valley, as well as a safe line of retreat or withdrawal should either become necessary. On the other hand, a march towards Frederick, though not shielded by any natural defenses, would certainly alarm Lincoln's government much more. Lincoln was deeply fearful for the safety of his capital, and neither he nor his army commander would be able to discern what Lee's goal would be—Washington, Baltimore or Harrisburg.

After pondering his two options, Lee chose the latter. One of the purposes of his invasion was to throw a scare into the

Lee's cavalry crossing the Potomac on 6 September. The invasion of Maryland would be driven back in less than two weeks.

Federal government, and this would be more readily accomplished by a movement to Frederick. In addition, the positioning of his own army near Frederick would enable him to react more quickly to take advantage of any Union mistakes in deployment, as he had done at the end of the Second Bull Run campaign. Nor could he overlook the prospects of obtaining provisions, shoes, and other much needed supplies from the wealthy town of Frederick. Lastly, if he suffered any discomforture near Frederick, he would still be able to move west of the mountains and take control of Hagerstown.

Once this decision was made, Lee began to mass his army near Leesburg, with the intention of crossing the Potomac at nearby White's Ford. He wanted to retain the initiative he had won in the recent campaign, and did not even wait for the arrival of all the reinforcements that were on their way to join him.

The actual crossing into Maryland began on 4 September, spearheaded by two brigades of D.H. Hill's newly arrived division. Most of Jackson's Corps crossed at White's Ford on the 5th and Longstreet's brigades followed on the 6th or 7th. Because of the backlog of troops wanting to cross at White's

Ford, Walker's division crossed at Cheek's Ford, some seven miles upstream.

The actual river crossing was a momentous event for many of the troops. In more than one instance, regimental bands struck up the air "Maryland, My Maryland." One of Kershaw's South Carolina men remarked that "Never before had an occurrence so excited and enlivened the spirits of the troops as the crossing into...Maryland. It is said the Crusaders, after months of toil, marching, and fighting on their way through the plains of Asia Minor, wept when they saw the towering spires of Jerusalem, the Holy City, in the distance; and if ever Lee's troops could have wept for joy it was at the crossing of the Potomac." The river crossing was tough going for some troops, gingerly walking barefoot over the rocky ford. Some Texans complained that the water was so cold that all the ice houses in western Maryland must have been emptied into the river. Another blissfully recounted the relief of the cool river, saying, "The river was shallow and clear, and some of us dallied merrily in its bright waters, glad to be refreshed after the tedious, dusty marches of the past month."

Major Heros von Borcke, a German born volunteer officer on Jeb Stuart's staff, described the morning scene as follows:

> It was, indeed, a magnificent sight as the long column of many thousand horsemen stretched across the beautiful Potomac. The evening sun slanted upon its clear placid waters, and burnished them with gold, while arms of the soldiers glittered and blazed in its radiance. There were few moments, perhaps, from the beginning to the close of the war, of excitement more intense, of exhilaration more delightful, than when we ascended the opposite bank to the familiar but now strangely thrilling music, "Maryland, My Maryland." As I gained the dry ground, I little thought that I should recross the river into Virginia, under circumstances far different and far less inspiring.

Once across the Potomac, Lee headed straight north to Frederick. He encamped on the night of 6 September at Monocacy Junction, an important stop on the Baltimore and Ohio Railroad. Control of the Junction was an important step in severing Washington's connections with the west. Lee also had plans to destroy a section of the Chesapeake and Ohio Canal,

Lee's troops crossing the Potomac into Maryland at White's Ford. The people of Maryland would not be as responsive to the Confederacy as Lee hoped.

which was an important supply route, but its locks proved to be too difficult a nut to crack.

To further buoy the spirits of his men once they crossed the river, Lee issued General Orders No. 103 on 6 September, in which he announced Kirby Smith's victory at Richmond, Kentucky, on 30 August: "This great victory is simultaneous with your own at Manassas. Soldiers, press onward! Let each man feel the responsibility now resting on him to pursue vigorously the success vouchsafed to us by Heaven. Let the armies of the East and the West vie with each other in discipline, bravery, and activity, and our brethren of our sister States will soon be released from tyranny, and our independence be established upon a sure and abiding basis."

Lee pushed on the next day to Frederick, which his troops had peacefully occupied the day before. Except for the Unionists who stayed in their basements, the town was a hubbub of activity. Major von Borcke related: "Entering the good city of Frederick, I found it in a tremendous state of excitement. The Unionists living there had their houses closely shut up and barred; but the far greater number of citizens, being favorably disposed to the Confederate cause, had thrown open their doors and windows and welcomed our troops with the liveliest enthusiasms. Flags were floating from the houses, and garlands of flowers were lying across the streets. Everywhere a dense multitude was moving up and down, singing and shouting in a paroxysm of joy and patriotic emotion, in many cases superinduced by an abundant flow of strong liquors."

Lee took special care that his own troops should not become intoxicated, and that his men would not participate in looting or pillaging—a far cry from the attitude of both sides, particularly Sherman and Sheridan, later in the war. Guards were placed at all the saloons and key businesses, and all purchases were made in gold or Confederate script.

The citizens of Frederick were impressed by Lee's restraint and the conduct of his men, but they were far from impressed by the ragged condition of the Confederate troops. Most of the southern soldiers had been marching and fighting ever since they left Richmond several weeks earlier, and they were dirty, exhausted, and much in need of clothing, even shoes. Nor had they been eating particularly well—their rapid advance on Manassas had outstripped their supply lines, and many of the men as well as the horses had been subsisting on green corn plucked from the fields. At least here in Frederick they were able to cook their corn and bathe and wash their clothes. One Southern soldier noted that "In all those weeks we had no change of clothing and were literally devoured by vermin....a prize fighter trains about two months to get himself in perfect condition, but we had been training for nearly two years, and the men were skin, bone and muscle."

Lee and both of his chief lieutenants, Longstreet and Jackson, set up their headquarters in a beautiful oak grove about two miles south of Frederick. It should be noted that none of the three generals were in the best physical shape as they pondered

Overview of Frederick, Maryland, home of Barbara Fritchie.

the next stage of the campaign. Longstreet was wearing slippers because his feet were sore, and Lee had both his wrists in splints for the past week since he tripped and fell on his hands while on a reconnaissance on 31 August; as a result of the injury he could not ride his horse and had to travel by ambulance during most of the Antietam campaign. Jackson was also bruised from an accident. The day after he crossed the Potomac, his horse shied and rolled over on him. Stonewall was so stunned he could not move for half an hour, and his staff feared that his back or spine was broken. He, too, had to spend some time in an ambulance, and was still stiff from his injury.

On 8 September, Lee chose to deliver an address to state his aims to the people of Maryland:

> It is right that you should know the purpose that brought the army under my command to the limits of your state....The people of the Confederate States have long watched with deepest sympathy the wrongs and outrages that have been inflicted upon the citizens of the South by the strongest social, political, and

Lee's troops ate so much unripe corn in Maryland that some called this invasion the "green corn campaign." This diet caused stomach distress for many, and contributed to the army's heavy straggling.

commercial ties. They have seen with profound indignation their sister State deprived of every right and reduced to the condition of a conquered province....our army has come among you, and is prepared to assist you with the power of its arms in regaining of the rights of which you have been despoiled....No constraint on your free will is intended; no intimidation will be allowed within the limits of this army, at least. Marylanders shall once more enjoy their ancient freedom of thought and speech....It is for you to decide your destiny freely and without constraint. This army will respect your choice, whatever it may be; and while the Southern people will rejoice to welcome you to your natural position among them, they will only welcome you when you come of your own free will.

Lee gave the people of Maryland the choice of joining with him or staying with the Union. Unfortunately for the Confederates, most chose the latter course. The numbers of new recruits Lee expected to join his army never materialized. Maybe a couple hundred at best joined the Confederate standard, certainly crushing Lee's expectations; and many of these soon deserted the ranks after a few days in the Rebel army.

There were many reasons for the notable lack of help from many Marylanders. The Southern sympathies that Lee had counted upon were upheld by citizens in the eastern part of the state around Baltimore. Out in western Maryland, most people stuck with the Union. Those who were either neutral or stood by the Southern cause might have been turned away by the ragged appearance of the Confederate troops that has already been mentioned. One citizen of Frederick wrote of their strange appearance and manners, "They were the dirtiest, lousiest, filthiest, piratical-looking cut-throat men I ever saw. A most ragged, lean, and hungry set of wolves....Many of them were from the far South and spoke a dialect I could scarcely understand. They were profane beyond belief and talked incessantly." Many Marylanders also believed, despite Lee's words, that the Army of Northern Virginia was only going to stay in their state for a short time. Once the Rebels left, those who had supported them would be at the mercy of vengeful Unionists. Not even pro-Southern Governor Enoch L. Lowe showed up to support the Rebels and their aims to liberate his own state.

Worse still, the Army of Northern Virginia had actually lost troops due to a crippling plague of stragglers. Some soldiers just could not keep up with the rest of the army after the intense campaigning of the previous month and the current breakneck pace. Others had simply remained on the Virginia side of the Potomac, refusing to cross the river, on the reasoning that they had enlisted to defend the South, not to invade the North. Once

Confederate straggling before Antietam was the worst of any of Lee's campaigns, and cost his army about one third of its strength.

across the river, the Army of Northern Virginia's crippling lack of shoes began to tell as men's feet, used to the soft dirt roads of Virginia, were painfully cut and scraped as they marched on the hard, rocky roads of Maryland. One soldier complained that while his heart was brave he was cursed with "unpatriotic feet." This combined with the rampant diarrhea, dysentery and hunger served to force many other men to fall from the ranks.

All told, Lee claimed to have lost from 8,000 to 10,000 men

from straggling. To avoid losing those who could not keep up to capture, the Provost Marshal was ordered to collect these masses of individuals and direct them to Winchester in the Shenandoah Valley to be reorganized and brought back into the rest of the army at a later date. Their loss did not bode well for the future success of the campaign.

Straggling

All armies on the march suffer from straggling to some degree or other. There are always those troops who are sick or weak, have sore feet, or must drop out to answer the call of nature. Technically any man so leaving the ranks must have a pass, and there was supposed to be a guard at the end of each unit to check for passes and unauthorized dropouts. However, armies that are moving quickly do not always have time to follow proper procedures, particularly when the troops are exhausted or unit command structure has broken down.

Even though McClellan did not push his troops at any stage of the campaign, his army still suffered noticeably from straggling. General Halleck addressed the issue in a letter sent to McClellan on 7 October, twenty days after the battle of Antietam:

> Straggling is the great curse of the army, and must be checked by severe measures....I think, myself, shooting them in the act of straggling from their commands, is the only effective remedy that can be applied. If you apply the remedy you will be sustained here....The country is becoming very impatient at the want of activity of your army, and we must push it on....There is a decided want of legs in our troops....The real difficulty is they are not sufficiently exercised in marching; they lie still in camp too long. After a hard march one day is time enough to rest. Lying still beyond that time does not rest the men. If we compare the average dis-

tances marched per month by our men for the last year, with that of the rebels, or with European armies in the field, we will see why our troops march no better. They are not sufficiently exercised to make them good and efficient soldiers.

Though straggling in the Union ranks was no more than usual for a campaign of this size, straggling in Lee's army was so great that it severely hampered his ability to fight. It is estimated that Lee crossed the Potomac with 50,000 to 55,000 men, yet barely 40,000 were present at Antietam.

Traditionally four principal reasons have been offered for the heavy Confederate straggling during the Antietam campaign.

First is the lack of shoes. The troops that had fought near Richmond in June and July had marched to Manassas in August and now were being sent into Maryland in September. Their footwear simply wore out, and there was not enough at hand to reshod them. Douglas Southall Freeman points out that most of all the Southern troops, with the significant exception of Jackson's foot cavalry, were not used to much marching and their feet were just not as tough and calloused as they would be later in the war. Hence many had to drop out of the ranks because they could simply walk no farther.

A second cause of excessive straggling was stomach distress caused by the diet of fruit and green corn most of the men ate while on the march. The army quickly outstripped its supply wagons, and during most of the campaign had to live off the land—which was indeed a major reason why Lee had begun the campaign in the first place. As a result, the principal staple for most of the troops was green corn picked fresh from the fields. The corn was safe enough to eat when it was parched, which the men usually had time to do in the morning and when they made camp at night. However, when the hungry troops ate corn right out of the fields, they developed serious diarrhea that made them leave the ranks often until they just became too weak to continue. Years after the invasion some of the troops still called Antietam "the green corn campaign."

Another discomfort for the men has not been much emphasized in many histories. It seems that the two weeks before the battle of Antietam were unusually hot and dry. Weather reports from down-river at Georgetown showed an average high temperature reading of over 80 each day at middle afternoon, with one day reaching 88. Local newspapers called September 1862 one of the driest months in memory, and soldier accounts agree that everyone was choking in dust, so much so that comrades could hardly recognize each other.

A third cause for the straggling has been overemphasized through the years. Some sources claim that a large number of troops, particularly those from Western North Carolina, had no interest in invading the North, and simply refused to cross the Potomac. This reason may have been valid for a number of individuals, but analysis of regimental strength figures at the battle does not show that the North Carolina

troops suffered from straggling losses any more than units from other states. In fact, the smallest units on the field were mostly from Virginia. It might be more accurate to argue that a large number of Virginians were simply tired from all the campaigning and decided to sit this one out, even at the risk of being shot for desertion.

These three reasons collectively account for a fair number of the stragglers, but do not hit the heart of the problem. The real issue seems to have been a breakdown in both morale and discipline during the campaign. The recent major battles had made casualties of the best and most devoted fighters, and had also caused a great number of casualties among the line officers and non-commissioned officers. Many new commanders were not experienced at enforcing discipline on the march, did not know how to care for their column, and could not distinguish between the skulkers and the sick. As a result, many more troops than usual were able to get away with falling out of line and not returning.

The ultimate cause of much of the straggling, then, appears to have been a loss of morale. Throughout the campaign the roadsides were frequented by numerous soldiers who had fallen out from their commands and were in no hurry to return. They had been fighting and marching much more than they had ever anticipated when they first enlisted, and many of the men were simply tired out. In the days after Antietam General John R. Jones sent about 6000 stragglers back to their commands, and said that the roads all the way to Winchester were still "full of stragglers." In some cases, troops were seen to throw away their shoes "so they would have an excuse for being away." Jones also noted that the "number of officers back here was most astonishing." Brigadier General Dorsey Pender noted on 19 September, "In one of my regiments the other day six out of ten officers skulked out....More than half my brigade went out the same day."

The Confederate army during the Antietam campaign was not the well oiled machine of devoted troops that we usually imagine it to be. It was in fact composed quite differently from the force that Lee took into Pennsylvania the next summer. Some of the troops were seeing their first battle, while others had seen too much fighting. The spirit of the army was not totally in support of yet another campaign, and the army's glue—the non-commissioned officers and officers—were not strong enough to hold it together, crippled as they were.

This is not to say that large numbers of Lee's troops deserted or went over to the enemy. Far from it.

Many simply got tired, or dropped out because of diarrhea, lack of shoes, or other reasons, and discipline was not strong enough to bring them immediately back to their commands. But most did return eventually, once they rested up or dealt with whatever problem was ailing them. In this regard, Lee's army was not a lot different from the volunteer troops who fought for George Washington—they were loyal and would not hesitate to put their lives on the line, but they were also human and free spirited, and sometimes needed time to tend to their personal needs before returning to the ranks.

The end result of this straggling was the loss of one-third of Lee's manpower, attrition that almost brought the end of the army at Antietam, and, sadly, those who were present to fight at Antietam comprised the best and most loyal troops of the army—troops that bled and died in record numbers while their weaker hearted brethren sat by the roadsides in the rear.

The Confederate Invasion of Kentucky

Lee's decision to invade Maryland after Second Bull Run may have been influenced in part by an invasion that was already underway by General Braxton Bragg and Kirby Smith into the border state of Kentucky. Bragg, who was based at Chattanooga, and Smith, who was based at Knoxville, formed their cooperative plan for many of the same reasons that influenced Lee to cross

the Potomac—they wanted to outmaneuver the enemy and drive the Yankees out of their immediate front, and then "liberate" a border state, in the process obtaining fresh recruits and much needed supplies.

Kirby Smith began the invasion first when he departed Knoxville on 14 August with about 9,000 men in three divisions. He successfully bypassed the Union garrison at Barboursville, Kentucky, and then won a victory at Richmond on 30 August. This success enabled him to occupy Lexington on 1 September, whereupon he began moving north against Covington, located across the Ohio River from Cincinnati.

Meanwhile, Bragg began his wing of the invasion on 28 August. He reached Glasgow, Kentucky, on 13 September, and marched north to capture Munfordville on 17 September, the day of the battle of Antietam. Instead of pushing on to unite with Smith, Bragg spread his army out in the center of the state from Bardstown to Harrodsburg in order to better gather up supplies and recruits. At the end of the month he conferred with Smith, who had been forced to pull back from Covington because of the strong defenses encountered there. One of the invasion's major objectives was fulfilled on 4 October when Bragg set up Richard Hawes as provisional Confederate governor of the state.

On 1 October Buell led his 60,000 men out of Louisville in four columns, searching for the Confederate forces known to be 30 or 40 miles to the east and southeast. Like McClellan in the Antietam campaign, Buell was not aware that he greatly outnumbered the enemy. Nor was he aware that there was a large gap between Bragg's 23,000 at Bardstown and Smith's 9,000 near Frankfort.

After a week of inconclusive maneuvering, about half of Buell's command engaged half of Bragg's force along Doctors Creek near Perryville on 8 October. The Confederates managed to gain some initial successes before Union Major General Phil Sheridan secured his line and launched a successful counterattack. Due to freakish atmospheric conditions (called "acoustic shadow"), Buell and two of his corps commanders did not hear the battle raging only three miles away and so did not march to Sheridan's aid until late in the day. Nevertheless the battle resulted in a Union victory that forced an end to the Confederate invasion of the state.

To be certain, Bragg and Smith met more success in their invasion of Kentucky than Lee did in Maryland. Their combined campaign of almost two months lasted much longer than Lee's three week long campaign, and covered much more ground than Lee did. Bragg also succeeded in installing a new Confederate governor in Kentucky, something that Lee was unable to do in Maryland. Even so, both invasions failed for much the same reasons—both faced much larger, well supplied Union armies, and, neither succeeded at garnering the amount of supplies and fresh recruits that had been anticipated. Other than Lee's capture of Harpers Ferry, the greatest success the two invasions achieved was to throw a serious scare into much of the north during the first half of September. To some observers, especially those in Europe, it looked as if the tide of the Confederacy was cresting and overwhelming all the Potomac and the Ohio. Their withdrawal on both fronts marked a significant turning point in the war. Never again would they enjoy such an opportunity for simultaneous success in both the eastern and western theaters of the conflict.

The Grand Ball at Urbana

While the rest of the Confederate Army encamped at Frederick from 6-10 September, the Confederate cavalry set up its headquarters at the nearby town of Urbana. J.E.B. Stuart was impressed with the welcome he had received so far in Maryland, and decided that he and his men should take a brief respite from the trials of warfare to hold a ball for his troopers and the local belles. He commandeered a large room in an abandoned ladies academy, and festooned its walls with regimental flags; the services of the regimental band of the 18th Mississippi were acquired to play the music. On 8 September, invitations were sent out and by that evening a large crowd of partiers had arrived to take part in the dance. Despite the gaiety of the occasion, cavalry officers left their swords nearby just in case of an emergency.

Master of ceremonies Major Heros Von Borcke (a German citizen serving with the Confederate cavalry) began the festivities with a polka. Turning to dance with his partner, he was introduced to the native customs as he recalled, "...my surprise was great indeed when my fair friend gracefully eluded my extended arms, and with some confusion explained that she did not join in round dances, thus making me acquainted for the first time with the fact that in America, especially in the South, young ladies rarely waltz except with brothers or first cousins and only in reels and contredanses with strangers."

The dashing cavalry troopers and their guests enjoyed dance after dance, until all were reawakened to the reality of war by a brisk fire of musketry and cannon that opened up in the distance. Immediately buckling on their sabers, the Confederates turned to their partners, bidding them to await their return before heading off into the darkness to do battle. When the soldiers finally returned, a woman screamed upon seeing the bloodied bodies of the wounded as they were brought into the building for care. Immediately, the ladies became "ministering angels," attending to the care of those unfortunate soldiers who had become casualties on the field of battle. One wounded Confederate smiled at the attention he received, declaring he would not mind getting hit any day with surgeons such as those attending him. When the grand ball finally ended, the soldiers escorted their partners home, keeping with them always the memories of one of the most pleasant experiences of the war.

Barbara Frietchie

One of the best known episodes of the Antietam campaign did not occur on the battlefield, but instead centered on a little old lady and her flag.

As the Federals entered the city of Frederick, an elderly woman of 96 years by the name of Barbara Frietchie could be seen gently waving an American flag to welcome the approaching troops. Touched by the scene, soldiers lifted their caps and cheered loudly, calling out, "God bless you, old lady!" "May you live long, you dear old soul!" The story of Frietchie's patriotism spread through the ranks, eventually reaching General Jesse Reno himself, who took the time to pay her a visit before he rode off to meet his death at South Mountain. Another citizen of Frederick, May Quantrall, was also seen waving an American flag before Stonewall Jackson. However, Confederate witnesses claim the general never saw her.

Evidently Frietchie's sudden status as a celebrity refused to remain in the ranks of the *Army of the Potomac*. The story of her waving the flag spread throughout the area. Like all good yarns, it picked up a little something more at every retelling. Eventually it reached a Washington novelist, Mrs. E.D.E.N. Southworth, who related the events to poet John Greenleaf Whittier. In putting the incident to lyrics, the account of an elderly woman waving a flag to welcome Union troops was transformed into a defiant flag waving before Jackson himself and his Rebel troops.

During and after the war, Confederate proponents were so disturbed by the poem that they heatedly disputed the validity of the work. Kyd Douglas wrote, "As for Barbara Frietchie, we did not pass her house....She never saw Stonewall Jackson and he never saw her. I was with him every minute while he was in town, and nothing like the patriotic incident so graphically described by Mr. Whittier in his poem ever occurred. The venerable poet held on to the fiction with such tenacity for years after, that he seemed to resent the truth about it." Unlike most of his comrades, Moxley Sorrel admitted that if Whittier's work did not contain much in the form of historical accuracy, it could still be appreciated for the fine lyrics of the author, "...the poet Whittier has told of Barbara Frietchie and Stonewall Jackson—a stirring poem in winning lines, but quite without fact at bottom. But that matters not in the least. The lines are good and we can well afford to throw in with all the hard words and abuse of those days, the poet's ideas about our Stonewall."

Despite Confederate objections to the basis of Whittier's poem, the poet absolutely refused to acknowledge that the story he was told was possibly false. He wrote in 1886, "The poem *Barbara Frietchie* was written in good faith. The story was no invention of mine. It came from sources which I regarded as completely reliable; it had been published in newspapers, and had gained public credence in Washington and Maryland before the poem was written. I had no reason to doubt its accuracy then, and I am still constrained to believe that it had

foundation in fact. If I thought otherwise, I should not hesitate to ex-
press it." True or otherwise, *Barbara*
Frietchie provides a glimpse of the
romanticism of the Civil War era.

Barbara Frietchie

by John Greenleaf Whittier

Up from the meadows rich with corn,
Clear in the cool September morn,
The clustered spires Frederick stand
Green-walled by the hills of Maryland.
Round about them orchards sweep,
Apple and peach trees fruited deep,
Fair as the garden of the Lord
To the eyes of the famished rebel Horde,
On that pleasant morn of early that fall
When Lee marched over the mountain-wall;
Over the mountains winding down,
Horse and foot, into Frederick town.

Forty flags with their silver stars,
Forty flags with their crimson bars,
Flapped in the morning wind: the sun
Of noon looked down, and saw not one.
Up rose old Barbara Frietchie then,
Bowed with her fourscore years and ten;
In her attic window the staff she set,
To show that one heart was loyal yet.
Up the street came the rebel tread,
Stonewall Jackson riding ahead.
Under his slouched hat left and right
He glanced; the old flag met his sight.

"Halt!"—the dust brown ranks stood fast.
"Fire!"—out blazed the rifle blast.
It shivered the window, pane and sash;
It rent the banner with seam and gash.
Quick, as it fell, from the broken staff
Dame Barbara snatched the silken scarf.
She leaned out the window-sill
And shook it forth with a royal will.
"Shoot if you must, this old gray head,
But spare your country's flag," she said.

A shade of sadness, a blush of shame,
Over the face of the leader came;
The nobler nature within him stirred
To life at that woman's deed and word:
"Who touches a hair of yon gray head
Dies like a dog! March on!" he said.
All day long through Frederick street
Sounded the tread of marching feet:
All day long that flag tree tost
Over the heads of the rebel host.
Ever its torn folds rose and fell
On the loyal winds that loved it well;
And through the hill-gaps sunset light
Shone over it with a warm good-night.

Barbara Frietchie's work is o'er,
And the Rebel rides on his raids no more.
Honor to her! and let a tear
Fall, for her sake, on Stonewall's bier.
Over Barbara Frietchie's grave,
Flag of Freedom and Union, wave!
Peace and order and beauty draw
Round thy symbol of light and law;
And ever the stars look down
On thy stars below Frederick town!

CHAPTER IV

Approach to Harpers Ferry

By 9 September it was clear to Lee that he could not remain much longer in Frederick. The main reason he had gone there was to collect provisions, and he was frankly disappointed at what had been garnered. The reason, as wrote President Davis that day, was that "many of the farmers have not yet gotten out their wheat, and there is a reluctance on the part of the millers and others to commit themselves to our favor." In addition, many of the farmers had been forewarned of the army's approach and had sent their horses and cattle to Pennsylvania for safe keeping. If he were to remain in Frederick much longer, he would have to rely increasingly on his awkward supply line that ran via Leesburg to Culpeper. This line, however, was very vulnerable to the enemy, especially now that the Union forces in Washington were at last on the move, as Lee had heard.

What Lee needed to do, he decided, was to move westward across the mountains to Hagerstown, which would become his base for securing more provisions and could be a launching pad for an incursion into the rich Cumberland Valley of Pennsylvania. In addition, Hagerstown offered the prospect of a much more secure line of communications via Martinsburg to the railroad at Staunton, the entire length of which would be guarded by the Blue Ridge Mountains.

There was one major monkey wrench impeding Lee's plan— the large Federal garrison at Harpers Ferry, just 12 miles southeast of Martinsburg and less that 20 miles southwest of Frederick, had not withdrawn when the Confederates crossed the Potomac, as Lee had anticipated, but was still remaining in place (see Chapter V). Now that his army was safely ensconced in Maryland, the Harpers Ferry garrison proved an attractive target that could be captured where it was or destroyed if it tried to flee. Once this garrison was eliminated, the Confederate supply line through the Shenandoah Valley would be secured.

Lee conferred with Stonewall Jackson about the situation, and the two agreed that a thrust against Harpers Ferry would be worth the risk, even if it meant dividing the army into several detachments in order to carry out the mission. By then McClellan was heard to have taken charge of the Union forces, and "Little Mac" was never known to move quickly. Lee felt he would have plenty of time to deal with Harpers Ferry and then move on to Hagerstown, without any likelihood of interference from the troops under McClellan.

Lee explained his reasoning to Major General John Walker, who would be one of the principals in the movement against Harpers Ferry. Walker recalled the speech in detail in an article he wrote for the *Battles and Leaders of the Civil War* series some 25 years later:

> At Cheek's Ford I overtook G.B. Anderson's brigade of D.H. Hill's division and crossed into Maryland with it. The next day we reached the neighborhood of Frederick. I went at once to General Lee, who was alone. After listening to my report, he said that as I had a division which would often, perhaps, be ordered on detached service, an intelligent performance of my duty might require a knowledge of the ulterior purposes and objects of the campaign.
>
> "Here," said he, tracing with his finger on a large map, "is the line of our communications, from Rapidan Station to Manassas, thence to Frederick. It is too near the Potomac, and is liable to be cut any day by the enemy's cavalry. I have therefore given orders to move the line back into the Valley of Virginia, by way of Staunton, Harrisburg, and Winchester, entering Maryland at Shepherdstown.
>
> "I wish you to return to the mouth of the Monocacy and effectually destroy the aqueduct of the Chesapeake and Ohio canal. By the time that is accomplished you will receive orders to cooperate in the capture of Harpers Ferry, and you will not return here, but, after the capture of Harpers Ferry, will rejoin us in Hagerstown, where the army will be concentrated. My information is that there are between 10,000 and 12,000 men at Harpers Ferry, and 3,000 at Martinsburg. The latter may escape toward Cumberland, but I think the chances are that they will take refuge at Harpers Ferry and be captured.

"Besides the men and material of war which we shall capture at Harpers Ferry, the position is necessary to us, not to garrison and hold, but because in the hands of the enemy it would be a break in our new line of communications with Richmond.

"A few days' rest at Hagerstown will be of great service to our men. Hundreds of them are barefooted, and nearly all of them are ragged. I hope to get shoes and clothing for the most needy. But the best of it will be the short delay will enable us to get up our stragglers—not stragglers from a shirking disposition, but simply from inability to keep up with their commands. I believe there are not less than from eight to ten thousand of them between here and Rapidan Station. Besides we shall be able to get a large number of recruits who have been accumulating in Richmond for some weeks. I have now requested that they be sent forward to join us. They ought to reach us at Hagerstown. We shall then have a very good army, and," he smilingly added, "one that I think will be able to give a good account of itself.

"In ten days from now," he continued, "if the military situation is then what I confidently expect it to be after the capture of Harpers Ferry, I shall concentrate the army at Hagerstown, effectually destroy the Baltimore and Ohio road, and march to this point," placing his finger at Harrisburg, Pennsylvania. "Well, I wish effectually to destroy that bridge, which will disable the Pennsylvania railroad for a time. With the Baltimore and Ohio in our possession, and the Pennsylvania railroad broken up, there will remain to the enemy but one route of communication with the West, and that very circuitous, by way of the Lakes. After that I can turn my attention to Philadelphia, Baltimore, or Washington, as may seem best for our interests."

Lee accordingly issued his now famous Special Orders No. 191, which is quoted here in full:

SPECIAL ORDERS, No. 191. HDQRS.
ARMY OF NORTHERN VIRGINIA
September 9, 1862.

I. The citizens of Fredericktown being unwilling, while overrun by members of this army, to open their stores, in order to give them confidence, and to secure to officers and men purchasing supplies for benefit of this command, all officers and men of this army are strictly prohibited from visiting Fredericktown except on business, in which case they will bear evidence of this in writing from division commanders. The provost marshal in Fredericktown will see that his guard rigidly enforces this order.

II. Major Taylor will proceed to Leesburg, Va., and arrange for transportation of the sick and those unable to walk to Winchester, securing the transportation of the country for this purpose. The route between this and Culpeper Court House east of the mountains being unsafe will no longer be traveled. Those on the way to this army already across the river will move up promptly; all others will proceed to Winchester collectively and under command of officers, at which point, being the general depot of this army, its movements will be known and instructions be given by commanding officer regulating further movements.

III. The army will resume its march to-morrow, taking the Hagerstown road. General Jackson's command will form the advance, and, after passing Middletown, with such portion as he may select, take the route toward Sharpsburg, cross the Potomac at the most convenient point, and by Friday morning take possession of the Baltimore and Ohio Railroad, capture such of them as may be at Martinsburg, and intercept such as may attempt to escape from Harpers Ferry.

IV. General Longstreet's command will pursue the main road as far as Boonsborough, where it will halt, with reserve, supply, and baggage trains of the army.

V. General McLaws, with his own division, and that of General R.H. Anderson, will follow General Longstreet. On reaching Middletown will take the route to Harpers Ferry, and by Friday morning possess himself of the Maryland Heights and endeavor to capture the enemy at Harpers Ferry and vicinity.

VI. General Walker, with his division, after accomplishing the object in which he is now engaged, will cross the Potomac at Cheek's Ford, ascend its right banks at Lovettsville, take possession of Loudoun Heights, if practicable, by Friday morning, Key's Ford on his left, and the road between the end of the mountain and the Potomac on his right. He will, as far as practicable, co-operate with General McLaws and Jackson, and intercept retreat of the enemy.

VII. General D.H. Hill's division will form the rear guard of the army, pursuing the road taken by the main body. The reserve artillery, ordinance, and supply trains, & c., will precede General Hill.

VIII. General Stuart will detach a squadron of cavalry to accompany the commands of General Longstreet, Jackson, and McLaws, and, with the main body of the cavalry, will cover the route of the army, bringing up all stragglers that may have been left behind.

IX. The commands of Generals Jackson, McLaws, and Walker, after accomplishing the objects for which they have been detached, will join the main body of the army at Boonsborough or Hagerstown.

X. Each regiment on the march will habitually carry its axes in the regimental ordinance wagons, for use of the men in their encampments, to procure wood, & c.

By command of General R.E. Lee:
R.H. CHILTON
Assistant Adjunct General

Lee's plan was a characteristically bold one, as it involved dividing his army into four detachments despite the fact that he had significantly less men than McClellan. Longstreet was to take about half the army and all the baggage trains to Boonsboro, which offered a good base for gathering supplies; the mountains between there and Frederick (the South Mountain and Catoctin Ranges) would offer an ample screen against any enemy advance or cavalry probe. Jackson was to take three divisions of about 14,000 men south across the Potomac at Martinsburg and then march east to Bolivar Heights, West Virginia, and invest Harpers Ferry from the west. Meanwhile McLaws' and R.H. Anderson's two divisions of about 8,000 men would occupy Maryland Heights, across the Potomac from Harpers Ferry. A third investing column, Walker's division of about 2,000 men, would recross the Potomac south of Frederick and then march west to occupy Loudoun Heights, located opposite Harpers Ferry on the east side of the Shenandoah River. Since Jackson's command had well over forty miles to cover, Lee figured that it would take two days for the trap to be closed.

As usual, Lee's more defensive minded subordinate Old Pete Longstreet had strenuous objections to this incredibly audacious plan. Arguing the risks involved were far too great, the General firmly stated the army was in no condition to make the planned long marches in enemy territory necessary to carry out the objective set. Furthermore, there was the threatening possibility McClellan might manage to get his army into fighting condition quickly, coming out to engage the vulnerable Army of Northern Virginia before it could be reunited. Instead, Longstreet urged caution and advised his commander to recoup the army's strength, recruit troops, and take in supplies.

Lee was not convinced by his subordinate's words of caution. He confidently believed his men able to achieve the monumental tasks set for them. Furthermore, Lee practically refused to believe McClellan possessed the initiative to advance from Washington with any great speed as he told General Walker after detailing his plans, "(McClellan) is a very able general but a very cautious one. His enemies among his own people think him too much so. His army is in a very demoralized and chaotic

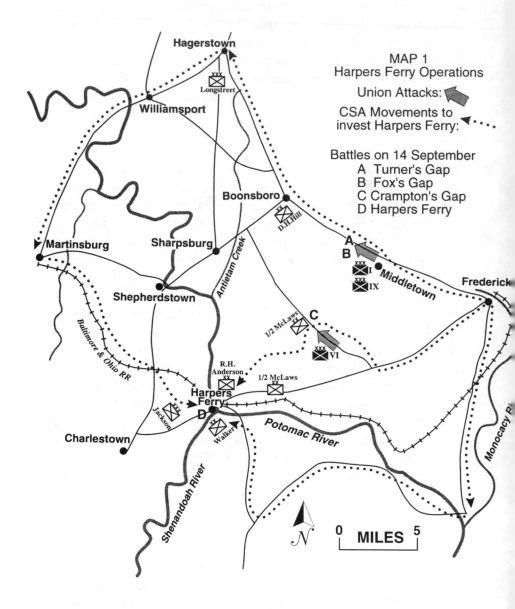

MAP 1
Harpers Ferry Operations

Union Attacks:

CSA Movements to
invest Harpers Ferry:

Battles on 14 September
A Turner's Gap
B Fox's Gap
C Crampton's Gap
D Harpers Ferry

condition, and will not be prepared for offensive operations—or he will not think it so—for three or four weeks. Before that time I hope to be on the Susquehanna."

Unlike Longstreet, Stonewall Jackson was eager for the Harpers Ferry operation. As with the flanking maneuver around Pope, it was his kind of campaign. Besides, as he jokingly told Lee, he had "impolitely" neglected his "friends" in the Shenandoah Valley for far too long.

On 9 September, Special Orders No. 191 detailing the commands for Harpers Ferry operations were dispatched to the appropriate commanders: Longstreet, Jackson, McLaws, R.H. Anderson, Walker, Harvey Hill, and Stuart. Though D.H. Hill had been detached from Jackson's command, Stonewall scribbled down a copy of the order, sending it on to his subordinate. While Hill received this copy, somehow, the one sent from headquarters never arrived. The next day, the Confederates were on the move, disappearing behind the protective cover of South Mountain with Stuart's troopers defending the approaches to the gaps and depriving their arch-foes, the Yankee cavalry, of any useful reconnaissance.

The Harpers Ferry operation got underway late on 9 September when Major General John G. Walker began leading his small division south towards the Potomac from Frederick. At about 2200 he arrived at the aqueduct that carried the Chesapeake and Ohio Canal over the Monocacy River. Here he paused to carry out a diversion—the destruction of the aqueduct, which daily conveyed a large amount of supplies (especially coal) eastward to Washington. The aqueduct, however, proved to be too tough a nut to crack. It was solidly built of granite and cement. Walker noted that "Not a seam or crevice could be discovered in which to insert the point of a crowbar, and the only resource was in blasting. But the drills furnished to my engineer were too dull and the granite too hard, and after several hours of zealous but ineffectual effort the attempt had to be abandoned. Dynamite had not been invented so we were foiled in our purpose."

Walker gave up on his attempt to destroy the aqueduct at 0300 on 10 September and went into camp a couple miles away. When he learned the next day that there was a Federal force at Cheek's Ford, his assigned crossing place on the Potomac, he took the initiative to pass the river at Point of Rocks. He completed his crossing by dawn of the 11th, and then, curiously, put his men into camp. He claimed in his campaign report and later that he did so because it was raining heavily and because the men were worn out by two days of hard marching, particularly by the night crossing. Walker seems to have been in no hurry to reach Harpers Ferry, as he covered only fifteen miles on the 12th before encamping at Hillsboro, five miles short of the goal. He then proceeded the next morning to occupy Loudoun Heights, which were occupied without opposition at about 1000 on 13 September.

Major General Lafayette McLaws had the shortest distance to cover of the three detachments Lee sent against Harpers Ferry—he had only 20 miles to cover between Frederick and his goal at Maryland Heights, located on the north side of the Potomac opposite Harpers Ferry. Nevertheless he took three days to reach his objective. He marched 12 miles on the 10th before encamping at Brownsville, near Crampton's Gap in the South Mountain. On the 11th he split his command. Part headed south to the Potomac at Weverton, while the remainder struggled south along the rocky woods of Elk Ridge directly towards the cliffs facing Harpers Ferry. The latter detachment's progress was so hindered by rough terrain that one Confederate recalled, "the men had to pull themselves up the precipitous inclines by the twigs and undergrowth that lined the mountainside, or hold themselves in position by the trees in front."

Stonewall Jackson's command had the toughest route to reach Harpers Ferry, a 51 mile circuitous trek through the Maryland and Virginia countryside. He left Frederick on the morning of 10 September and marched west along the Old National Road to Middletown and then Boonsboro, where he spent the night. The march was not a very cheerful one as the Rebels found themselves in unfriendly pro-Union territory. When the column reached Middletown, the men found the stores locked tight, their owners gone, and the houses likewise closed. Those citizens who did come out were not at a loss to show their pro-Union sympathies. As Stonewall Jackson rode through town, two young girls with red, white, and blue ribbons in their hair rushed before him, audaciously waving the Stars and

Stripes in his face. Instead of yielding to some sort of harsh reaction, Jackson chivalrously bowed, lifted his cap, and said, "We evidently have no friends in this town." Seeing a group of ladies wearing red, white, and blue cockades pinned to their blouses, a Confederate officer rode up to them, politely touched his cap in salute, and said, "If you will take the advice of a fool, you will return into the house and take off the colors; some damned fool may come along and insult you."

From Boonsboro Jackson headed west to the Potomac ford at Williamsport. His men recrossed the river on 11 September to the tune of "Carry Me Back to Ole Virginny," and were relieved to find themselves in friendly territory once more.

Before completing his march against Harpers Ferry, Jackson had first to deal with Brigadier General Julius White's Federal command of about 2,500 men stationed at Martinsburg, about 10 miles south of Williamsport. He hoped to capture the Yankee force without a fight by sending Lawton's and Ewell's divisions towards the back of the town while A.P. Hill marched directly there from Williamsport; White's possible escape route towards Harpers Ferry would be blocked by the 7th Virginia Cavalry. White, however, learned of Jackson's approach before all the Confederate troops were in position, and managed to escape safely to Bolivar Heights and Harpers Ferry. In his haste he left behind a large quantity of quartermaster, commissary and ordinance stores.

Jackson's cavalry occupied Martinsburg without incident on the morning of 11 September. In stark contrast to their experiences in Middletown, the Confederates found themselves welcomed by an adoring populace. J.F.J. Caldwell recounted the reception after the liberation of the town:

> We were enthusiastically received. In addition to the sutler's goods and government provisions, which were found in abundance, the citizens of the place brought us baskets of food, and invited large numbers of us to go home and dine with them. I doubt not I saw a ton of bread devoured that day. The thanks and words of encouragement we received from fair lips, and the more moving attention of fair eyes, perhaps deserve first place in the list of our enjoyments, but a soldier may be pardoned on the more substantial comfort of bread and meat.

The Lost Order

One of the greatest mysteries of Antietam and the Civil War is the origin of the lost copy of Special Orders 191 that fell into McClellan's hands and informed the Federal general of all the movements of Lee's army, so placing the Confederates in extreme danger. On 9 September, Lee dispatched his orders to the proper commanders, informing them of his intentions to divide the army to capture Harpers Ferry. Copies were drawn up by Lee's Assistant Adjutant General R.H. Chilton with one each going to Jackson (commanding the Harpers Ferry operation), Longstreet, D.H. Hill, J.E.B. Stuart, Lafayette McLaws, R.H. Anderson, John Walker, and staff officer Walter Taylor, who was in charge of dispatching casualties to Winchester, Virginia. Of these, the existence of only three is certain: Jackson kept his copy, Longstreet destroyed the order by ripping it apart and chewing on the pieces, and Walker pinned his copy to a pocket for safekeeping. The fate of those delivered to McLaws, Taylor, and Stuart is not readily known and Anderson denied ever receiving a copy. One mysterious copy found its way into the hands of Confederate staff officer Moxley Sorrel who upon seeing the succinctness of the orders professed some anxiety over the possibility of what to do with the paper should he be captured with it on his person.

Somehow the copy sent from Confederate headquarters to D.H. Hill fell into Federal hands. Its loss was unnoticed because Jackson had sent his subordinate a duplicate of the orders penciled by himself. Unfortu-nately, there is conflicting testimony as to whether Hill received a copy of Special Orders 191 from Lee's headquarters. No receipt for the order was ever returned to Chilton, although Lee's assistant adjutant general maintained he would have recalled if a courier returned without proper documentation proving Hill had received the order.

For many years after the war, Hill was blamed for the actual loss of the order. Some people claimed the cigars the order were wrapped in served as ample evidence of the general's guilt, since he was a notorious smoker. Hill steadfastly maintained his innocence, arguing he had never received any copy of Special Orders 191 save those sent from Jackson. He wrote "I went into Maryland under Jackson's command. I was under his command when Lee's order was issued. It was proper that order come through Jackson and not Lee....My adjutant-general made an affidavit, twenty years ago, that no order was received at our office from General Lee. But an order from Lee's office, directed to me, was lost and fell into McClellan's hands. Did the courier lose it? I don't know. Did Lee's staff officers lose it? I don't know." At any rate, he went as far as to argue that the lost order was actually a boon to the Confederate cause. Since the captured order placed Longstreet at Boonsboro, the Federals were inclined to believe his full force was on the mountain rather than merely Hill's weak command.

This mystery will probably never be unraveled because some of the most important facts still remain missing. Did Chilton receive a receipt? Did a courier give the dispatch to Hill or somebody on his staff? Unless more evidence is forthcoming, the lost order will probably remain one of the greatest unanswered enigmas of the Civil War.

CHAPTER V

The Fall of Harpers Ferry

Jackson's target at Harpers Ferry was the 10,000 man garrison posted there, under the command of Colonel Dixon S. Miles. Unfortunately for the Federals, Harpers Ferry itself was virtually indefensible, situated as it was on a point of land at the confluence of the Potomac and Shenandoah Rivers. The town was thoroughly dominated by higher ground on all sides; Maryland Heights, on the north side of the Potomac, rose to 1,450 feet; Loudoun Heights, to the southeast across the Shenandoah, rose to 1,250 feet; and Bolivar Heights, 650 feet high, was on the landward approach from the west, rising some 300 feet above the adjacent terrain.

Miles chose to post no troops on Loudoun Heights since he believed the terrain there was too rough for artillery; he also felt that any troops he sent there would be too easily dominated by the nearby higher ground on Maryland Heights. Indeed, Maryland Heights was actually the key to the entire situation, since it totally dominated Loudoun Heights and all the nearby terrain; enemy guns posted there could easily blast directly down into the town of Harpers Ferry. Miles chose to defend this key position with an ad hoc brigade of 2,000 men under command of Col. Thomas Ford of the *32nd Indiana*. He also set up a three gun naval battery (two 9-inch Dahlgren guns and a 50-pounder rifle) partway up the southwest slope of Maryland Heights, for the purpose of supporting his lines west of Harpers Ferry.

Miles posted the bulk of his command, some 7000 men, to guard the landward approach to Harpers Ferry from the west. The best position for them was along Bolivar Heights, a ridge that ran for one and one-half miles from the Potomac to the Shenandoah, about 2 miles west of Harpers Ferry. Bolivar Heights was about 300 feet above the surrounding terrain and had a clear field of fire against the probable lines of enemy approach. To complete his defenses, Miles stationed a 2,000 man reserve with a battery of 20 pound Parrott guns at Camp Hill, a 300 foot rise next to Harpers Ferry. Miles' strength figures do not include the 2,500 men under Brigadier General Julius White, who was stationed at Martinsburg, about 15 miles to the northwest.

Miles was aware of Lee's movement to the Potomac, and was justifiably concerned that the entire Confederate army was between him and Washington. His condition became more awkward when his direct telegraph line to the capital was cut on 6 September. Two days later Lee's army began to concentrate at Frederick, only 18 miles to the northeast, and the Rebels seemed intent on staying in Maryland for awhile.

Miles had indeed found himself in an awkward position when the Confederates concentrated at Leesburg and then began crossing the Potomac. On 5 September, he had received orders from Washington to be "energetic and active, and defend all places to the last extremity. There must be no abandoning of a post and shoot the first man that thinks of it." Later in the day General Halleck directed him to "Have your wits about you, and do all you can to annoy the rebels should they advance on you....you will not abandon Harpers Ferry without defending it to the last extremity."

Halleck's last ditch mentality is difficult to understand. He apparently believed that Miles' garrison was large enough to defend itself against any small or moderate sized enemy attack, and that any withdrawal would expose it to possible destruction, particularly the loss of the great amount of ordnance and supplies stored there. However, it should be pointed out that the large garrison—which was bigger than any corps with McClellan—could readily have slipped away simply by marching to the west anytime before 10 September. Halleck simply wanted to hold on to the post until it could be relieved by McClellan, which he hoped would happen soon. With this decision he unknowingly changed the whole course of the campaign. Lee

*Loudoun Heights, Va. is on the right, Maryland Heights on the left.
At the time of Jackson's siege the railroad bridge was in ruins and
there was a pontoon bridge nearby.*

had expected the garrison to be moved and when it was not, he
was forced to turn back to deal with it, so stalling his entire
advance.

Despite the growing threat the Rebel army posed to the
garrison at Harpers Ferry, Halleck sent only a reassuring dispatch telling Miles to hold, writing on 7 September, "Our army
is in motion. It is important that Harpers Ferry be held to the
latest moment. The Government has the utmost confidence in
you, and is ready to give you full credit for the defence it expects
you to make." Still, despite the harrowing situation, Miles did
little to prepare himself for the worst, only having a defensive
set of breastworks built on Maryland Heights. McClellan would
request Miles' men to reinforce his own army, writing Halleck
on the 10th, "Colonel Miles is at or near Harpers Ferry, I
understand, with 9,000 troops. He can do nothing where he is,
and could be of great service if ordered to join me." Initially, on
the 11th, Halleck refused, but the next day put Miles within the
command of the *Army of the Potomac*, telling him, "You will obey
orders General McClellan may give you. You will endeavor to

open communication with him and unite your forces to his at the earliest possible moment." Of course with Jackson moving to surround the town, there was little chance that Miles would ever have the chance to establish communications with the *Army of the Potomac.*

Miles was informed by his active cavalry of the three pronged Confederate advance against him as soon as it began to develop. He could do little but watch the trap begin to close in on 12 September, when he heard of Walker's advance to Loudoun Heights, and McLaws' movement down Elk Mountain toward Maryland Heights. He was also aware that a large force had crossed at Williamsport and was headed his way. This was confirmed later on the 12th when White's command began to arrive from Martinsburg. These were the only reinforcements Miles would receive before Jackson's trap closed. Though White was a brigadier general and outranked Colonel Miles, he deferred to Miles as commander of the Harpers Ferry Post, and so became only an observer to the events that were about to unfold.

The key action during the entire Harpers Ferry operation was a sharp and largely ignored fight on Maryland Heights that was fought on the morning of 13 September. Union skirmishers had made contact with McLaws' advancing troops at 1500 the day before, and the Federals were as prepared as they could be for the fight they knew would come in the morning. Colonel Ford, the Union commander, was not at all confident in his ability to hold the Heights, which he properly recognized to be the key to Harpers Ferry. Most of his regiments had previously seen only limited battle action, and one, the *126th New York*, had been in the army only six days. Nor were his defenses anywhere as strong as he would have liked. Though Union troops had occupied Harpers Ferry for many months, no defenses had been prepared on the Heights, and Ford had not had time to prepare any of substance. To make matters worse, Colonel Miles refused his request for some field artillery to bolster his lines; the only cannons he received were the three naval guns previously mentioned, and these were aimed in the opposite direction from the line of McLaws' advance.

The battle for Maryland Heights began at 0630 on 13 September when Kershaw's South Carolina brigade began advancing against Ford's line, and Barksdale's Mississippi brigade moved to turn the Union right. The Confederates found it very difficult to advance because of the rocky and steep ground, and sometimes had to cling to bushes on the incline while they loaded and fired. After they managed to drive back the Union skirmishers they met "a most obstinate and determined resistance" at their main line. The Confederates did all they could for the next three hours but still could not carry the position.

The fighting came to a climax at 1100 when Kershaw launched yet another assault. Colonel John Henigan of the 8th South Carolina fell badly wounded while waving the unit's flag. When he saw his troops begin to waver, he called out to them, "About face! Charge and take those works!" The South Carolinians rallied, and soon the Union line was in full retreat. It seems that the colonel of the *126th New York*, Eliakiam Sherrill, had been badly wounded in the jaw, and his loss totally unnerved the green regiment. The New Yorkers began streaming to the rear, and this in turn gave the acting commander of the *32nd Ohio* no choice but to order a retreat. Kershaw's men were surprised to see the blue line literally melt away, and Barksdale's troops were equally surprised when they finally got behind the right of the Union line, only to find its defenders gone.

It was at this point that Colonel Miles arrived at Ford's headquarters to see how the fighting was going. He was truly dismayed to see elements of the *126th New York* in full flight. Miles frantically tried to rally them and succeeded at stopping their flight only by having a company of formed infantry fix bayonets and begin driving the disorganized mass back towards the fighting. With difficulty a new line was formed on another crest about 400 yards behind the commander's original position. Miles then had a heated discussion with Ford, when Ford expressed doubt he could hold out any longer. Miles responded that "You can and you must," and then left to return to Harpers Ferry. He did, though, let Ford know that he could withdraw across the Potomac if his situation became desperate.

Ford felt a little more secure when seven companies of the *115th New York* arrived at about noon. However, the enemy soon advanced a heavy line of skirmishers to renew the fight, and by mid-afternoon it was clear to him that strong Confederate columns were pushing past both Union flanks. Ford was certain that there was no hope of holding the position much longer, so he ordered a withdrawal under the discretionary orders he had received from Miles late that morning.

Ford's withdrawal order was received with utter disbelief by the officers on the front line, who were unaware that they were about to be flanked. The commander on the crest, Lieutenant Colonel S.W. Downey of the *3rd Maryland Potomac Home Brigade*, refused to obey it until it was confirmed by his own adjutant 15 minutes later. Likewise Captain Philo D. Phillips of the *126th New York* also initially refused to obey the order: "The Rebels could be seen over the abatis and the breastworks in force; but as we were holding them in check at all points, it was a mystery why we should be ordered to fall back." However, when the other units in the line began to move out, Phillips found that he had no choice but to follow.

When Colonel Miles saw Ford's troops filing off the mountain towards the pontoon bridge over the Potomac, he exclaimed, "God Almighty! What does this mean? They are coming down! Hell and damnation! They are coming down! We must stop it!" But it was too late. Not only had Ford's men given up the heights, but they had also spiked three naval guns on the mountainside, as Miles had earlier ordered Ford to do if the position had to be abandoned.

It is interesting to speculate what might have happened had Miles elected to defend Maryland Heights with a stronger force. The Heights were the key to the Harpers Ferry defense because any Confederate cannons placed there could have blasted Harpers Ferry at will. Miles was clearly not expecting such a strong Confederate movement against that section, and he also may have been clinging too closely to his precise orders to defend Harpers Ferry proper. Be that as it may, it is clear from all accounts that Ford did not defend the Heights as ably as he might have. After the campaign he was tried and convicted for neglect of duty.

As Ford's dispirited men filed into Harpers Ferry, Miles knew that his situation was desperate—Walker's troops had started to appear on Loudoun Heights, McLaws would soon have artillery on the dominating heights of the Maryland shore, and Jackson's troops were beginning to form opposite his line on Bolivar Heights. His only hope was to try to hold on until McClellan could come to his relief. Unfortunately, his demeanor and physical pressure were not sufficient to instill any confidence from his troops. He was simply an aged West Point graduate who had seen 40 years of service, including active duty in the Mexican War. His reputation had been tarnished by charges of drunkenness at First Bull Run (of which he had been acquitted), and he had been annoyed at the advancement of former subordinates while he remained a colonel in charge of the *Railroad Brigade* based at Harpers Ferry. Miles certainly was not a source of inspiration for the troops—many of them green—who were now totally disheartened by the appearance of enemy forces on their front.

About all that Miles could do for now was to strengthen his lines on Bolivar Heights. In an act of desperation he called in Captain Charles H. Russell of the *1st Maryland Cavalry*, and ordered him to break through the enemy lines and try to reach "Somebody who had ever heard of the United States Army, or knew anything about the United States Army, and report the condition of Harpers Ferry." He told Russell to report that the garrison had subsistence to hold out for only 48 hours, and "if not relieved at that time, I will have to surrender the place." Russell left that night with an escort of nine cavalrymen, and managed to make it through to General McClellan by 0900 the next morning, when matters were taken out of his hands.

Although his operation was running behind schedule, Jackson chose not to force the issue by launching an infantry assault—Miles' line was too ably posted and amply defended. Instead, he decided to bring up all the cannons he could and force Miles to surrender by an overwhelming barrage of converging fire.

Despite Ford's bad feelings about the situation, his line held out as the afternoon progressed towards the evening. The enemy did not actually assault his front, but continued pressuring him. At about 1500 he found out why—the enemy was holding back while a brigade worked its way around his left. Ford knew that this would make his new line untenable, and "in obedience to the positive orders of Colonel Miles" ordered a withdrawal to

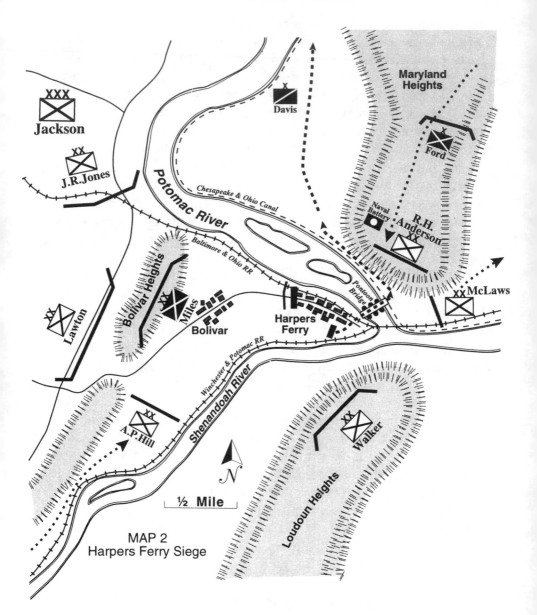

Maryland Heights

XXX Jackson

XX J.R.Jones

Potomac River

Chesapeake & Ohio Canal

Davis

Naval Battery

R.H. Anderson XX

Ford X

XX McLaws

Baltimore & Ohio RR

Bolivar Heights

XX Lawton

Miles XX

Bolivar

Harpers Ferry

Pontoon Bridge

Winchester & Potomac RR

Shenandoah River

A.P.Hill XX

Walker XX

Loudoun Heights

N

½ Mile

MAP 2
Harpers Ferry Siege

the other side of the river while there was still time to do so safely.

There was only sporadic skirmishing on Bolivar Heights on the night of 13-14 September as Jackson prepared to bring his cannons up. He certainly had an easier job than Walker and McLaws, whose men had to cut paths through the woods and drag their artillery pieces one by one over rocks and rough terrain. By 1000 on the 14th, Walker with great difficulty had five rifled pieces in place on Loudoun Heights, and by 1400 McLaws had three 10-pounder Parrotts and one 3-inch ordnance rifle ready on Maryland Heights.

Jackson was unwilling to open his artillery bombardment until all his guns were in place, and he was experiencing difficulty communicating with McLaws and Walker through the medium of signal flags. At length Walker grew impatient at waiting since 1000 to open the fight. At midafternoon he paraded two of his regiments in full view of Miles' opposing troops. When this display drew Union fire, as he knew it would, he responded with his cannons, and the barrage was begun. Soon Jackson's guns on School House Ridge, opposite Bolivar Heights, opened fire, as did McLaws' pieces on Maryland Heights.

The suddenness of the bombardment caught the Union troops totally by surprise. Captain Edward Ripley of the *9th Vermont* wrote, "I saw two, three, four, half a dozen puffs of smoke burst out...a crash, then another and another, and columns of dirt and smoke leap into the air, as though a dozen young volcanoes had burst forth. In an instant the bivouac turned into the appearance of a disturbed ant-hill. Artillery, infantry and cavalry were mixed in an absurd and laughable melee as the panic increased." A captain in the *125th New York* wrote that "our regiment was caught napping and lounging around....we saw we were at their mercy, to remain was to be slaughtered, so we ran like hounds to get under cover of the mountainside."

While Miles' infantry dashed for cover, the weight of the Confederate artillery concentrated on the Union battery at Camp Hill. Walker's guns on Loudoun Heights were particularly active, and within two hours the Federal guns were silenced. During all the firing there were not actually that many casualties, but the effect of all the noise and firepower was enough to unnerve a great number of the Yankee defenders, particularly the raw troops—just the goal Jackson wanted to achieve.

Not all the Union infantry spent the afternoon cowering in the many ravines that crisscrossed Bolivar Heights. At noontime Colonel Frederick D'Utassy of the *39th New York* had asked Colonel Miles for permission to try to retake Maryland Heights. Miles disdainfully refused him, but D'Utassy proceeded to cross the river on his own. He took four companies of his regiment and managed to recapture the site of the disabled naval battery without any difficulty just after the Confederate cannonade started. Instead of proceeding farther uphill to see how much infantry was supporting McLaws' guns, D'Utassy thought it best to gather up four disabled field guns and all the gunpowder he could and return to Harpers Ferry. Curiously, Miles did not reprimand D'Utassy for his freelance expedition. Nor did he think of attempting to mount a larger attack for the recovery of Maryland Heights. Instead he waited out his fate in his current position, determined to fight until he ran out of shells or food.

The glow of the Confederate campfires on all the heights around Harpers Ferry that night further demoralized Miles' men and convinced them that the end was near. A few Yankees, however, were not about to submit to captivity. At about 1900 Colonel Benjamin F. Davis of the *8th New York Cavalry* presented Colonel Miles with a plan for the bold escape of all the post's cavalry troops. His successful dash to freedom is presented in the accompanying sidebar.

A short while into the cannonade, Jackson realized that artillery fire alone would not be able to force the enemy garrison into submission. Late in the afternoon he directed A.P. Hill to take his "Light Division" of six brigades and move to the Shenandoah River, with the goal of turning Miles' left flank. Hill did not reach his objective by nightfall, and his men had to stumble over the unfamiliar terrain in the darkness. The Yankees were well aware of Hill's advance, but made no effort to stop it, like a deer mesmerized by a stalking tiger. In the absence of any enemy resistance, Hill was able to bring two brigades to within 150 yards of the Federal left flank. He knew that the enemy

Major General Thomas J. "Stonewall" Jackson was promoted to Lieutenant General three weeks after the battle. His capture of Harper's Ferry was the single largest Confederate capture of Union troops in the war.

would be hard pressed in the morning, and so did Jackson. At 2015, Stonewall sent a note to Lee, "Through God's blessing, the advance, which commenced this evening, has been successful, and I look to Him for complete success tomorrow. The advance has been directed to be resumed at dawn tomorrow morning."

As the dawn rose on the fateful day of 15 September, an ominous mist covered the town of Harpers Ferry, mercifully shielding it from the watchful eyes of the cannoneers on the heights surrounding the town. Miles' Federals found the respite a short one as the fog was slowly burned away by the rising sun. The Rebel guns, now numbering at least 50, opened fire almost at once. One Confederate artilleryman noted of the commencement of the bombardment, "Simultaneously the great circle of artillery opened, all firing to a common center, while clouds of smoke, rolling up from the tops of the various mountains, and the thunder of the guns reverberating among them gave the idea of so many volcanoes." Once again, the embattled Yankees scrambled to reach whatever cover they could find in the face of the falling exploding shells. The unfortunate troops on Bolivar

Heights found themselves raked by a barrage from Hill's guns set up on their left during the night. The day's prospects for Miles did not bode well.

At about 0800, the fire from the Union guns began to slacken as the last supply of long range ammunition was expended. Rather than risk a needless effusion of blood, Miles prepared to surrender. To the great satisfaction of the Confederates and the horror of the Federals the white flag was sent up. Despite the odds against them, some Yankees wanted to fight it out; Captain Philo D. Phillips of the *126th New York*, believing help was on its way, rushed out to Miles pleading, "For God's sake, Colonel, don't surrender us....Our forces are near us. Let us cut our way out and join them." Miles merely replied such action was impossible. "They will blow us out of this in half an hour." After Jackson's guns silenced in honor of the white flag, Miles and Binney approached the Confederate lines to seek terms. The colonel said passively, "Well, Mr. Binney, we have done our duty, but where can McClellan be? The Rebels have opened up on us again; what do they mean." Indeed, some battery commander had not paid attention to the truce and had continued to fire. By pure chance, a shell exploded right before Miles with a piece of shrapnel tearing away part of his leg. Seeing their commander fall, Captain Phillips grumbled, "Good," writing later, "The rest felt it if they did not say it." The wound would prove mortal; as the colonel passed away, he was confident that he had done his duty, and as an old soldier was willing to die.

General White at once took his place, and rode up to give the surrender, attired splendidly in a fine dress uniform with a gleaming sword sheathed in its scabbard. Conversely, Jackson appeared in garb weathered from many months of campaigning. A reporter from the *New York Times* noted, "He was dressed in the coarsest kind of homespun, seedy and dirty at that; wore an old hat which any Northern beggar would consider an insult to have offered him, and in his general appearance was in no respect to be distinguished from the mongrel, bare footed crew who follow his fortunes." After receiving White, Jackson had Hill work out the surrender while he prepared to put his army on the road to join with Lee. The magnanimous Confederates offered generous terms to the defeated Federals; all personal property and side arms of the officers were to be retained by their owners while all troops were to be paroled, agreeing not to fight until exchanged.

Upon hearing news of the surrender, McLaws' men in Pleasant Valley let out a mighty roar, prompting a Federal picket to jump up on a rock to inquire what all the racket was about, shouting, "What in hell are you fellows cheering for?" To which he got the reply, "Because Harpers Ferry has gone up, damn you!" "I thought so," grumbled the Yank. Exultant over the surrender, Stuart told Von Borcke, "My dear Von, is not this glorious? You must immediately gallop over with me to congratulate Stonewall on his splendid success." When he met with Jackson, the General could only say, "Ah, this is all very well, Major, but we have much hard work before us."

A bountiful stash of supplies was gathered to equip the Southern army, including 13,000 small arms, 200 wagons, 73 cannons, as well as plenty of ammunition and food. Starved Confederate soldiers rushed to get what they could of the available supplies of food and clothing, greedily grabbing meat, hardtack, sugar, coffee, shoes, undergarments and blankets. One biblically minded South Carolinian drew an allusion to the sight saying, "It really looked like Pharaoh's lean kine devouring the fat."

Looking on in dismay, the Yankees could only curse their humiliating plight. One New Yorker openly wept, crying out, "Boys, we have no country now." Another captive, a veteran of the fight on Maryland Heights, bitterly remarked, "Rather than let this happen, I gladly would have left my bones on the field."

As Jackson rode through the town, Northern soldiers crowded the roadways to get a look at the man who had bagged them. Throughout the mass of soldiers, admiring shouts of "Boys, he's not much to look at, but if we had him we wouldn't have been caught in this trap" and "Ah! If we had him we should whip you in short order" were heard from troops who had been his enemies. As soldiers from both sides mingled together, Yankees and Rebels marveled at each other's appearance. The Federals well groomed and washed in clean, almost pristine uniforms; the Confederates dirty, ragged, and foul smelling. The observer from the *New York Times* wrote, "I've heard much of the decayed appearance of Rebel soldiers, but such a looking crowd! Ireland in her worst straits could present no parallel and yet they glory in their shame." Of the Federals, Blackford recalled they looked as though they had just stepped out of a bandbox with their clean uniforms, whiter shirts, and polished boots. Both factions found the time to trade jokes as one Reb called out noting the pale complexion of his Northern adversaries, "I say, Yank, what kind of soap do you fellows use? It has washed the color out of your faces." A cocky Yankee quickly retorted, "You don't look like you ever used soap of any sort," winning a hearty laugh from all around.

All told the Federals had lost a total of 12,500 men as prisoners to the Confederacy; 44 had been killed and 173 wounded during the entire affair with most of the casualties suffered during the fight on Maryland Heights. Jackson suffered sparingly, losing only 286 men in killed and wounded; most of these were also suffered on Maryland Heights. The magnitude of Jackson's success has been largely neglected because it fell so closely to the great battle of Antietam, which was fought only two days later. It was in fact the greatest single capture of Federal troops the Confederates made in the war, not to mention all the cannons and supplies. After the capture of Harpers Ferry, Lee could well have withdrawn to Virginia and called the campaign a success. But he had greater goals in mind.

Recriminations for the loss of Harpers Ferry ripped through the Union army and the government even before the campaign ended. On 25 September, just 10 days after the surrender, a special commission met in Washington to investigate what happened. It was headed by Major General David Hunter, and in fifteen days of inquiry asked 1800 questions of 44 different witnesses. The investigation concentrated on the orders and behavior of Colonel Miles, but he could not be made to bear the full burden of guilt because he had fallen at his post. Instead, the commission made Colonel Ford the scapegoat for his failure to defend Maryland Heights adequately. It also censured General McClellan for failure to move quickly enough to relieve the post. In this they were right, but that is another story.

John George Walker (1822-1893)

Unlike most of his comrades, Missourian John Walker received his education outside West Point in the Jesuit College in St. Louis. He entered the army after he received a commission in 1846. A captain when the Civil War broke out, Walker threw in his lot with the Confederate States, becoming a lieutenant colonel in the 8th Texas Cavalry. By the summer of 1862, he was commissioned a brigadier and took command of a division in Lee's army. He served with Jackson during the campaign in Maryland, and was charged with taking Loudoun Heights during the operation against Harpers Ferry. After being promoted to the rank of major general, he was shipped out west to join the Trans-Mississippi Department and led the Texas Infantry Division. Walker helped Kirby Smith to thwart the designs of the hapless Nathaniel Banks. He then commanded the District of West Louisiana and the District of Texas, New Mexico, and Arizona before the end of the war. After fleeing briefly to Mexico, he returned to serve the Federal Government as Consul-General to Colombia and commissioner in the Pan-American Convention.

The Great Escape of Grimes Davis

When the situation for the Federals at Harpers Ferry was growing exceedingly dim on 14 September 1862, a few officers were not about to meekly submit to their fate. Among them was the commander of the *8th New York Cavalry*, Lieutenant Colonel Benjamin "Grimes" Davis, a Mississippian loyal to the Union. With Stonewall Jackson's Confederates bombarding the garrison from the heights surrounding the town and resistance seemingly futile, Davis and his fellow troopers decided to attempt a breakout rather than be trapped in an ignominious surrender. Davis informed the garrison's commander, Colonel Dixon Miles, of his decision, and argued for the merits of the action. Miles was forced to give his approval once Davis made it clear he was determined to go with or without his commander's assent.

At 2000 that night, all the Federal cavalry at Harpers Ferry, consisting of 1,500 men of the *1st Maryland*, *1st Rhode Island*, *12th Illinois*, *8th New York*, and a detachment of the *Maryland Home Brigade*, set out across a pontoon bridge over the Potomac into the night's inky blackness. Since the moon was not out that evening, the Federal movements were concealed from detection by McLaws'and Richard Anderson's troops atop Maryland Heights. The cavalry took a winding road from the base of Maryland Heights towards Sharpsburg, and proceeded in a column almost 12 miles in length across the Maryland countryside, their only source of illumination the sparks of horseshoes striking the pavement of the road. An area native knowledgeable about local roads led the way, enabling the Federals to sneak their way through Confederate lines without being detected. Still, there was plenty of room for error. One company threatened the success of the entire mission when it made a wrong turn and ran into a Rebel picket. The men managed to get back on the right track, however, before the enemy discovered them.

The long trek through the night was as exhausting as it was tense, with men slumping in the saddle to get a few minutes of sleep before forcing themselves awake again to stay on guard for enemy pickets. Upon entering Sharpsburg, the Federals stumbled on a few Confederates, but managed to escape unharmed. Fortunately, a friendly local citizen informed Davis and his men of the position of a large enemy detachment near Hagerstown. They turned off to the west to avoid this force, and continued on into the early morning until they reached the Hagerstown-Williamsport Road,

where the far off creak and rumble of wagon wheels could be heard. They had stumbled upon a file of enemy wagons with a cavalry escort. Davis cleverly applied an ingenious ruse to take possession of the supply train. With his blue uniform disguised by the darkness, the Mississippian employed the accent of his native South to fool the cavalrymen, who believed him to be a friendly officer. When the cavalry halted, Davis directed the wagons off onto a road which led into Pennsylvania. As the train was escorted away, the Federals surprised their unsuspecting Confederate counterparts and drove them off through the countryside. When daylight illuminated the surroundings, the Confederate teamsters were shocked to find themselves surrounded by Yankee cavalry. As he crossed into the safety of Pennsylvania on the morning of the 15th, Davis counted in his possession some 91 wagons belonging to General Longstreet's reserve ammunition train. Thus, the Mississippian brought a bright chapter to the otherwise miserable Federal stand at Harpers Ferry in September of 1862.

Standing with the Colors

Perhaps the object of greatest importance to a Civil War regiment was the battle flag flown in combat. The flag served as a means of identification, direction, and a rallying point for a unit, and maintained a great deal of symbolic value as well. Banners usually bore the list of battles the regiment had fought in, and

were emblems of honor, to be flown at all times throughout any engagement; to lose them was the utmost disgrace. As a result, it was a distinction to serve as a color bearer; soldiers displayed great bravery while wielding their flags despite imminent danger or wounds. At Antietam, a corporal of the *8th*

Pennsylvania Regiment continued to wave his regiment's colors despite a broken leg and an advance of the enemy. He called out to his comrades not to desert the flag, until he was shot through the head by a Confederate soldier.

Troops were also known to risk their lives to capture enemy standards. During Hooker's attack, Lieutenant Lewis C. Parmelee of the *2nd U.S. Sharpshooters* was killed near the Hagerstown Road by six or seven bullets from Rebel rifles as he attempted to capture a fallen Confederate flag as a trophy.

When the Federal garrison surrendered at Harpers Ferry, a few regiments escaped further dishonor by preventing the loss of their flags as trophies for the Confederates through various cunning maneuvers. One regiment tore their banner to bits, each soldier keeping a piece. Corporal Omar S. Lee managed to save the flag of the *32nd Ohio* by wrapping it around himself under his clothes.

Understandably, there was always a high rate of mortality among color bearers. Due to their importance to the fighting effectiveness of the regiment and distinctiveness as a target, the flags made good targets for enemy soldiers. At Antietam, the 1st Texas lost eight color bearers during the battle; the *9th New York* also lost eight men carrying the flag into battle; the Hampton Legion lost four in succession while attacking Gibbon's men. Thus there is no wonder that enthusiasm to serve as color bearer waned among soldiers on both sides.

CHAPTER VI

McClellan Gets a Break

*A*s noted in Chapter II, Major General George B. McClellan did almost a miraculous job at reorganizing the *Army of the Potomac* and restoring its morale in the first few days after he assumed command on 2 September. (As Lincoln told his secretary, John Hay, even if McClellan would not always fight himself, "he excels in making others ready to fight.") He began shifting troops to the northern outskirts of Washington as early as 3 September, in order to be more ready to meet any move Lee might make on the capital from that quarter. When he learned that Lee was crossing the Potomac in force, McClellan shifted the bulk of his army to the Maryland side of the Potomac on 5 September, even as he was reorganizing his corps and absorbing new regiments into them. The *II, X,* and *XII Corps* were stationed to guard the northwestern approaches to Washington, with the *I* and *VI Corps* in reserve. The *II, IX,* and *XI Corps* were left in Virginia to hold the line from the Chain Bridge to Alexandria.

In the next few days, McClellan slowly advanced his frontline troops to the northwest when it became clear that Lee was not going to advance on Washington but was headed into western Maryland and possibly even Pennsylvania. On 7 September, "Little Mac" himself took to the field and joined the troops at Rockville. McClellan later claimed that his decision to take to the field with his army was one of great personal jeopardy, since he had been ordered only to "have command of the fortifications of Washington and of all the troops for the defense of the capital," and had not been specifically directed to take to the field. He later wrote that "I fought the battle of South Mountain and Antietam with a halter around my neck. If the *Army of the Potomac* had been defeated and I had survived, I would, no doubt, have been tried for assuming authority without orders and probably been condemned to death."

McClellan clearly overstated his personal position in order to bring more attention to himself, or to detract attention from his failure to destroy Lee at South Mountain and Antietam. Lincoln and Halleck were clearly aware of what he was doing, even if they dreaded the idea of his leading another army into combat again. The administration was simply in no position to say no to the commander, be he prima donna or not. They had perhaps hoped to use McClellan to reorganize the army and then transfer it to the command of someone else, perhaps Burnside, if he could be persuaded to accept. But the swiftness of Lee's invasion forced them to ride with McClellan. As historian Edward J. Stackpole colorfully put it, "When the house is on fire, the owner is not likely to throw obstacles in the path of the fireman, even though he may not think well of him."

One of the better organizational changes McClellan ordered was the creation of a centralized cavalry division under the command of Brigadier General Alfred Pleasonton. Previously, he had used his cavalry only piecemeal, with regiments and battalions assigned to various corps and divisions for scouting and courier service. The first really effective use of Federal cavalry in the Virginia theater was probably *Bayard's brigade* during the Second Bull Run campaign. Before setting out against Lee, McClellan formed a new cavalry division of five brigades, four of which contained two regiments, while the fifth had four. The organization would be the nucleus of the fine cavalry corps that would serve so well in the Gettysburg campaign and later. For the moment, though, the strength and experience of the Yankee horsemen was no match for their Confederate counterparts, nor was Pleasonton any match for Jeb Stuart.

In setting out to make contact with the enemy, McClellan decided to divide his army into three wings: the *I* and *IX Corps* under Burnside, on the left; the *II* and *XII Corps* under Sumner in the center; and the *VI Corps* and *Couch's division* of the *IV Corps* under Franklin on the right. The *V Corps* under Porter

*President Lincoln visiting McClellan at Porter's headquarters, lo-
cated on the Grove Farm, 3/4 mile west of Sharpsburg, on 30 October. Lincoln was greatly annoyed that McClellan did not pursue
Lee's army back to Virginia right after the battle.*

would form a reserve, and Pleasonton's newly arrived cavalry
division would lead the way. These troops totaled over 85,000
men, significantly larger than Lee's force of about 50,000 (but see
sidebar on Pinkerton's numbers). McClellan decided to leave
the *III Corps* behind in Washington because it had suffered so
severely in the Peninsula and Second Bull Run campaign; he
also left the *XI Corps* behind simply because it was the weakest
and least trusted of his commands. These and other new,
unassigned, and garrison troops in Washington totalled over
26,000 men, all under their new commander, Major General
Nathaniel P. Banks.

McClellan sent Pleasonton's troops out ahead of his infantry,
and they first made contact with Stuart's horsemen on 7 September at Poolesville. Three days of constant skirmishing followed

as Stuart effectively employed his regiments on a 20 mile arc from New Market, Maryland, to Edwards Ferry and very effectively screened Lee's command at Frederick. It was during this period that Stuart held his noted ball at Urbana (see sidebar).

On 9 September McClellan began moving towards Frederick, but at the cautious rate of 10 miles a day. He advanced on a broad front from the Potomac northward in order to allay the administration's fears that Lee might slip around either flank and attack the capital or Baltimore. Couch followed the Potomac watching the river fords, and marched via Poolesville and Bainesville to Lickville, which was reached on 13 September. Franklin headed up through Dawsonville and Bainesville, and reached Buckeyestown on the 13th. Sumner's wing followed the Old National Road and reached Frederick on the 17th, where he was joined by *Burnside's Corps*.

In heading west, troops from the *Army of the Potomac* toiled along the Maryland roads, kicking up the familiar choking dust clouds, a symbol of an army on the move. The march caused some to reflect on the dramatic differences between their appearance now and a year earlier when the romance of war still prevailed. De Trobriand noted:

> What a contrast between the departure and the return! We had started out in the spring, gay, smart, well provided with everything. The drums beat, the bugles sounded; the flag, with its folds of immaculate silk, glistened in the sunshine. And we were returning before autumn, sad, weary, covered with mud, with uniforms in rags. Now the drummers carried their cracked drums on their backs, the buglers were bent over and silent; the flag, riddled by the balls, torn by shrapnel, discolored by the rain, hung sadly upon the staff without color.

Still, many a Yankee was happy to be campaigning on friendly ground for a change. One soldier wrote home, "I shall always remember the march through Maryland as among the most pleasant of my experiences as a soldier. The roads were splendid and the country as beautiful a country as I ever saw. It has but little of the desolate appearances of the devastated Old Dominion, but everywhere landscapes of exquisite beauty meet the eye. Pretty villages are frequent, and pretty girls more so, and instead of gazing at passing soldiers with scorn and contempt, they were always ready with a pleasant word and a glass of water."

As the *Army of the Potomac* arrived in Frederick, the city had seemingly changed its allegiances with the Federal arrival. The Yankees were received in the same resplendent fashion as the Rebels had been, as David L. Thompson of the *9th New York* wrote, "The city was abloom with flags, houses were open everywhere, trays of food were set on window sills of nearly all the better class of houses, and the streets were filled with women dressed in their best, walking bareheaded, singing, and testifying in every way the general joy."

John Gibbon recalled:

> I did not much believe before coming here that there was so much Union feeling in the state as had been shown towards us. As the troops passed through Frederick, the houses were covered in U.S. flags and the whole population seemed to turn out to welcome us. When General McClellan came through he was overwhelmed by the ladies, they kissed his clothes, threw their arms around his horse's neck and committed all sorts of extravagances. Those who saw it say there never could have been such a scene witnessed in this country since Washington's time....The people come out and speak to us as we pass and show their delight at the idea of the rebels being driven out of the state. There is no question of the loyalty of this part of Maryland.

Despite their reception, the Yankees often took advantage of the Marylanders, foraging throughout the area, stealing food and other items when it suited them, so defaming their reputation when compared with the better behaved Southerners. Some officers attempted to curb such crimes. In one instance a soldier stole two bundles of hay from a barn in the vicinity of Frederick only to run into the disapproving George Gordon Meade who ordered him to return the stolen booty immediately. The soldier audaciously grumbled, "General, I suppose I will have to obey your order, but if you were not wearing shoulder straps, I'll be damned if I would." To this, Meade immediately dismounted from his horse, threw down his coat and gruffly commented, "Now, young man, the straps are out of the way, you take that straw back." Taken aback, the soldier grabbed the bundles and returned them immediately.

McClellan was hailed as a savior by many when he reorganized the **Army of the Potomac** *after the disaster at Second Bull Run.*

Two soldiers of the *XII Corps'* *27th Indiana* were up to more honest pursuits as their command went into bivouac in a camp abandoned by the Confederates just three days earlier. Corporal Barton W. Mitchell and Sergeant John M. Bloss were lounging around when the former discovered a stuffed envelope lying in the grass. Opening it up, he found a most pleasant discovery, three cigars wrapped in a piece of paper. Though no doubt excited by their find, the two soldiers took the time to examine the cigars' wrapper only to marvel at what was to become the biggest discovery of the war. The sheet of paper was in fact Special Orders 191 signed by Lee's Adjutant General Colonel R.H. Chilton and contained the movements of the entire Rebel army.

The astute soldiers took the paper to their company captain, Peter Kop, who sent it on to the *27th's* skipper Silas Cosgrove. Cosgrove then gave it to Alpheus Williams and his aide Colonel Samuel E. Pittman. Fortunately for the Federals, Pittman, an acquaintance of Chilton, recognized the handwriting and verified the document as an original. Thus, the orders made their way into the hands of General McClellan just as he was receiving a group of prominent citizens. It was the greatest good fortune that any general could desperately hope for in wartime; the complete plans of the adversary. Even better that this stupendous discovery was the knowledge that his enemy was incautiously divided, practically inviting the Federal commander to beat him in detail. As Confederate staff officer Moxley Sorrel noted, "Had Lee whispered into the Federal General's ear his inmost plans, the latter could have asked for nothing more than the information brought to him on that fatal paper." If McClellan could only take advantage of his find, the Army of Northern Virginia could be totally crushed and the war brought a lot closer to a conclusion.

The jubilant commander informed Lincoln of his magnificent find at 2400 on 13 September:

> I have the whole rebel force in front of me, but am confident, and no time shall be lost. I have a difficult task, but with God's blessing will accomplish it. I think Lee has made a gross mistake, and will be punished for it. The army is in motion as rapidly as possible. I hope for great success if the plans of the rebels remain unchanged....I have all the plans of the rebels, and will catch them in their own trap if my men are equal to the emergency.

John Gibbon happened to stop in on Little Mac as he was beginning to plot Lee's demise. Though he did not show him the order in its entirety, McClellan displayed Chilton's signature and confidently stated, "Here is a paper with which if I cannot whip Bobbie Lee,' I shall be willing to go home....Tomorrow we will pitch into his centre and if you people will do two good hard days marching I will put Lee in a position he will find hard to get out of."

Thus McClellan came to possess Lee's orders along with the unparalleled opportunity to crush the Army of Northern Virginia. Still, the Yankees would have to move quickly; the orders were four days old and it was already one day past the moment when Jackson's forces were to be arrayed around Harpers Ferry. In drawing up his plans, McClellan opted to send Franklin's men through Crampton's Gap to come up in the rear of McLaws in order to save the garrison at Harpers Ferry if that was still possible. The rest of the army, with the *IX Corps* leading the

Allan Pinkerton, head of McClellan's secret service, continually overestimated Lee's strength and so contributed to McClellan's hesitation to commit all his forces at Antietam.

advance, was to pitch forward through Turner's Gap and interpose between Lee's divided units in order to gobble up the scattered detachments as they presented themselves. In a communique to Halleck, McClellan plainly stated the army would move out early the next day and make forced marches to save the beleaguered garrison at Harpers Ferry. But despite his enthusiasm, the general did not move as fast as would be expected under the circumstances. If he had faith in his men as he wrote in his dispatches, he would have had them on the road the night of the 13th rather than waiting till morning of the next day. Had the Federals marched that night they would have found the gaps unguarded and Lee's army invitingly open to destruction. By waiting until the morning of the 14th to get under way, they allowed the Rebels to take proper measures to safeguard themselves from an attack.

In fact, Little Mac was actually luckier than he had reason to believe. On 10 September, Lee divided his forces once more in response to rumors of a menacing Federal force coming down from Pennsylvania. Longstreet was dispatched with Lee to Hagerstown while Harvey Hill remained in Boonsboro, the sole defense of the Southern army should McClellan come suddenly bursting through South Mountain—but then Lee had no reason to expect him so soon. In fact, Lee had left the vital passes unguarded as a lure to bring the *Army of the Potomac* away from the security of Washington and force McClellan to extend his vulnerable supply line. He then hoped to bring the enemy to a pitched battle on terms favorable to the Confederates.

The Numbers Game

A major reason for McClellan's slowness during the campaign and his reluctance to engage Lee on 16 or 18 September was his firm belief that the Confederate army had many more men than it actually did. All his sources seemed to indicate that Lee had crossed the Potomac with at least 100,000 men, and on 9 September his cavalry chief reported Jackson had 80,000 and Longstreet 30,000, all near Frederick. The numbers all seemed reasonable, since McClellan had been told that Lee had defended Richmond with 200,000 men earlier in the summer, and it did not seem reasonable that the Confederate commander would have invaded Maryland with less that 120,000 men. These figures understandably gave McClellan reason to pause, since he had only about 85,000 men with which to conduct the campaign. In this light, his hesitancy to push Lee before or after the battle of Antietam can be better understood.

McClellan's inaccurate intelligence concerning Lee's strength came about because there was no organized CIA or G-2 such as more recent armies have had. In those days strength figures were all gathered second hand from enemy newspapers, deserters, or civilians who had seen troops march by. None of these were precise or accurate, and evaluation of conflicting sources was left to the general himself, not to a specialized department.

McClellan's difficulty in particular was aggravated by the fact that he relied extensively on contracted civilians to gather intelligence data—specifically Allan Pinkerton, later the founder of the Pinkerton Detective Agency. Pinkerton employed a system of spies but consistently overestimated Confederate strength. He also is known to have made simple computational errors, and had the bad practice of always accepting the higher number when any figures conflicted. Pinkerton's inflated numbers served only to give McClellan still more reason to believe that Lee had 100,000 men at Antietam, when the Confederates actually had barely 40,000.

CHAPTER VII

South Mountain

By 13 September, Lee was already concerned about the success of his Maryland campaign—Jackson's siege of Harpers Ferry was running behind schedule and McClellan was already approaching the Catoctin Mountain passes. The Union cavalry, now reinforced by infantry, was beginning to push Stuart's cavalry screen back. In addition, an officer sent by D.H. Hill to Turner's Gap reported seeing a large number of enemy campfires at Middletown. Lee became concerned about the security of the pass and directed Hill to secure it. Hill responded by posting two brigades (Colquitt's and Garland's) at Turner's Gap while the rest of his division moved to Boonsboro.

Lee then received a severe jolt on the night of 13-14 September when a Southern informer arrived with news that McClellan had found a copy of Lee's orders. The informer had been at McClellan's headquarters when the order was brought in, and realized the gravity of the situation; he risked his own life to pass through the Union and then Confederate pickets in order to inform Lee of the danger.

Lee now had to make a quick decision on how to respond to the crisis. Longstreet, who had not favored dividing the army in the first place, suggested falling back to Sharpsburg, where his wing would be able to flank any Federal force going to the aid of Harpers Ferry. Lee, however, decided to act otherwise—he would boldly support D.H. Hill's division at Turner's Gap and so give Jackson the additional time he needed to force Harpers Ferry to capitulate. McClellan was still McClellan, and there was

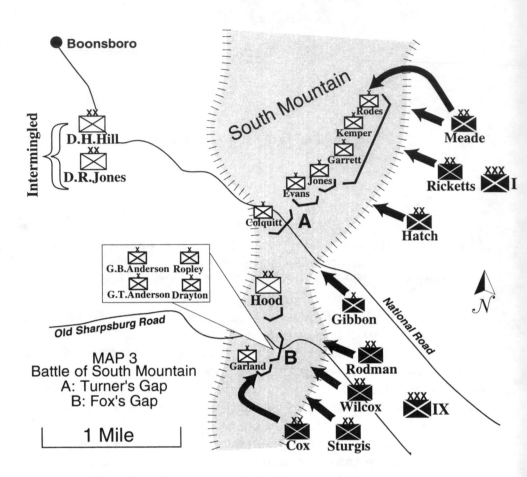

MAP 3
Battle of South Mountain
A: Turner's Gap
B: Fox's Gap

1 Mile

a strong chance the enemy would still not proceed aggressively, in spite of their recent good fortune.

Early on Sunday, 14 September, D.H. Hill rode to South Mountain to make his first real examination of the ground he was to defend. The terrain looked like a very awkward place to hold a battle, even for the defenders holding the mountain heights. Most of the slope consisted of heavily wooded clefts, ravines and hollows, all of which made even routine military formations difficult, if not impossible. Remarkedly, some farmers had managed to carve out a living on the tangled mountain side, and a few cultivated fields and lanes with wood and stone fences interspersed the mountain side.

Hill was made considerably anxious by the large amount of ground he was going to cover in the face of a Yankee advance. The most important feature of his position was the pass at Turner's Gap. The old National Road ran from Frederick over the Cacoctin Mountains through Middletown and through South Mountain before going on to Boonsboro and western Maryland. A mile to the south, the Old Sharpsburg Road climbed through another pass called Fox's Gap. Just before this small gorge, a farm road went off in a circuitous route before heading up an eminence just above Fox's Gap and continuing across the summit to link up with the Old National Road at Turner's Gap. To the north, the Old Hagerstown Road veered off from the National Road at the small town of Bolivar, swinging off to the north before rejoining it at Turner's Gap.

The Federal advance against Hill's position had begun at 0600, led by *Pleasonton's cavalry* and Colonel Eliakin *Scammon's brigade* of the *Kanawha Division* of the *IX Corps*, accompanied by division commander Brigadier General Jacob D. Cox, As the next column advanced, Cox met Colonel Augustus Moor of the *28th Ohio*, walking towards the Federal lines. Moor had been captured by the Confederate cavalry during a skirmish at Frederick, and had just been paroled. Moor honored the terms of his parole when he learned of Cox's plans to advance and did not tell Cox of the number of Confederate troops he faced. However, he did exclaim, "By God! Be careful!" which was enough warning for Cox.

Hill was even more disturbed that he saw only a few cavalry-

D.H. Hill was a superb division commander but had difficulty getting along with his peers and had to be transferred out of Lee's army. He was not a relative of A.P. Hill, but he was related to Stonewall Jackson by marriage.

men in the pass facing an imminent Yankee assault. He had expected to find Stuart and several regiments in position, but Stuart had moved most of his command to Crampton's Gap in order to protect the rear of McLaws' command on Maryland Heights. He had left behind only a token 200 men and an artillery battery under Colonel Thomas L. Rosser. Worse still, the shouts of Federal commanders and the movements of Union troops could be heard by the enemy now pressing up the mountain. Hill recognized the danger at once and readied his men to receive the assault. Colquitt's brigade of 1,100 men was placed in a good defensive position behind a farmer's stone wall along the National Road in order to hold Turner's Gap. Garland's brigade of 1,000 men was ordered to the right to hold the road that ran from Fox's Gap toward the Old National Road. Hill also sent for reinforcements from Boonsboro, the 4th Georgia and all of G.B. Anderson's brigade.

Now forewarned that the enemy was probably in force on the heights ahead of him, Cox called up *Moor's* old *brigade* under Colonel George Crook to follow Scammon as he proceeded up the Old Sharpsburg Road towards Fox's Gap. All in all, Cox was taking some 3,000 men on the advance. After sending a dispatch to his corps commander Jesse Reno, he turned his affairs to the battle at hand. Pleasonton's troopers were already skirmishing heavily with the enemy. Cox sent Scammon up the Sharpsburg Road about 0730, and half an hour later placed *Crook's brigade* to his left. Part of Crook's command was sent to the left along an old farm lane from the Old Sharpsburg Road with orders to find and turn the Confederate right. The flanking force advanced with bayonets fixed and often had to move single file through the tangled wood of laurel trees. The terrain caused some units to break apart and fight as clumps and individuals against the Confederate skirmish line. By 0900 Crook's men reached a pasture in front of Garland's prepared line. A heavy fire fight ensued, and the first Federal charge met a hammering storm of grape and canister from several well placed Confederate cannons.

As Scammon and Crook engaged the main portion of Hill's line, the *11th* and *23rd Ohio* were sent to flank the Confederate left. Their goal was to reach higher ground that would enable them to achieve a plunging fire on the enemy. Meanwhile the *23rd Ohio*, commanded by Lieutenant Colonel Rutherford B. Hayes (later President of the U.S.) had succeeded in flanking Garland's right rear.

Garland's brigade was being pressured at both ends of its line when Cox ordered another frontal assault on the stone wall that formed the Confederate center. At this crisis Garland was struck down by a fatal wound. At once the 12th North Carolina, located at the center of the line, began to waver, as much from the loss of Garland as from the ferocity of Cox's charge. The completion of the Federal attack then broke through the stone wall, and the Confederates' center disintegrated, with the flanks crumbling soon after.

Those who could fled down the western mountainside leaving some 200 of their fellow soldiers prisoners in the Yankee hands. Faced with the advancing Federals, Rosser's cavalry and his battery were also forced to fall back to a new position where his field pieces could still blast the enemy advancing up the lane.

View of Boonsboro, Maryland, with South Mountain and its gaps in the distance.

For a moment, it seemed that all Cox needed to do to sweep all the Confederates off South Mountain was to swing Scammon's and Crook's men north towards Colquitt's position at Turner's Gap, and roll up Hill's flank. By 1000 the victorious Yankees had reached a farm owned by Daniel Wise, located on the north side of the Old Sharpsburg Road. Hill had sent two guns there to try to block the oncoming enemy, and they unleashed a tremendously destructive fire on the Ohioans. To deter any attempt to rush the guns, Hill set up a line of staff officers, couriers, teamsters and cooks to present the appearance of a strong infantry line standing in support of the guns. Fortunately for the Confederates, the advancing Yankees were themselves exhausted from the climb and heavy fighting, and were also low on ammunition. Cox was bluffed, and decided to pull the troops back. If anything more was to be done, reinforcements would be needed. By 1100, the fighting ceased on this front except for occasional artillery firing, as both sides awaited reinforcements and the chance to renew the conflict.

Hill was also lucky that Cox did not press the attack more strenuously on Colquitt's brigade posted in Turner's Gap. It appears that Cox was content with putting up only a demonstration there while he threw most of his weight against Garland's command in Fox's Gap. To be certain, Colonel Colquitt was quite relieved that the enemy made no determined effort to advance, since his troops were a bit winded from being rushed so quickly into position.

From his vantage point atop South Mountain, Hill could see hordes of Union troops moving towards both Fox's and Turner's Gap, and he renewed his call for reinforcements from the remainder of his division. His orders from Lee had been to hold Boonsboro, but he now felt he had no choice but to abandon the town in order to be able to hold on to the South Mountain passes. He later wrote, "I do not remember ever to have experienced a feeling of greater loneliness. It seemed as though we were deserted by all the world and the rest of mankind."

While Hill waited frantically for his reinforcements to come up, Cox was also awaiting troops that had been promised for his support. Attacking *IX Corps* commander Jesse Reno had put his entire command in motion at 0800 when he heard about the strength of the enemy position on South Mountain. Brigadier General Orlando *Wilcox's division* was dispatched from Middletown at 1030 but managed to get lost on its way to the front when it was misdirected towards the wrong pass. He did not arrive on Cox's front until between 1300 and 1400. Wilcox was posted on Cox's right, and the two commands were further reinforced by the arrival of the two remaining divisions of the *IX Corps*, under Brigadiers Samuel P. Sturgis and Isaac Rodman. Oddly, there was no Union advance even when the entire corps reached the field. Wing commander Ambrose E. Burnside refused to attack until Hooker's *I Corps* came up.

To many soldiers on both sides, the sight of the Federal army on the move was incredibly awe inspiring. One soldier of the *125th Pennsylvania* recalled, "....through the shimmering heat waves we could see lines of infantry—which looked like ribbons of blue—being rushed to the front; the rays of the sun glinted from musket barrel and bayonet and polished brass cannon batteries....It was a panoramic moving picture." Even Harvey Hill was impressed by the spectacle as he watched this mighty host draw closer, calling it both "grand and sublime," invoking the phrase of a Hebrew poet, "Terrible as an army with banners."

While Burnside took his time marshaling his battalions, breathless and tired reinforcements came rushing to Hill's aid. The first to arrive was Brigadier General George B. Anderson's brigade, which had been called up that morning. He moved into position by 1400 along the line given up by Garland. His counterattack on Cox's line was repulsed, and this position of the Confederate line did not fully stabilize until Ripley's brigade came up at about 1500. Robert Rodes arrived at about the same time with his Alabama brigade and was directed to a knoll to the north of the National Road, where the Old Hagerstown Road rose up South Mountain.

During the afternoon a number of reinforcements also reached Hill's line from Longstreet's command near Hagerstown. Some units were exhausted from marching 17 miles in 9 hours, leaving a line of stragglers in their wake.

Hill directed the arriving brigades of Colonel George T. Anderson and Brigadier General Thomas F. Drayton to the right to fend off Reno's newly arrived corps. Ripley attempted to launch an assault, and directed his own, Anderson's and Drayton's brigades to move against Cox's men. Unfortunately, Ripley's brigade somehow managed to get lost, so leaving a hole in the rest of the line. The Federals promptly exploited it and put the Confederates under a vengeful fusillade that forced them back. Ripley's command was not the only Confederate unit to have difficulty moving into position. Kemper's and Garnett's brigades of Longstreet's command got lost on their way to reinforce Hill's left at Turner's Gap. By the time they made it through all the rough terrain and found their assigned location, their troops were much too exhausted to be very combat effective.

General Lee himself neared the battlefield at about 1500 while riding with the van of Longstreet's column. When he passed the valiant fighters of Hood's brigade, some shouted to have their commander returned to the post he had been forced to vacate because of his quarrel with Brigadier General Nathan Evans mentioned in Chapter I: "If there's any fighting to be done by the Texas brigade, Hood must command it." To this, Lee raised his

Major General Jesse Reno, killed at Fox's Gap while commanding IX Corps.

hat and called out, "You shall have him, Gentlemen." As the gallant Texan thus took to the field once more to lead his troops into battle, a wild shout went up from the Texans. One Confederate wrote, "the cheers deepened into a roar that drowned out the volley of a hundred cannons that were then vengefully thundering at the gap."

While Reno was conferring with Burnside at the foot of the mountain, General McClellan rode up to get an appraisal of the situation. The generals decided to renew the attack in three prongs—the *IX Corps* would move against Fox's Gap, most of the *I Corps* would follow the old Hagerstown Road against the left flank of the Confederate troops at Turner's Gap, and *Gibbon's brigade* of western troops would advance up the National Road against the right flank of the forces in Turner's Gap.

It was late afternoon by the time the Federal attack was renewed. However, before McClellan's attack was fully mounted, Hood's and D.R. Jones' newly arrived divisions pitched into Reno's men on the slope below Fox's Gap in a ferocious counterattack. As the fighting raged on near sunset,

General Reno rode forward to take a personal look at the situation. He was giving some personal instructions to the *51st Pennsylvania* when a sudden volley from Hood's troops cut him down. Reno was carried to the rear with a wound he knew was mortal. On the way he happened to see General Sturgis, and called out cheerfully, "Haloo, Sam, I'm dead." His tone was so natural, Sturgis thought he was making some sort of morbid joke and replied, "Oh no, General, not so bad as that I hope." "Yes, yes," lamented Reno, "I'm dead, good by."

Cox then took command of the *IX Corps*, and launched another furious offensive against the Rebel line, driving within half a mile of Turner's Gap. Oliver C. Bosbyshell of the *48th Pennsylvania* recalled of the furious musketry, "Shot was answered by shot, sixty rounds of ammunition per man was expended, and some of the boys were so excited they forgot to withdraw their ramrods...." However, the momentum was not enough; the Federals slowly ground to a halt even though they were so close to their goal, and the battle puttered out into the growing darkness of the night.

Meanwhile Hooker had at last launched his attack on Turner's Gap at about sunset. His preparations had been delayed by the length of time it took his long columns to come up on the few approach roads and form in the rolling fields at the base of the mountain. *Meade's* and *Hatch's divisions* led the way against the left of Hill's line.

As the men of the *21st New York* approached the enemy line, an old woman vainly attempted to warn the troops away. "Don't go up there," she cried waving her arms, "There are hundreds of them up there." It took some time to get men into proper formation with one brigade getting entirely lost in the thick woodland of the area. Once on the move, all that lay in their path was the 1000 man brigade of Rodes' Alabamians.

Brigadier General Truman Seymore of *Meade's division* was directed to move his brigade around the enemy left in order to flank Rodes' face. He was checked by the 6th Alabama under John B. Gordon. Though the Federals pressed Rodes with overwhelming odds, the Confederates managed to hold on desperately. To protect their cannons, Rebel gunners pulled them back to reload in safety before sending them back up to the front to fire once more. In this mighty contest, the color bearer of the *76th New York* rushed ahead of his regiment and shoved his flagpole into the ground, challenging his compatriots, "There, boys, come up to that," only to receive an enemy bullet in the skull. Finally, *Hatch's division*, now under Brigadier General Abner Doubleday after Hatch fell wounded, managed to turn the Confederate right at a cornfield near the summit.

All of a sudden, Rodes' command was flanked. Colonel B.B. Gayle of the 12th Alabama was caught up in the Federal advance on his regiment, but refused to surrender, crying out, "We are flanked, boys, but let us die in our tracks." He was soon shot down, his body riddled with bullets. Hooker had finally managed to crush the Rebel left, only to fall short of his goal as darkness fell forcing the fight to an uncertain conclusion. After nightfall the Rebels managed to unleash one last terrific volley, scattering some Federals. Their officers tried to calm their unnerved men, and called out, "Why, boys, what are you running for? We've beaten the enemy. Three cheers for victory!"

There was one more Federal attack launched that day—*Gibbon's western brigade* assault against Colquitt's line, which was located behind a strong defensive position in the gorge through which the National Road passed as it traveled over South Mountain. Some of the Confederates were fortunate enough to find protection behind a stone wall running to the south from the road. After receiving his orders to move out, Gibbon placed his two regiments, the *19th Indiana* and the *7th Wisconsin*, in double columns with the rest of the brigade coming up in support. After some annoying picket fire, the troops were torn by shell and canister as they continued their march; seven unfortunate men were cruelly taken out by one blast. The Black Hats fired away defiantly at the Confederate line as the *7th Wisconsin* attempted to flank the enemy, only to receive an enfilading fire itself from a detachment of Southerners concealed in some woods. After throwing in the rest of his men, Gibbon advanced his line forward once more, driving the Confederates from the wall back to their main line. As the Federals pressed against Colquitt's command at Turner's Gap, the Rebels could be heard taunting their foe, "O, you damned Yanks, we gave you hell again at Bull Run!"

Union artillery moving into position at the battle of South Mountain.

The Black Hats responded in kind and cried out, "Never mind, Johnny, its not McDowell after you now. Little Mac and Johnny Gibbon are after you now." The two forces slugged away into the coming night; when they could not see their targets anymore through the darkness, men aimed at the flash of firing guns.

Thus ended the battle of Turner's Gap. The Confederates suffered harshly, losing around 2,300 men, while the Federals lost some 1,800. McClellan wrote to Halleck, "After a very serious engagement, the corps of Hooker and Reno have carried the heights commanding the Hagerstown Road. The troops behaved magnificently....It has been a glorious victory." In actuality, McClellan did not have much reason for such optimism. Hill's masterful defense upon South Mountain against huge numbers of Federals had managed to impede McClellan's plans to crush Lee's army while it was still divided. In effect, Harvey Hill had brought his commander a present he desperately needed, time to capture Harpers Ferry and reunite his divided command.

While Burnside's wing fought at Turner's and Fox's Gap, William B. Franklin took on what promised to be a far easier contest at Crampton's Gap, five miles to the south. Franklin had been ordered to try to relieve Harpers Ferry, and indeed might have done so had he acted more decisively.

Fortunately for the Confederates the Federals of the *VI Corps* were moving with a slowness that belied the importance of reaching Harpers Ferry before it could fall into enemy hands. Though Franklin had taken to the road around 0600, he had stopped at the town of Jefferson to wait for Darius *Couch's division* which had mysteriously disappeared from the vicinity. After it was located Franklin resumed his march and reached the town of Burkittsville before Crampton's Gap at around 1200, only to find 1000 Confederate troops entrenched defiantly behind a stone wall at the base of the mountain.

It took some three hours to get the attack going and even then the Yankees made things more difficult than they needed to be. While Franklin could be a tough fighter at times he was certainly not the most imaginative officer in the Union army. The Confederate detachment before him so occupied his attention, he ignored the possibility of using his overpowering numbers, 12,300 men, to easily outflank his enemy by moving through the Brownsville Gap to the south. Union commanders merely planned for a full frontal assault.

The only Confederate troops initially holding the Gap were about 300 cavalrymen and two batteries under the command of Colonel Thomas Munford. More cavalry might have been available, but Stuart, who had just abandoned Turner's Gap, had moved on to Harpers Ferry in order to aid Jackson's troops there. Munford was supported by a few infantrymen from Malone's Virginia brigade; the bulk of this brigade, plus Semmes' Georgia brigade had earlier been sent by McLaws to guard Brownsville Gap, two miles south of Crampton's, and protect the rear of the troops on Maryland Heights that were not operating against Harpers Ferry. As soon as he heard that a large column of Federal troops was moving against Crampton's Gap, he sent Howell Cobb's Georgia brigade to Rosser's aid.

With Major General Henry W. *Slocum's division* on the right and Major General William F. *Smith's division* on the left, the Federals advanced against the comparatively tiny line of Munford and Mahone, who were anxiously awaiting reinforcements from Cobb's brigade. *Slocum's division* bore the brunt of the attack, forming up in line and firing away at the enemy 300 yards away from behind a rail fence. Eventually, the Yankees, tired of the fight, decided to break it up with an all out attack. All of a sudden the Bluecoats silenced their rifles and the shout of "Charge" went up. The Confederate position at the wall was easily overwhelmed and crushed; those who were not captured made a hasty retreat for the summit. As the Federals swept up the ridge, their ascent was slowed as the Rebels peppered the advancing line with well placed shots from behind trees and boulders. Of the carnage and debris from the battle lying before their advance, one Federal recalled:

> Their dead strewed our path, and great care was required, as we passed along the road, to avoid treading upon the lifeless remains which lay thickly upon the ground. On every side the evidence of the fearful conflict multiplied. Trees were literally cut to pieces by shells and bullets; a continual procession of rebel wounded and prisoners lined the roadsides, while knapsacks, guns, canteens, and haversacks were scattered in great confusion.

Munford's men withdrew slowly and with heavy losses to the top of the crest, where they were gladly reinforced by Semmes' and Cobb's newly arrived brigades. These troops, though, were unable to stop the enormous numbers of advancing Yankees. Soon McLaws himself approached the scene with still more reinforcements from Kershaw's and Barksdale's brigades. He had been assured earlier by Jeb Stuart that the fighting in the gap was just a cavalry action, but had a bad feeling about it and moved most of his division up to support Munford. When he neared the pass, he found utter mayhem, with infantry, cavalry and wagons all thronged in retreat. Howell Cobb rushed up to warn him and his staff, "Dismount, gentlemen, dismount, if your lives are dear to you! The enemy is within fifty yards of us. I am expecting their attack every moment." McLaws managed to extricate most of his men, but not without the loss of 400 men

The Confederate retreat from South Mountain.

from 17 different units, including three flags—the largest single such loss in Lee's army up to that point in the war.

Undaunted by the desperateness of the situation, McLaws gathered up what troops he could and threw up a thin defensive line across Pleasant Valley; most of the infantry formed around Brownsville, while the cavalry withdrew to Rohrersville. The sight of these troops was enough for Franklin, who evidently believed that he was confronted by a larger Confederate force. He was also apprehensive about the possibility of the main body of Lee's army striking his right or rear if he pushed ahead too far. As a result, he decided to halt for the night. The *VI Corps* had lost 545 men that day and had inflicted an approximately equal number of casualties on the Confederates.

Even McClellan realized that the road to Harpers Ferry could now be easily opened. At 0100 on 15 September, the commander directed Franklin to advance via Rohrersville, seize Pleasant Valley, and hurry to Miles' relief. Had he moved promptly at dawn, Franklin might well have saved Harpers Ferry, which was only six miles away. Instead, he was daunted by McLaws' show of force, and responded to McClellan at 0850 that he believed Harpers Ferry had already surrendered, since he heard no more firing from that quarter.

There is no doubt that McClellan's delay in ordering his

115

troops to move after the discovery of Lee's lost order, and also Franklin's hesitation at Crampton's Gap, spoiled the North's golden opportunity to crush Lee's army and save the Harpers Ferry garrison. Even so, the battles on South Mountain at Fox's, Turner's and Crampton's Gaps on 14 September were all closely fought as the Confederates were strained to the maximum and barely managed to hold on with the aid of their bravado and last minute reinforcements. The Union troops carried the field at all three engagements, but found themselves unable to reap the benefit of their victories because of the hesitation of their commanders.

Daniel Harvey Hill (1821-1889)

South Carolinian Daniel Harvey Hill embarked on a short military career after graduating from West Point in 1842, only to take up an unglorified post as teacher in a military school in North Carolina. He returned to the military to fight for the Confederacy, and led the 1st North Carolina Regiment in one of the South's first major victories at Big Bethel. Promoted to the rank of major general, Hill served under Joseph E. Johnston and later Robert E. Lee in the Peninsula campaign, where his troops met a bloody repulse in an attempt to storm Federal positions at Malvern Hill.

During the Antietam campaign, Hill held out against incredible odds battling the Union *I* and *XII Corps* to a standstill at South Mountain with his lone division, thus buying precious time for Lee's army to reunite and make a stand near Sharpsburg. Despite his heavy losses there, he also fought well at the Bloody Lane at Antietam.

Hill's cantankerous nature caused him to be separated from the Army of Northern Virginia, and he was assigned to the Department of North Carolina after Antietam. Even so, he won promotion to lieutenant general and was sent west to lead a corps under Braxton Bragg at Chickamauga. His criticism of Bragg won him not only the lasting enmity of that general, but of Bragg's good friend Jefferson Davis as well. After being removed from command as a result of charges brought against him by Bragg, Hill managed to return to command to see some service at Petersburg and in North Carolina with Joseph E. Johnston.

The conclusion of the war allowed Hill to return to more academic pursuits. He wrote on the great conflict and also became president of the University of Arkansas. Hill was brother-in-law to his illustrious comrade, Stonewall Jackson.

Sharpsburg

The town of Sharpsburg was founded in 1763 by Colonel Joseph Chapline, who had owned a large amount of land in the vicinity since 1753. It was named after the proprietary governor of Maryland, Joseph Sharpe. The town consisted initially of only four houses, the sturdiest of which was a combination blockhouse and Indian trading post. By the time of the battle in 1862 (when the town was 99 years old), some 1,300 residents lived in Sharpsburg and its many nearby farms. Most were tradesmen or farmers with solid German names such as Rohrbach, Mumma, Otto and Poffenberger. Some were workers on the Chesapeake and Ohio canal, or the Antietam Iron Works, located at the mouth of the creek. Most were pro-Union, like many of their neighbors in western Maryland, though a few favored the South. When the battle began, almost all local residents fled or took shelter in their basements, not to reappear until the morning of the 19th. Almost every building in the village was damaged by artillery fire on the 16th and 17th. The most seriously damaged of all the local farms was that of Samuel Mumma, whose house was deliberately burned at the orders of Confederate General Ripley so that Union sharpshooters would not use it as a post. All the other farms suffered heavy crop and fence damage, and also were used as hospitals. The town today retains all its rural character, and is refreshing to visit, since it is not overgrown with motels and fast food franchises. It consists of one long Main Street with a number of small cross streets, and still has many battle era buildings. Its principal church, St. Paul's Episcopal, was so damaged that it had to be razed and replaced in 1871. The famous Dunker Church near the West Woods was destroyed by a storm in 1921, and was rebuilt in 1962. Many of the key farmhouses retain their wartime appearance, including D.R. Miller's, Roulette's, Piper's, Pry's (McClellan's headquarters), and the Otto and Sherrick houses.

CHAPTER VIII

Sharpsburg

On the night of 14 September Lee was relieved to know that D.H. Hill's valiant defense of the South Mountain gaps had saved the entire Confederate army from piecemeal destruction at the hands of an unexpectedly aggressive Union army. Even so, he knew in his heart that the entire nature of the campaign had been changed, and the army was still in dire jeopardy. D.H. Hill was directed to pull back his bloodied troops and their supports to Sharpsburg, where they would be joined by the rest of Longstreet's command; from there they could withdraw in safety to Virginia if the enemy did not press too closely. Because of Franklin's penetration of Pleasant Valley, Lee directed McLaws to make preparations to withdraw to Virginia any way he could, regardless of what was happening at Harpers Ferry.

Lee's spirits were raised somewhat when he received a message from Jackson that Harpers Ferry would possibly capitulate the next day. If Harpers Ferry could be taken, something positive could be garnered from the campaign. All he needed to do was to occupy McClellan for another day. This he decided to do by forming a defensive perimeter behind Antietam Creek. New orders went out to McLaws to march north to Sharpsburg along the River Road; he should cross the Potomac only if really necessary. Longstreet and D.H. Hill would move for the moment to Keedysville, a village about halfway between Sharpsburg and Boonsboro, in order to slow down McClellan if he pushed his advance. They would then fall back behind Antietam Creek once McLaws' march was secured.

The whitewashed walls of the Dunker Church made the building stand out noticeably against the background of the West Woods. The church was rebuilt after being destroyed by a storm in 1921.

That night Lee's divisions made an as-yet rare night march. D.H. Hill and Longstreet managed to disengage from South Mountain without enemy detection and headed for Keedysville with their wagons in advance. (It was at this point that a number of Longstreet's wagons were captured by Grimes Davis' Union cavalry as they fled from Harpers Ferry—see sidebar). Davis' sudden inclusion and uncertainty about the situation at Harpers Ferry persuaded Lee to march his troops past Keedysville to Sharpsville. McLaws was sent his third set of orders to cross to Harpers Ferry if the town had surrendered, in order to best escape Franklin's advance.

The area around Sharpsburg yielded a fine defensive position for the Confederate army that precluded the need for building trenches and extensive breastworks. A turnpike ran due south from Hagerstown and followed a low ridge line as it approached Sharpsburg. Along the rise was a large patch of woods bordering the western side of the Hagerstown turnpike: the West Woods.

A small white structure that might be mistaken for a one room schoolhouse stood before the southern portion of this woods. This austere building belonged to a pacifistic German Christian sect called the Dunkers. Across from the unpretentious house of worship was an intersection in the Hagerstown Turnpike where the Smoketown Road turned off to run northeast through a plot of trees: the East Woods. Overlooking this ground to the northwest was a prominence called Nicodemus Hill. Interspersed throughout the area were a series of pleasant farms and cultivated fields belonging to families of German stock that had settled in the area. To the east, the Antietam Creek meandered south, cutting through the Maryland countryside as it approached the waters of the Potomac. There were three immediate crossings over the stream available: the Upper Bridge with a road leading to the town of Keedysville, the Middle Bridge maintaining the Boonsboro Road, and the Rohrbach Bridge that connected the road running from Sharpsburg to Rohrersville.

The countryside was rolling and offered plenty of protection behind rises, trees, limestone outcroppings, and farmers' fences. However, the ground also came with a price that could prove to be disastrous. The Potomac snaked just a few miles behind Sharpsburg, a mighty obstacle to any withdrawal. Since the only nearby crossing was at Boteler's Ford near Shepardstown, Lee readily and knowingly risked ultimate disaster in choosing to make a stand at Sharpsburg. If he should at any time be forced to retreat, a quick and orderly passage across the Potomac would be close to impossible.

In setting up his army's position, Lee had part of his force head to the north of the town; east of the Hagerstown Road Hood took the left flank just above the Dunker Church, followed by Hill's division, and Evan's Independent Brigade, with D.R. Jones' division extended along a line south of Sharpsburg. Since the Antietam was neither wide enough nor deep enough to

A section of the Sunken Road (Bloody Lane) after the war.

provide a natural defensible barrier, Lee chose to contest a Federal crossing of the stream only at the Rohrbach Bridge. In deciding to make his stand, Lee only had some 15,000 men immediately at hand against what he knew to be a largely superior Union force.

The Confederate general believed McClellan would stall just long enough for Jackson to arrive with the rest of the Confederate army. Even then, the odds would be at least two to one against Lee, but the men of the Army of Northern Virginia had faced an overwhelmingly superior force before only to humiliatingly best their foe. It was indeed a bold decision for Lee to stay and fight, a decision reached only through utter contempt of McClellan's fighting ability.

As the sun rose on South Mountain on the 15th, the Federals were exposed to sights of frightful carnage from the contest of the previous day. However, most men were heartened by their first substantial victory in quite a while. As one soldier noted in viewing the debris left behind in the wake of the Confederate retreat, "The summit and westerly side of the mountain, down which the Confederates fled, gave proof of the extreme panic which seized them at the close of the battle; guns, blankets, and equipments were scattered about the ground in great profusion.

O.J. Smith's barn, about 1 1/2 miles northeast of the Bloody Lane, housed wounded of II Corps after the battle. Every barn for some distance was pressed into use as a hospital.

It was encouraging to our soldiers to witness these indications of the retreat of their valiant old enemy of the Peninsula, who, less than two months before had put them in the same awkward plight, and caused them untold hardships."

Upon learning of the Battle of South Mountain, Lincoln sent a dispatch to his general to provide encouragement, "God bless you, and all with you. Destroy the rebel army if possible." Ultimate victory appeared at hand, Lee was on the run, his army had not yet united and there was still time to bag him if the Federals could just move fast enough.

Despite the necessity of moving quickly to catch the fleeing enemy while still without Jackson, McClellan did not attempt to drive his troops with all due haste. It was not until 1500 that the first Union troops of *Sumner's corps* arrived on the field near Sharpsburg. As McClellan joined his men there, he and Fitz-John Porter looked over the enemy defenses and received some shots from the Confederate artillery across the stream. McClellan had no way of perceiving how many Confederates lurked behind the opposing ridges, and honestly believed that Lee had more men on hand than he ever could have. Rather than gambling to bring the enemy army before him to battle while it was still weak, Little Mac stubbornly decided to plan safely, and wait until the rest of his troops came up before deciding on any aggressive action. An attack could always wait until the next day. By the end of the 15th, most of the Federal army had gone into camp at Keedysville to the northeast of Sharpsburg.

As dawn broke on the 16th, the monotonous deep thud of cannon fire opened up across the countryside as gun commanders from both sides duelled with each other, seeking out their targets. Frederick L. Hitchcock of the *132nd Pennsylvania* watched the artillery contest, writing later:

> The ball opened soon after daylight by a rebel battery, about three quarters of a mile away, attempting to shell our lines. Our division was massed under the shelter of a hill. One of our batteries of 12-pounder brass guns promptly replied, and a beautiful artillery duel ensued, the first I had ever witnessed at close quarters. Many of us had crept up to the brow of the hill to see the "fun," though we were warned that we were courting danger in so doing. We could see columns of rebel infantry marching in ranks of four, just as we marched "en route," and as shell after shell of our guns would explode among them and scatter and kill we would cheer. We were enjoying ourselves hugely until presently some additional puffs of smoke appeared from their side, followed immediately by a series of very ugly hissing, and whizzing sounds, and the dropping of shell amongst our troops which changed the whole aspect of things. Our merriment and cheering were replaced by a scurrying to cover, with blanched faces on some and an ominous, thoughtful quiet overall.

As a Confederate battery fired away a young newly commissioned lieutenant, excited by the fire, rode up amongst the gunners shouting, "Let 'em have it." Irritated by this youthful show of exuberance, the cannoneers gave the officer icy stares, silently telling him they would "let him have it" if he did not get out of their way.

Lee assumed his bold bluff was paying off when he saw McClellan's troops slowly march up and form into position on the west side of Antietam Creek. At noon he received the news

McClellan spent most of the battle at his headquarters at the Pry house, located on the east bank of Antietam Creek, one mile east of the Bloody Lane.

he had been longing to hear—Harpers Ferry had surrendered, and Jackson's brigades (including McLaws' endangered division) were on their way to Sharpsburg, less A.P. Hill's division, which was staying behind to recover from its battle losses, secure captured supplies, and parole enemy prisoners.

Any reasonable general would have rejoiced at the capture of Harpers Ferry and withdrawn the army across the Potomac from Sharpsburg. Lee, though, was not about to surrender the initiative he had held ever since the beginning of the Seven Days battles, no matter how weakened his troops were by marching, straggling, and fighting. It is certain that he felt in his heart that he would out general McClellan; he was sure that the Union general would not commit all his forces at once, and would probably telegraph his punches, which could be readily defeated by strong defensive terrain and limited counterattacks. But Lee's decision to remain and fight was also greatly influenced by another belief his admirers are seldom ready to admit—the belief that his valiant troops were somehow invincible, definitely better than their opponents. It was a not unfounded trust, one drawn on previous battle successes, but one that would lead to terrible losses here on the banks of the Antietam as it would later on Cemetery Ridge at Gettysburg—and had already on the slopes of Malvern Hill.

Two Uncanny Cannon Shots

Confederate General James Longstreet was fond of recalling two extraordinary cannon shots he personally witnessed during the war. The first occurred at Yorktown, where he saw a Southern gun drop a shot right on the table of a Federal engineer who was drawing up a map. Longstreet's second favorite shot came during the battle of Antietam. It seems that Harvey Hill was surveying the battle from a ridge that was under intermittent enemy artillery fire. Hill refused to dismount, though his comrades, Generals Lee and Longstreet, readily did so for fear of drawing enemy fire. Longstreet warned Hill, "If you insist on riding up there and drawing the fire, give us a little interval so that we may not be in the line of fire when they open on you." Sure enough, Captain Stephen H. Weed serving with the *5th New York Artillery* spotted the mounted officer and aimed one of his cannons at the easy target, firing off a shot. Longstreet noticed the flash and smoke emanating from the Yankee gun as it unloaded its deadly missile, and turned to Hill to say, "There is a shot for you." The shell was so accurately fired that, after hanging in the air for two or three seconds, it landed right in front of Hill's horse, cutting off both of the animal's forelegs. His mount fell upon its bloody stumps, and Hill found himself ignominiously stuck in the saddle, unable to free himself.

General Lee Loses His Temper

While engaged in supervising his forces during the immense conflagration at Sharpsburg, General Robert E. Lee stumbled upon one of his soldiers straggling from the ranks. Not only had the contemptible individual deserted his comrades in their hour of need, but he had also violated the orders prohibiting foraging as he was attempting to drag a pig he had killed back to camp. Lee was incensed by this shameful spectacle, and had the man arrested on the spot; he ordered him to be turned over to General Jackson to face immediate execution. Jackson received the unfortunate skulker in the thick of battle, and decided the man could hardly be killed when his lines were so outnumbered and so hard pressed. Instead of fulfilling Lee's order, Stonewall had the man armed with a musket and sent him forward to where the fighting was thickest. Though a straggler and a thief, the soldier gave a good account of himself, surviving the battle after displaying much gallantry. He thus escaped his death sentence, and became known as the man who lost his pig, but "saved his bacon."

CHAPTER IX

Opening Blows

Dawn on 16 September brought Lee another tense morning as he boldly faced the growing Federal army across Antietam Creek while anxiously awaiting the arrival of Stonewall Jackson's victorious troops from Harpers Ferry. He played his bluff well, and by actively employing his limited number of long range cannons managed to persuade McClellan's troops to remain as quiet as they had been on the previous day. Lee's patience paid off at noon when Generals Jackson and Walker rode up to report that their three divisions would soon be arriving. Their appearance almost doubled Lee's meager strength, and increased the morale of his other troops already on the field. Furthermore, it meant that McLaws, Dick Anderson, and A.P. Hill would not be far behind. Lee was greatly heartened to see Jackson's arrival, and further deepened his resolve to stay and fight. He sent Jackson's two divisions (Lawton's and J.R. Jones) to support Hood's command on the left of the army's line, and Walker was ordered to place his command behind the army's right before daylight the next morning (17 September).

McClellan had most of his army on the field by noon on 16 September and at length developed his plan of battle: he would send the *I, II,* and *XII Corps* against the Confederate left, while Burnside's *IX Corps* would take on the enemy right in the vicinity of Rohrbach's Bridge. Porter's *V Corps* would hold the middle and strike Lee's center at the right moment, and drive the Confederate army into the Potomac. Almost as an after-

Major General Joseph Hooker had been in command of **I** Corps *less than a week when he was wounded in the foot at Antietam. He would lead the* **Army of the Potomac** *to defeat at Chancellorsville eight months later.*

thought, he ordered Franklin's *VI Corps* to come up from Pleasant Valley and join the rest of the army.

McClellan's plan was sound, particularly given the fact that he so greatly outnumbered Lee's haggard command. All he had to do was to ensure that his three wings attacked in reasonable unison, so as to bear their weight on the Confederate line all at one time. The greatest weakness in his plan was the breakdown of his wing structure that he had employed throughout the campaign. Hooker's *I Corps* was stripped down from *Burnside's wing,* now on the army's left, to spearhead the attack on the right. This shift essentially left Burnside as a wing commander without a wing; he was personally affronted by the apparent devotion and continued to act as a wing commander nonetheless, leaving corps command to Brigadier General Jacob Cox, who had been a division commander until Reno's death at Fox's Gap two days earlier.

It is also unclear why McClellan chose for his two leading attacks to be launched by the troops that had been most heavily engaged at South Mountain, the *I* and *IX Corps*. Nor is it clear whether he expected to achieve more success on the left or on the right. His initial battle report to General Halleck ably conveys his confused thinking at the time:

> The design was to make the main attack upon the enemy's left—at least to create a diversion in favor of the main attack, with the hope of something more, by assailing the enemy's right-and, as soon as one or both of the flank movements were fully successful, to attack their center with any reserve I might have in hand.

The battle of Antietam may well be said to have begun at 1400 on 16 September when Major General Joseph Hooker led his *I Corps* from its camp at Keedysville and marched across the upper bridge over Antietam Creek to the Hagerstown Pike two miles north of Sharpsburg. The corps was led by *Meade's division* of *Pennsylvania Reserves*, which ran into a strong Confederate picket line towards dusk. The inconclusive fighting died off in the darkness, and the Federals withdrew to a bivouac on the Samuel Poffenberger farm near the North Woods. Hooker then prophetically informed his men, "We are through for tonight, gentlemen, but tomorrow we fight the battle that will decide the fate of the Republic."

This initial skirmish in actuality achieved nothing except to telegraph to Lee where the first Union assault would fall on the next day. In fact, Hooker would spend several restless hours fearing a Confederate counterattack in the dark against his isolated position; it was not until midnight that his supporting troops, Mansfield's *XII Corps*, came up and encamped a mile to the northwest. Strangely, Lee does not appear to have taken extra steps to strengthen his left, even though it was clear that the Federals were going to attack there in force. All he really did was to allow the men of Hood's two brigades, who had borne the brunt of the evening's skirmishing, to withdraw and cook a good hot meal, a pleasure they had not enjoyed for several days. Hood's withdrawal to the West Woods left Lawton's division in the East Woods as the troops closest to the enemy lines.

That night the soldiers on both sides sought an uneasy rest, and slept on their rifles, prepared to go to battle at a moment's notice. At first the men had to contend with the booming artillery, as cannoneers attempted to get their last shots of the day in on their foe. Vautier described the effect of the night's cannonade, "Every time a piece was discharged the flash of a gun illuminated the surroundings, producing an effect similar to sheet lightning; and when the other fellows sent their howling compliments back, the flash of their exploding shell fitfully lit up the ranks, and the broken particle went buzzing around in search of victims." As if to compound the discomfort of the anxious troops on the field, a chilling rain swept across the countryside during the night. Captain William Harries, of the *Iron Brigade*, recalled the freezing effect of the dampness, "I slept very little. The night was chilly, there seemed to be a cold sensation creeping up and down my spinal column. I could not have felt more cold in that region if a chunk of ice had been drawn up and down my back." The palpable tension between the opposing forces constantly burst out during the night as picket fire opened up the front lines. The apprehension also led to a great deal of confusion; in Burnside's command, two whole regiments fell into disorder after an unfortunate trooper from the *103rd New York* stumbled onto the regimental dog and then into a stack of muskets, setting off an alarm of a possible attack.

Dawn on 17 September 1862 was wet and musty, offering a low mist that obscured the fences of both sides. Hooker's plan of attack was quite simple—he would drive south along the Hagerstown Pike to high ground covered by the West Woods; his mile wide front would stretch from the Pike on the right to the East Woods, and would aim straight for the now famous Dunker Church, whose whitewashed walls were clearly visible to all against the greenery of the West Woods, once the mist lifted.

Hooker and Mansfield together had over twice as many men as the two divisions of Jackson's Corps that faced them in the West and East Woods. Jackson's old division, now led by D.J. Jones, occupied the West Woods for one-half mile west of the turnpike.

The Stonewall Brigade, now under the helm of Colonel A.J. Grigsby, and Jones' brigade led by Colonel Bradley T. Johnson, held the front with Taliaferro's brigade, under Colonel E.T.H.

Dead Confederate artillery horses from S.D. Lee's artillery battalion, which fought near the Dunker Church.

Warren, and Starke's brigade in support. Lawton, with Ewell's old division, was posted on Jones' right angling to the south towards the Smoketown Road, with Lawton's old brigade, now under Colonel Marcellus Douglas, extended east from the turnpike through the southern edge of the Miller cornfield. Brigadier Henry T. Hays' brigade, and Trimble's brigade, led by Colonel James A. Walker, set up before the East Woods on the Mumma farm. General Ripley's brigade from Harvey Hill's division was on the far left with his brigade to protect the flank and support Stuart's Horse Artillery under Major John Pelham on Nicodemus Hill. Most of the Confederate artillery strength was massed on the high ground before the Dunker Church where it could draw a good bead on the approaching Federals. All in all, the Confederate left presented a barrier of 7,700 men three-fourths of a mile in length, a mighty obstacle to any Federal advance.

As soon as the mist had cleared and enemy positions could be seen, the artillery on both sides opened up fiercely. Pelham's and

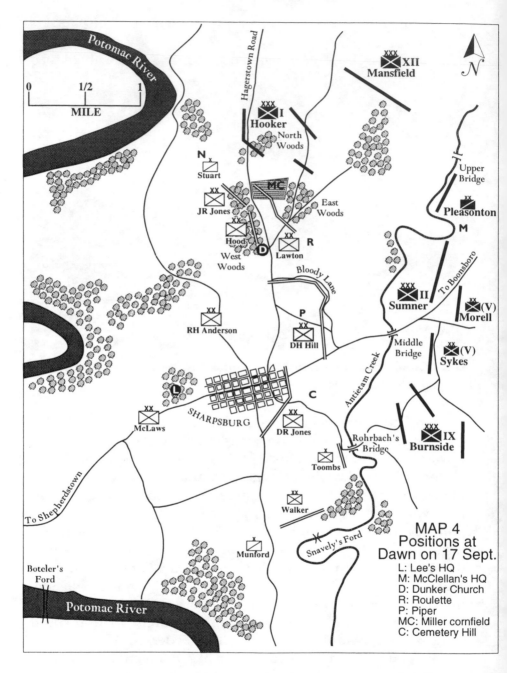

MAP 4
Positions at
Dawn on 17 Sept.
L: Lee's HQ
M: McClellan's HQ
D: Dunker Church
R: Roulette
P: Piper
MC: Miller cornfield
C: Cemetery Hill

Lee's guns hit all the Federals in range; Hooker's guns and the 20-pound Parrotts of McClellan's reserve artillery, located on heights across the creek, opened up in reply. The effectiveness of the Union cannons, and especially the range of the pieces placed east of the Antietam, would cause the Confederates to remember Antietam as the day they were subjected to "artillery hell." One shell struck a member of the 4th Georgia in his cover in the West Woods and sent a piece of his skull hurling into the ranks behind him. Another shell fell in the ranks of the 3rd North Carolina, killing and wounding 16 men all at once. After watching Pelham's Southern gunners tirelessly discharge barrage after barrage from Nicodemus Hill, a cannoneer of the *1st Rhode Island Artillery* wrote that their fire gave the hill an appearance of "...an active volcano belching forth flame." During the almost incessant shelling, a Pennsylvania battery had a good scare when a shell exploded near the muzzle of a gun and felled three men before lighting off the fuse just being loaded into a cannon. The Yankee holding the deadly missile acted quickly to save himself and those around him by painfully extinguishing the fuse with his bare hand.

By 0600, the *I Corps* of Joseph "Fighting Joe" Hooker was in motion against Jackson's line, thus inaugurating what was to become the bloodiest day in all of American History. *Ricketts' division* took the offensive into the East Woods and the Cornfield. Duryea led the advance by moving south towards D.R. Miller's cornfield through a heavy bombardment from Stuart's guns. Hooker noticed the sun glinting from the bayonets of some of Lawton's skirmishers in the Cornfield and prepared to assault the Confederate battle line behind them: "Instructions were immediately given for the assemblage of all my spare batteries, near at hand, of which I think there were five or six, to spring into battery to the right of this field, and to open up with canister at once. In the time I am writing every stalk in the Northern quarter and greater part of the field was cut as closely as could have been done with a knife, and the slain lay in rows precisely as they had stood in their ranks a few moments before. It was never my fortune to witness a more bloody, dismal battlefield. Those that escaped fled...as there was no resisting this torrent of death-dealing missives."

RALLYING BEHIND THE TURNPIKE FENCE.

Sketch of the fighting along the Hagerstown Pike near the Miller Cornfield.

When the torrential volleys of canister ceased, Duryea's men entered the sea of carnage and headed for their goal at the Dunker Church. Marcellus Douglass and his Georgia brigade were lying prostrate in the pasture to the south of the Cornfield, and awaited the approaching Union line. When he saw Federal bayonets poking up from the corn, Douglass advised his troops to pick out a row of stalks, aim closely at it, and fire when the order was finally given. As the blue line emerged from their cover, the Confederates let loose a mighty fusillade. All of a sudden there was a crackle, flash, and the acrid gray smoke from the ignited black powder covered the field. Now came the painful screams and moans of scores of Yankee wounded. Mauled but undaunted, the Federals redressed their lines and came on again, advancing over the bodies of fallen comrades to within 250 yards of the enemy. For a while, both lines blasted away at close range, each volley taking deadly effect. One soldier described the musketry as a "tremendous murdering fire." With men falling fast, those fortunate enough not to get hit had the good sense to forget romantic notions of bravado, and immediately scattered for cover.

Colonel James Walker advanced his brigade on Duryea's flank only to get hit in turn by enfilading fire from Federals within the East Woods. Since part of the 21st Georgia had failed to advance,

Walker approached them to urge them on, and was astonished to find most either dead or wounded. Duryea's command also suffered tremendously; roughly one-third of his men fell casualty and those still standing were exhausted and running low on ammunition. Faced with no other choice, Duryea ordered his men to fall back in retreat through the Cornfield.

When he saw his battle flag lying in the field under a pile of dead, J.C. Delancy of the *107th Pennsylvania* called to two of his comrades, Captain H.J. Sheafer and Private James Kennedy, to retrieve the colors in the face of an advancing Confederate line. All ran back to recover the flags as quickly as possible and speedily fled to the rear. Though the enemy troops behind the Yankees called for the Pennsylvanians to surrender, they did not fire.

After Duryea's men abandoned the field, his supports, Hartsuff and Christian, finally arrived to take up the attack. Both brigades were suffering from the loss of commanders, which hampered their effectiveness in combat. Harstuff's brigade advanced to find itself the target of Rebel cannoneers, but the first shots flew harmlessly over the heads of the advancing Federals. However, the aim of the guns quickly improved: explosions landed closer and closer to the brigade line. While taking stock of the ground before his command, Harstuff fell badly wounded from enemy shrapnel, and brigade command fell on Colonel Richard Coulter of the *11th Pennsylvania*. He eventually gained control of his new brigade, and followed Duryea's path through the Cornfield, where he received the same terrible fire as his predecessor. One Yankee observed: "Never did I see more rebels to fire at than that moment....It was magnificent and it was war." A member of the *13th Massachusetts* remembered, "The rebels fired first but we being so near, many of the balls went over our heads, but still many took effect. We halted and commenced firing immediately. Men now commenced to drop on all sides; I remember now, as I stood loading my gun, of looking up the line and seeing a man of *Company D* who I was quite intimate with throw up his hands and fall to the ground; one last struggle and that was all."

Lawton at last took to the offensive in order to drive the Yankees from this front. Hays' crack brigade, the Louisiana

A Union charge through the Miller Cornfield which saw very heavy casualties on both sides.

Tigers, with difficulty led the way joined by some of Douglass' Georgians. The Confederates pressed the new Union line back through the Cornfield. Once again both lines began firing away at close range. As soldiers in the *12th Massachusetts* fell, the rest of those standing continued to close in on the colors until the size of the unit was just that of a mere company. Both Northern and Southern batteries began to fire case shot, which tore huge holes in the ranks. The Confederates suffered horribly, with the Tigers taking 60 percent of the casualties. The Federals fared not much better. After taking heavy casualties, Coulter opted to retreat. Following the fight, the *12th Massachusetts* could only count 32 of the 345 men brought into action. Later in the day the rest of the command filtered in, and the regiment found it had actually lost 220 of its numbers.

As *Christian's brigade* was going in, the men were no doubt disgruntled from being forced to go to battle without having time to fill canteens with desperately needed water to wet their parched throats. Nor had they been allowed to cook breakfast to fill their empty stomachs, or even to shake the dirt off their uniforms. They moved forth in columns of division, with officers barking out orders for the brigade to move first to the right and then to the left. As Vautier recalled, "...we thought they were making a show of us for the benefit of the rebel artillery." Even so the movements were executed, "as quietly as on parade." A flustered Colonel Coulter rode up to Christian, and implored him, "For God's sake come help us out." The troops were put in motion once more; all the while ever present Confederate shells came screaming down upon the Federals, kicking dirt high up into the air. The historian of the *88th Pennsylvania* noted of the bombardment:

> The hideous noise made by those projectiles as they screamed through the air was indescribable; it appeared to the blue masses in that advancing host as if all the devils infernal had been incarnated and assembled on this horrible field, with the power to make the most terrible noises that were ever heard. At any rate, the appalling sound was enough to terrify the heart of the bravest and cause the blood to chill in one's veins.

Even Colonel Christian was completely terrorized by the cannon fire. Openly displaying the "white feather," he fled his command and left his men to face open combat on their own. Colonel Peter Lyle of the *90th Pennsylvania* then advanced to the edge of the woods and assumed Christian's position.

Meanwhile, the *Iron Brigade* was going into action on the Federal right. Gibbon advanced his troops in columns of division until he deployed them in line of battle before the North Woods, with the *6th Wisconsin* regiment taking the lead. Under heavy fire from the Confederate artillery, the brigade pushed south along the Hagerstown Turnpike and reached the Miller farm. The Rebel guns severely punished the *Iron Brigade* as Rufus Dawes of the *6th Wisconsin* recalled, "We had marched ten rods when whizz! bang! burst a shell over our heads; then another; then a percussion shell struck and exploded in the very center of the moving mass of men. It killed two and wounded 11. It tore off Captain David K. Noyes' foot and cut off both arms of a man in his company."

The *6th Wisconsin* saw what appeared to be an enemy force bearing down on its right, and opened fire, quickly dispatching the supposed threat. In fact, the "enemy" located on the flank of the regiment were two companies from the same unit deployed there to protect the flank, which now remained invitingly open. The Westerners would cruelly discover this error when Grig-

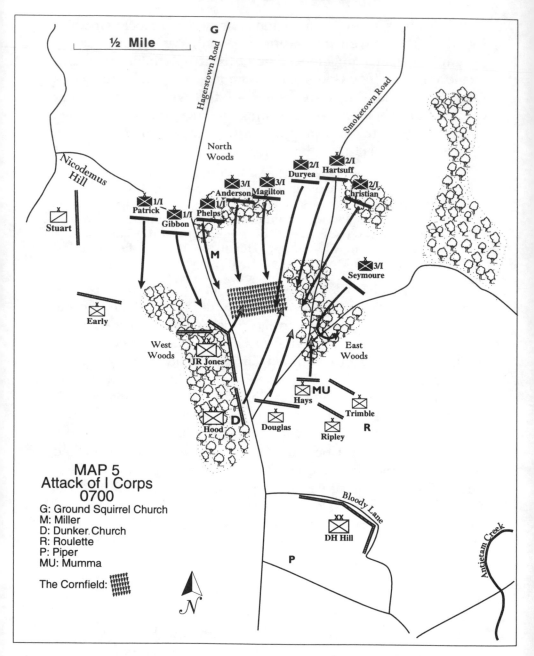

½ Mile

G: Ground Squirrel Church
M: Miller
D: Dunker Church
R: Roulette
P: Piper
MU: Mumma

The Cornfield:

MAP 5
Attack of I Corps
0700

sby's Virginians, who had been lying down before the West Woods for concealment and protection, rose up to throw a staggering volley into their line. Captain William E. Brown received a musket ball in the mouth while shouting orders to his men. Dawes recalled of the attack, "Men, I cannot say fell; they were knocked out of the ranks by the dozens."

Gibbon dispatched the *7th Wisconsin* and the *19th Indiana* to meet this attack by taking the right of the *6th Wisconsin* on the west side of the turnpike. *Patrick's brigade* also went in as support. Together, these reinforcements forced Grigsby's Virginians to slowly fall back into the West Woods. Of the advance Dawes recalled, "There was on the part of the men, great hysterical excitement, eagerness to go forward, and a reckless disregard for life, of everything but victory."

Now supported by the *2nd Wisconsin* on the left and also by *Phelps' brigade*, Gibbon renewed his offensive down the turnpike, only to run headlong into a massive destructive fire in the Cornfield from Lawton's Georgians who previously had met Duryea and Coulter. Dawes described the frantic scene, "Men and officers of the New York and Wisconsin are fused into a common mass, in the frantic struggle to shoot fast. Everybody tears cartridges, loads, passes guns, or shoots. Men are falling in their places or running back into the corn."

Starke brought up his and Taliaferro's brigades to reinforce the wavering Confederate lines. The new troops fell and lay down an unmerciful fire upon the Blackhats. The Westerners were forced to fall back into the cornfield, where they regrouped and counterattacked.

Starke now found himself in a desperate situation. The *7th Wisconsin* and *19th Indiana*, joined by *Patrick's brigade*, swept through the West Woods and hit Starke's Confederates in the left and rear while the rest of the *Iron Brigade* played havoc with their front. The Rebel brigades fell back, and Starke himself fell mortally wounded when struck three times by enemy bullets. As the Blackhats drew south toward the objective of the Dunker Church, the situation grew all the more serious for Jackson's line. If something was not done quickly, the entire Army of Northern Virginia would be in great peril. Dawes recalled, "The men are firing and loading in demonical fury and shouting and

Rare photograph of some members of the Texas Brigade during the summer of 1862.

laughing hysterically, and the whole field before us is lying with Rebels fleeing for life, into the woods. Great numbers of them are shot while climbing over the high post and rail fences along the turnpike. We push over the open fields halfway to the little church."

Fortunately, Jackson had a superb reserve at his command to throw at the oncoming Federals. It was one of the toughest units in the whole Army of Northern Virginia: Hood's division. The desperate call for help went out just as Hood's men were settling down to their first hot meal in days. They were cooking fistfuls of moistened flour on their ramrods to make a crude sort of bread. Hood's men stuffed down whatever could be eaten, and grabbed their rifles and ran into position. At 0700, the ghastly haunting cry of the Rebel yell came from the woods in front of the advancing Federals. All of a sudden, 2,300 howling mad Southerners of Colonel William T. Wofford's and Colonel Evander M. Law's brigades exploded from the West Woods, firing a withering volley that, in the words of Rufus Dawes, cut like a "scythe" through the Federal line. The Union soldiers not only

John B. Hood was perhaps Lee's most aggressive division commander. But this aggressiveness destroyed the Army of Tennessee in 1864. He was badly wounded in the arm at Gettysburg and lost a leg at Chickamauga.

stopped, but fled to the rear as quickly as possible over the mounting carnage of the day's fight, the enemy close on their heels. The Federal batteries did their best to check the oncoming horde, firing case shot at increasing short ranges.

Now Hooker found his own command in desperate peril. He at once committed his reserve, *Anderson's* and *Magilton's brigades* of *Meade's division*, and also sent for assistance from Mansfield's *XII Corps*. Meanwhile Wofford pressed against the Federal right under Gibbon, Phelps, and Patrick, and drove them back to the Cornfield to the west. One soldier in the *24th New York* called out to his men, shouting, "Hold on boys, I have a load in my musket that I want to fire before I go." As he turned to empty his gun, a load of grapeshot tore off his leg. The 4th Texas, 18th Georgia and the Hampton Legion wheeled to the left in the corn, and advanced on those of Gibbon's men who were rallying around *Battery B* at the northern edge of the Cornfield. When he saw the colors of the Hampton Legion fall after a third bearer was struck down, Major D.H. Dingle grabbed the flag and shouted, "Legion, follow your colors!" Lieutenant Colonel M.W. Gary of the Hampton Legion described what happened next in his official report: "The words had an inspiring effect, and the men rallied bravely under their flag, fighting desperately at every step. He bore the colors to the edge of the corn near the turnpike road, on our left, and, while bravely upholding them within 50 yards of the enemy and three Federal flags, was shot dead."

Battery B fired canister at a feverish pace and with deadly effect at the advance of the Confederate line. In his haste, one battery sergeant failed to get out of the way of his piece as it recoiled after firing and was crushed under a wheel. Each blast struck the rebels like a huge shotgun, tearing gaping holes in the formation. With every shot, torn caps, broken rifles, and ripped haversacks filled the air. In one instance, an arm was torn off its owner, and thrown into the air some thirty feet. Gibbon noted that one of the cannons was elevated too high, and rushed to the gun to turn the elevating screw down. The gunners fired double shots of canister as the Confederates drew closer, and eventually began to force them to fall back.

Meanwhile, on the northern edge of the Cornfield, the 1st Texas had advanced beyond any support and was rushing headlong into disaster. Robert Anderson and the *Third Brigade* of *Meade's division* were awaiting the Texans in opposition behind a low fence. As the unknowing Texans approached to close quarters, the Pennsylvanians fired a blaze of musketry that decimated the entire Confederate line. Those who survived the killing volleys fled for cover, leaving 186 out of 226 of their comrades behind. The 1st Texas had lost a total of 82 percent casualties in only a few minutes.

A Yankee who went out to grab the fallen regimental flag of the 1st Texas found the standard surrounded by 13 corpses.

The counterattack against Hooker's left in the East Woods and Cornfield was led by Law's 4th Alabama, 21st Georgia and 5th Texas, which were soon supported by Colquitt's, Garland's (under Colonel D.K. McRae), and Ripley's brigades from the Confederate center. During their advance, Law's troops saw a foolhardy Union officer urging on his troops from a white horse. All of a sudden, the unanimous call went up to "shoot the fool!" because he was such a clear target. Despite the many shots aimed at him, the officer remained unscathed.

The Confederates received a "lively cannonade and shelling when they entered the East Woods and engaged *Christian's brigade*." In the tremendous fire, a lieutenant in the 4th Alabama had his head taken off by a shell that spattered all those around him with brains, blood and gore. Still, the Confederates pressed on in a din so loud that officers were forced to communicate by hand gestures. Soon the Union brigade had to fall back, with the *90th Pennsylvania* protecting the rear. As the regiment retreated slowly, its color bearer walked backwards to ensure he would not receive an ignominious death from Rebel bullets in the back. *Magilton's brigade* of *Meade's division* came up to try to block the Confederate advance, only to melt away in the face of the furious assault of the Confederates.

On the Union left Gibbon was also forced to retire as he faced a new threat in his rear; Early's brigade had been ordered up by Jackson and was moving from Nicodemus Hill towards Gibbon's rear. The *Iron Brigade*, along with *Patrick's* and *Phelps' brigades*, found themselves in severe danger of being flanked. Though hard pressed, the Yankees made a hasty retreat to the Miller farm to set up a new defensive position.

The troops on both sides were exhausted and had suffered horribly in just an hour and a half of heavy fighting. Already the I Corps had lost almost a third of its numbers, some 2500 men. Hood could have spoken for the entire Confederate left when he replied to a questioner asking where his command was, saying, "dead on the field." Jones' division had 33 percent of its soldiers in butternut killed or wounded; the strength of Lawton's division was cut in half with his old brigade losing 554 men out of 1150 of those going into combat. The majority of officers had fallen from wounds. Hood's repulse cost the 4th and 5th Texas, and the 18th Georgia roughly half their men while the Hampton Legion and the aforementioned 1st Texas were completely decimated. While the fight was effectively over for Hooker's troops, Jackson's men had two more Federal corps to contend with.

At about 0730, Major General J.K.F. Mansfield arrived with the 7,200 men of the *XII Corps* to reinforce Hooker. Though Mansfield was a veteran officer, this was his first time commanding a unit this size. Most of his men were rookies as well; a good many had fought with Banks at Cedar Mountain, but at least half had never been in combat before. This being the case, Mansfield had his men approach the field in tight compact lines.

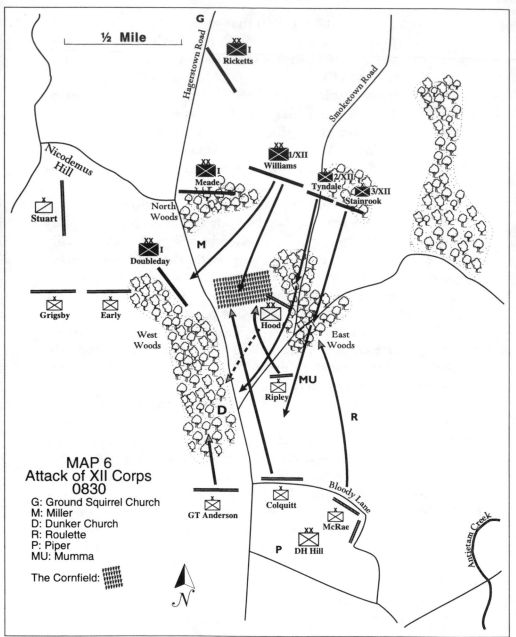

½ Mile

Hagerstown Road

G

XX I
Ricketts

Smoketown Road

Nicodemus
Hill

XX 1/XII
Williams

XX I
Meade

XX 2/XII
Tyndale

XX 3/XII
Stainrook

X
Stuart

North
Woods

M

XX I
Doubleday

XX
Hood

East
Woods

X
Grigsby

X
Early

West
Woods

MU

X
Ripley

R

D

MAP 6
Attack of XII Corps
0830
G: Ground Squirrel Church
M: Miller
D: Dunker Church
R: Roulette
P: Piper
MU: Mumma

The Cornfield:

X
GT Anderson

X
Colquitt

Bloody Lane

X
McRae

P

XX
DH Hill

Antietam Creek

N

Major General Joseph K. Mansfield, commander of XII Corps, *was mortally wounded just as his command was entering action.*

Though this maneuver ran the risk of incurring increased casualties from exploding shells, Mansfield believed it was essential to keep all the troops, especially the newer soldiers, under the watchful eyes of the officers to ensure that the weak of heart would not break out to the rear once in combat. To give confidence to the troops, the general shouted words of encouragement: "Ah, boys. We shall do a fine thing today. We have got them where we want them. They cannot escape by the skin of their teeth."

As the commander of the *XII Corps* approached the field, a flustered Hooker rode up to him requesting immediate assistance because the Rebels were breaking through his lines. The *XII Corps* approached the battle via the Smoketown Road, and entered the East Woods from the northeast. The depleted Rebels of Law's and Hill's detached brigades wisely fell back in the face of this new threat; one Confederate later said the soldiers' fighting instinct told them it was time to "git up and git." Many of Law's men were extremely low on ammunition; men with only two cartridges in their belts gave one to a comrade without any at all. Despite being low on ammunition and men, the Rebels gave the Yankees a tough time of it. As Mansfield's Federals drove through the wood they encountered irritating sniper fire from Rebels who dodged from tree to tree or from behind rocks, fallen branches and wood piles.

Mansfield tried his best to get his troops into position in the East Woods, despite the blanket of smoke covering the area and the fire from the woods and corn. When he saw the *10th Maine* firing into the Cornfield, Mansfield supposed they were accidently shooting at some of Hooker's men who were attempting to retreat to safety. He interposed himself between what he believed to be friendly forces, and rode before the Maine regiment calling out, "You are firing into your own men." The men argued the contrary, and persuaded the general to scrutinize the opposing force. He at once recognized his mistake and exclaimed, "Yes, Yes, you are right." Just then his mount collapsed after receiving a bullet from the enemy's guns. Another shot hit Mansfield in the chest and gave him a wound that was to prove mortal.

Command of the *XII Corps* devolved upon Alpheus Williams, who approached Hooker to get an appraisal on the situation that awaited him. While they were conversing, a shell struck Fighting Joe in the foot, and forced him to be carried from the field. Williams tried to rally his command in the confusion caused by

Mansfield's loss, only to meet a shattering fire from D.H. Hill's brigades which had just come up from the Confederate center.

Williams' new command had difficulty coping with the ferocity of Hill's attack. One soldier of the rookie *125th Pennsylvania* turned to his comrade next to him in order to discover why he was being so quiet. He was aghast to find his compatriot's skull pierced by a bullet with his brains oozing out. Eventually, Williams decided to divide his command in order to reinforce the depleted commands of Meade and Gibbon; he sent *Crawford's brigade* to join the lines near the Miller farm and ordered Gordon to take a position to the north of the Cornfield. When they saw Crawford's reinforcements, the remnants of the decimated *5th Pennsylvania Reserves* gave a few mighty cheers, calling out, "God bless you boys!" While it moved into position before the Cornfield, the *27th Indiana* lost its two most famous celebrities: Corporal Bloss and Sergeant Mitchell, the finders of Lee's lost order, were both wounded.

On their part, the Confederates had increasing difficulties in dealing with the new threat posed by the *XII Corps*. The Yankees defiantly held against a counterattack conducted by Hill's brigades. Garland's brigade, which had not yet recovered from the licking it took at South Mountain, fled from the field when it was flanked on the right.

The fighting still continued to sway back and forth across the Cornfield. The next division to enter the fray was that of General George S. Greene, son of the famous hero of the Revolutionary War, Nathanael Greene. Lieutenant Colonel Hector *Tyndale's Brigade* took Hill's troops in flank, and drove them from the field into the West Woods. The 6th Georgia lost 226 out of 250 men during the attack. A few members of the Peach State Regiment were attempting to make a stand before the oncoming blue lines, when one called out, "Let's get out of here!" A comrade who saw a number of Georgians remaining on the ground, replied, "We have a line, let them come." The soldier in favor of fleeing informed his misinformed friend that the men around him were all dead or wounded and proved his statement by shooting a nearby corpse, after which he said, "The sooner we get out of here the better."

A soldier of the *8th Ohio* came upon a Confederate who had

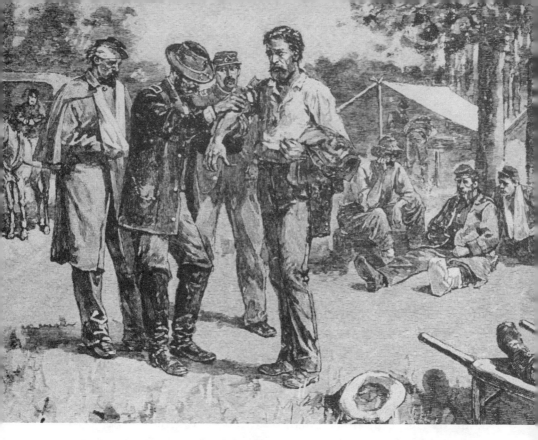

Civil War hospitals were primitive by any standard. The preferred way to treat a limb wound was amputation with or without anesthesia.

his face partially blown away but was still alive. He halted amidst the fighting long enough to give his unfortunate enemy a drink before he moved on. Greene's men pressed forward through the Cornfield, and moved to the south to take position on the plateau in front of the Dunker Church, which had been Hooker's objective for the day. A member of the *111th Pennsylvania* recalled the heavy fighting there:

> Without nervousness or haste the men monotonously loaded and discharged their pieces, and the officers walked back and forth shouting orders....Every moment men went down, some with wounds so slight that they were unheeded, some disabled for life, and some to rise no more. Throats were parched from thirst. Faces were blackened with smoke, lips smeared and cracked with powder from bitten cartridges. The guns were so hot that their brass bands were discolored. Belts sagged loosely over empty

Clara Barton did not hesitate to help in the field hospitals at Antie-tam right after the battle ended. She later helped mark the graves of the prisoners who died at Andersonville.

stomachs. Hands were swollen with the incessant use of the ramrod. Shoulders were lamed by the recoil of pieces.

Jacob E. Miller of the *111th Pennsylvania* was hit in the stomach and died while desperately trying to shove his exposed intestines back into his abdomen cut open by the hideous wound.

151

Somehow, the *125th Pennsylvania* from *Crawford's division* managed to get up into the West Woods right above the Dunker Church. The Federals were on the verge of seizing the day, if they could just take advantage of their good fortune. By 0900, the plucky soldiers from the Keystone State were seemingly assured of possible success because reinforcements were approaching the field.

Mansfield's Corps lost 1800 men in the fight against Lee's left, which had already been weakened by Hooker's initial assault. The Union foothold needed only to be exploited. McClellan, though, was not prepared to commit his corps in tandem and so reap maximum benefit from his numbers. Instead, he allowed his corps to be thrown into battle piecemeal, one at a time, destroying the absolute power their combined numbers could wield. In the end, Hooker and Mansfield essentially wound up fighting separate battles, and both were badly chewed up in the process. While McClellan failed to press attacks against the Confederate line in other areas, Lee shunted reinforcements to blunt his enemy's assaults before they could seriously threaten his position. He would use the same tactic to meet McClellan's next assault, by Sumner's *II Corps*.

Joseph Hooker (1814-1879)

Joseph Hooker was born in Hadley, Massachusetts, the son of a captain in the Revolutionary War. He attended the Hopkins Academy before going on to receive instruction in the art of warfare at the United States Military Academy (Class of 1837). He saw his first action in the Second Seminole War, and then made a name for himself in the campaigns of Generals Zachary Taylor and Winfield Scott in the Mexican American War, where he won all brevets from first lieutenant to lieutenant colonel. Hooker abandoned his military career and resigned his commission to take up farming. The Civil War caused him to return to active service, and he soon was given command of a division in Heintzelman's *III Corps*. During the Peninsula campaign, Hooker won his sobriquet "Fighting Joe" from a misinterpreted press dispatch which read "Fighting—Joe Hooker." The belligerent general lived up to his name at Second Manassas, Antietam, and Fredericksburg, as a corps and then wing commander. When Burnside was relieved from the command of the *Army of the Potomac*, Lincoln entrusted Hooker with the command of the army on 26 January despite the general's penchant for political opportunism; he basically told a reporter that a dictator should assume power in Washington to win the war. When he heard this, Lincoln sternly told Hooker, "Only those generals who gain successes can set up dictators. What I ask of you now is military success, and I will risk the dictatorship."

Whatever his aims might have been, Hooker's aspirations were shattered when he lost his nerve at the battle of Chancellorsville, suffering a tremendous defeat at the hands of Lee. Though relieved of command, his military career was rejuvenated when he was ordered to lead the *XI* and *XII Corps* in the West, and he won a great victory at Lookout Mountain. During the Atlanta Campaign, Hooker believed he was deprived of proper praise and commendations for his efforts, and asked to be relieved. He spent the rest of the war serving in various administrative posts.

Civil War historian Francis W. Palfrey probably best assessed Hooker when he wrote, "As an inferior, he planned badly and fought well; as chief, he planned well and fought badly."

The Union's Best: The Iron Brigade

Probably the toughest Federal brigade in the Civil War was a unit comprised solely of Westerners and called the *Iron Brigade* or the Black-hat Brigade. On 15 October, 1861, four regiments from western states, the *2nd, 6th, 7th Wisconsin*, and the *19th Indiana* were organized into a brigade under Brigadier General Rufus King. This unit was the only unit in the east comprised solely of men from the west. It was not until an officer from the Regular Army, North Carolinian John Gibbon, assumed control of the command that it acquired the distinctive characteristics that would make the brigade famous. While Gibbon put his raw troops through rigorous drill and ruled with iron discipline to turn them into real soldiers, he had the men wear a uniform different from that of the ordinary Federal fighting man. A long blue frock coat with a turned up light blue collar, light blue trousers and dressy white gaiters set them apart. Unlike the rest of the troops in the Union army, these westerners wore black hardee hats instead of the kepi, thus giving the unit one of its nicknames. Only the *7th Wisconsin* had seen previous combat when the brigade faced its first real fight at Groveton on 28 August 1862. Going into battle against the elite of the Confederacy, Jackson's Brigade, the Westerners performed their duties valiantly, losing 731 men (a 33 percent casualty loss) during a stand up fight.

While serving in *Hooker's corps* in Maryland, the brigade advanced unsupported against the Rebel center at South Mountain on 14 September, again giving a good account of themselves. McClellan reportedly saw the fight and asked Hooker what brigade was fighting on the heights before them. When told it was *Gibbon's Brigade* of Western men, the general commanding mused, "They must be made of iron." To this, Hooker claimed, "By the Eternal, they are iron! If you had seen them at Bull Run as I did, you would know them

to be iron." Though this story may be somewhat too fanciful to be true, the unit's tenacity in combat did win the Western unit the title of the *Iron Brigade* sometime after South Mountain or its next big fight, Antietam. The Blackhats were involved in Hooker's drive on Jackson's left on 17 September, and managed to press back the Confederates only to be forced to retreat by the countercharge of Hood's brigade. Despite this setback, the Westerners held together on the field, eventually repulsing the attack and holding the line after *Sedgwick's division* collapsed in the West Woods. To replenish the ranks of the *Iron Brigade* after the costly fights from Groveton to Antietam, Gibbon requested and got another Western regiment, the *24th Michigan*.

The *Iron Brigade* was not fiercely engaged at Fredericksburg and Chancellorsville. It faced its ultimate test in the greatest battle of the war, Gettysburg. When it entered action at McPherson's Ridge on the first day of the battle, some of the opposing Confederates were heard to exclaim, "Here are those damned black hatted fellers again." The Westerners managed to completely crush Brigadier General J.J. Archer's brigade and captured Archer himself, the first general officer ever captured from Lee's army. When the reinforced Confederates began to drive back the Federal right, the Brigade's reserve regiment under Colonel Rufus Dawes was committed to the fray. The *6th Wisconsin* assisted in the destruction of Brigadier General Joseph R. Davis' brigade, at the railroad cut. When finally forced to give ground, the Blackhats did so grudgingly, ensuring that the enemy paid for every step it took. The Westerners lost 1,200 of their number in the fight, a 63 percent casualty loss, the fourth highest toll of all Union brigades engaged in the battle.

The *Iron Brigade* served for the rest of the war until its conclusion at Appomattox, but lost its distinctive character after Gettysburg. Easterners, substitutes and conscripts were added to its rolls, men poorly received by the proud veterans who had seen and done so much together. Some of the old regiments were also either detached or consolidated, leaving the unit a mere shadow of its former glory. Still, the *Iron Brigade* had forged a legacy that would live forever after both Federals and Confederates had laid aside their arms in peace.

Hood's Texas Brigade

One of the most notorious fighting units in the Confederate Army was a brigade of Texans who first won fame under the command of Kentuckian John Bell Hood. The soldiers of the 1st, 2nd, 4th, and 5th Texas regiments absolutely refused to submit to the rigorous discipline of army training. Early in the war, the 1st Texas crossed the Potomac without orders to give the Federals in Washington, D.C., a good natured scare. Later joined by the 18th Georgia, the Hampton Legion and 3rd Arkansas, the brigade's first real engagement was at Eltham's Landing on the Peninsula where they routed Franklin's Yankees as they attempted to make a landing. The commander of the Confederate forces, Joseph E. Johnston had originally intended Hood's brigade to engage the enemy lightly. He complained to their commander, "General Hood, have you given an illustration of the Texas idea of feeling an enemy gently and then falling back? What would your Texans have done, Sir, if I ordered them to charge and drive back the enemy?" To which his subordinate replied, "I suppose, General, they would have driven them into the river, and tried to swim out and capture the gunboats." The Texans served in the Seven Days and at Second Bull Run, and won a fearsome reputation amongst the Yankees for their destructive charges. Hood's men won the battle of Gaines Mill with a desperate charge, and their counterattack across the cornfield at Antietam shattered Hooker's initial attack on the Confederate left.

After seeing service in the bloody campaigns of Fredericksburg, Chancellorsville and Gettysburg, the brigade headed west to join Bragg's Army of Tennessee only to find the Western ways of combat, which one soldier described as "stand-up and-fire or lie-down-and-shoot," ill suited them. At the great battle of the West, Chickamauga, the brigade displayed its patented style of charging as it participated in the fatal breakthrough of the *Army of the Cumberland*'s line. Upon returning to the Army of Northern Virginia, the depleted ranks of the Texans served with Lee until the final surrender at Appomattox. There, only some 600 of the 5,300 men that had served

with the brigade remained with the colors.

Clara Harlowe Barton

With the tremendous number of casualties resulting from the Civil War, leaders on both sides found themselves at a loss to provide proper care for wounded soldiers. Early in the conflict, a clerk in the Patent Office, Clara Barton, sought to meet this concern though she had no prior medical experience. Shocked by the lack of medical supplies and treatment available for the wounded on the field of battle and during their removal to hospitals, Barton inaugurated efforts to collect bandages and food for casualties by advertising in the newspaper the *Worcester Spy*. She committed herself to administer aid to the wounded and dying on the battlefield, and saw her first service during the Peninsula campaign.

At the battle of Antietam, Barton provided surgeons with desperately needed bandages and anesthetics. She tended to the wounded in the field, and was nearly a casualty herself when a bullet pierced her sleeve and killed the soldier she was attending. Though hardly acquainted

with the art of surgery, Barton later used a pocketknife at a soldier's request to remove a musket ball from his cheek and ease the pain of his wound.

Barton later expanded her duties to include the creation of a program to locate soldiers missing in action. Lincoln himself gave personal approval to the plan giving her the title of "General Correspondent of the Friends of Paroled Prisoners."

In this post, she interviewed freed prisoners to locate those soldiers not accounted for in battle who might be held in Southern jails. Her duties also included scouring newspapers to find names of lost troops in the lists of the discharged from hospitals, service and enemy prisons. Among her achievements was the preparation of a list of the Federal dead at the terrible prison at Andersonville.

Following the war, Barton continued to champion the cause of health care, her efforts culminating in the establishment of the American Red Cross.

Hospitals at Antietam

Throughout the terrible conflict, all available barns and houses were converted into hospitals as thou-

sands of wounded men were brought in from the lines to be attended by surgeons. Those who could be taken care of frequently faced amputation as the only means to care for their wounds.

The scene at the field hospital must have been a horror to behold. Doctors worked all day and were literally covered in blood as they went about their gruesome tasks. Limbs cut from patients were thrown into large piles or stacked like cordwood. Throughout the hospitals men could be heard wailing miserably over their fate and from their pain. Parched with thirst, they cried for water and those fortunate enough to receive a canteen quickly guzzled its contents. Others, thinking of loved ones at home, cried out, "Why was this war begun? Lord have mercy on my dear family. Must I die and never see them again?"

Many singular experiences forever lingered in the minds of the soldiers that witnessed them. John Vautier of the *88th Pennsylvania* recalled seeing comrade Lorenzo Wilson arrive in a field hospital with his leg almost entirely shot off except for a thin layer of skin holding it together. When asked about his condition he replied, "Boys, I've got it." In a Confederate hospital, a Southern gunner was brought in with a terrible leg wound. Though the attending surgeon wanted to amputate the limb, the cannoneer just pointed at a pistol at his side, saying defiantly, "You see that? It will not be taken off while I can pull a trigger." A rookie lieutenant of the *35th Massachusetts*, was treated for his wounds and when he learned he was to recover, exclaimed, "Oh isn't this rich! Only a month away from home and back there again with wounds; got in a big battle, and victory; and all the girls running after

me, and all the fellows envious." Captain James A. Martin, who had fled from the battlefield at Second Manassas, said after losing his leg at Antietam, "Now when I get back to Baltimore, if anybody says I was a coward, I can tell them that if they were willing to go where I was and stay as long as I did, they may call me a coward...." Alas he would not get the chance, as he died a month later in Frederick. Some Confederates were brought off the field by their enemy and found themselves in Union field hospitals. After one member of the *14th Indiana* had his leg removed, he was placed near a Rebel who was complaining that the Yankee doctors were ignoring the Southern wounded. The Hoosier morbidly recalled that when the soldier was placed on the amputating table "he was treated as the others when the time came." A member of the *9th Massachusetts* recalled this scene which occurred shortly after the battle,

A boy, about fourteen years old, was one day undergoing the process of amputation. He lay upon the stage, dressed in his rebel uniform, his face pale, and his large blue eyes gazing wonderingly around. His injured leg was stretched before the surgeons, who were carefully feeling it about the wound—a black break the size of a nickel cent. A sign from one of the doctors, and the instruments were brought and placed upon a large box that once contained army clothes, but now was partly filled with bandages besmeared with blood. The surgeon selected one of the instruments; a cloth was held before the nostrils of the white-faced boy; the surgeon began his work. The skin of the white leg was cut; in a little while the bone was off, the skin laid over, the bandages applied, and the whole bound carefully up. "It is fin- ished," said the doctor, as he wiped the blood off from his hands. He said truly; the work was finished. The boy was dead.

CHAPTER X

Advance of II Corps

At 0720 Major General E.V. Sumner was directed to move his *II Corps* to the support of the stalled Federal right wing. However, McClellan let him advance initially with only two of his three divisions (*Sedgwick's* and *French's*). McClellan was reluctant to dismiss all his tactical reserve on that wing and ordered *Richardson's division* to wait until it was relieved by *Morell's division* on the *V Corps*. Though Morell was encamped only a mile away, it would take him two hours to move up. As a result, Sumner was unable to advance into action with only 11,000 of his 15,400 men. The two *II Corps* divisions crossed the Antietam to the south of the northern bridge, and came onto the battlefield below Hooker's and Mansfield's positions.

As they approached the battle, the noise of firing sounded to one Yankee like a "rapid pouring of shot on a tin pan." Sumner had been told that *I* and *XI Corps* were holding their own against the enemy, and so was astonished to find the remnants of a mighty bloodfest cast about the field: muskets, soldiers' belongings, torn cartridge papers, and the slaughtered bodies of the dead and wounded of both sides. It appeared to him as though both sides had been driven off the field or completely annihilated, leaving the *II Corps* completely alone to face an unseen enemy.

Sumner concluded he was above the Union and Confederate positions, and decided to push off to the west, hoping to get on the Rebel flank and then wheel around to the south to roll up the rest of the enemy's line. Sedgwick was directed to take the lead

French's division *of II Corps advancing across the Roulette farm to attack the Sunken Lane at the height of the battle.*

with his brigades formed into three compact parallel lines about 60 to 70 yards apart, thereby packing a potentially powerful sledgehammer-like blow. Brigadier General Willis A. *Gorman's brigade* took the front, followed by Brigadier General Napoleon Jackson Tecumseh *Dana's brigade* and Brigadier General Oliver O. *Howard's brigade* of Philadelphians. This maneuver was not without risk; the stubby lines of *Sedgwick's division* were extremely vulnerable to flank attack, should they ever face the misfortune of becoming exposed. Sedgwick's only available support was *French's division*, which followed 20 minutes behind. However, French soon veered off course to the southwest, so losing sight of Sedgwick's column and leaving Sedgwick's flanks totally unsupported.

Sedgwick's division headed towards the West Woods just north of the Dunker Church. The men of the newer regiments bit their lips and gritted their teeth as their eyes gazed upon the terrible aftermath of battle and anticipated the grim fate that awaited them. Some just could not take the pressure and performed what veterans called the "cannon quick step," fleeing for the rear. They provided a welcome new target for Stuart's Horse Artillery, which had been giving the Federals trouble all day. Anthony W. McDermott of the *69th Pennsylvania* in *Howard's brigade* noted of the fire,

> The range of the Confederate artillery upon our lines was most accurate and destructive; every conceivable article of destruction that could be used was hurled against us—solid shot, shell, spherical case, grape and canister and judging by the tearing sound through the air, the general opinion was that railroad iron, nails, etc., were belched from the cannon's mouth, so that our men jocularly claim that whole blacksmith's shops were discharged from their guns against us.

Colonel Edward Hines noticed that the men of his *19th Massachusetts* regiment were becoming increasingly unnerved by the shelling, and put his troops through the manual of arms drill in full view of the Confederate guns. This unusual measure had the desired effect of restoring the men's confidence before they pushed on.

Sedgwick and Sumner rode up front with their men, willing to undergo whatever horror their men might experience. The only opposition to their advance was the thin battered commands of Jackson's wing, which seemed hardly able to put up much opposition in the face of Sedgwick's 5,400 bearing down on them. However, help was on the way from several sources. McLaws had finally arrived from Harpers Ferry at sunrise and was even now advancing to support the left. Since the Federal left flank and center were as yet not seriously engaged, Lee decided to dispatch George T. Anderson's brigade to Jackson at 0730. He also sent orders for General Walker's division, posted below the Rohrbach Bridge, to head north to join the fight on the left; he arrived there sometime around 0900. These three commands were moving up from the south, just as the unknowing Sumner was entering the West Woods. Meanwhile, the remaining Confederates fell back before the oncoming enemy, and set up a last ditch defense beyond the West Woods.

Jubal Early, who commanded the only organized force in the

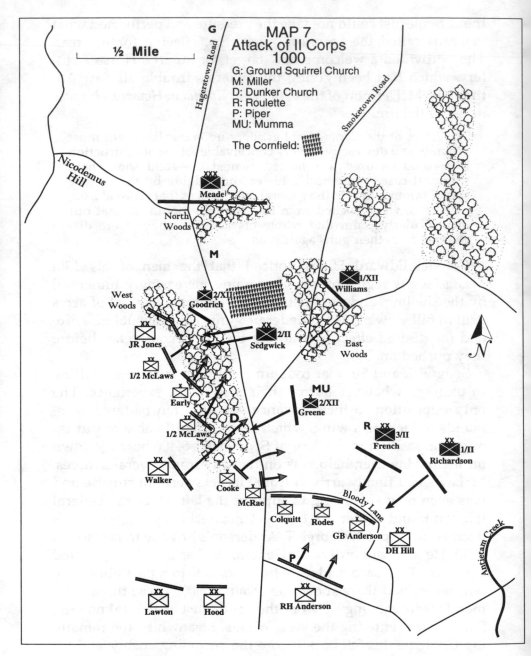

MAP 7
Attack of II Corps
1000

G: Ground Squirrel Church
M: Miller
D: Dunker Church
R: Roulette
P: Piper
MU: Mumma

The Cornfield:

½ Mile

area, realized the desperateness of the situation and prepared to launch a counterattack.

The Federals were deceived by the ease with which they pushed Jackson's exhausted troops back and paid no attention to their flanks. This allowed McLaws, Walker and G.T. Anderson to come up unnoticed and form on Sedgwick's exposed left flank. The Rebel reinforcements after a little confusion set up with Anderson and Kershaw on the right, Barksdale in the center, and Semmes on the left, with Brigadier General Robert Ranson's brigade in support. Their advance upon the unsuspecting Federals was easily concealed behind the trees, gullies, and limestone outcroppings of the West Woods.

General Sumner was talking with Lieutenant Colonel John W. Kimball of the *15th Massachusetts*, when a shocked major gave a shout of alarm, "See the Rebels!" Sumner turned to the Federal left to see the imminent danger, only to exclaim, "My God! We must get out of this." All of a sudden the woods on Sedgwick's left exploded in a destructive blast of Confederate musketry; the *72nd Pennsylvania* on Howard's left totally disintegrated under the fire. Shots fired from the Confederate front lines tore through the troops in Sedgwick's first line, and doubled their effectiveness when they slew men in the rear ranks as well. Many stunned regiments collapsed as troops began to desert their positions, fleeing in panic. Because the enemy swept into Howard's rear, the Yankees only avenue of escape was to the north. Pelham's busy guns then opened fire on all the troops that came fleeing north out of the woods.

The situation in the West Woods quickly became untenable for those who attempted to stay and fight. Gorman was preoccupied with applied pressure from Early's and Colonel Andrew Grigsby's men; some of the Confederates came to within 15 yards to unleash their fire on the uneasy Federal line. Despite the intense salvos of musketry, Federal commanders tried to bring some kind of order to the growing chaos. Sedgwick was hit by a bullet while attempting to wheel his men around, but refused to leave, only to have another knock him off his mount. It took a third wound to finally force him to leave the fight. Dana himself was also wounded, but he adamantly refused to abandon his men in their time of need.

At this point the noise of the musketry was becoming so deafening that even Bull Sumner's voice could not be heard over the din. Howard recalled his commander's difficulty in attempting to give orders over the racket, "The noise of the musketry and artillery was so great that I judged more by the gestures of the general (Sumner) as to the disposition he wished me to make than by the orders that reached my ears." Originally, the men of *Howard's brigade* mistakenly thought Sumner had ordered a charge and immediately fixed their bayonets, cheering wildly, only to be told by the general, "Back, boys, for God's sake, move back! You are in a bad fix!" As the predicament quickly worsened, the first two lines attempted to weather the fire; however, the brigade of Philadelphians in the rear fell apart, and retreated from the terrible slaughter. The men of the *59th New York* managed to pull together to return fire, but through a tragic mishap unleashed a fusillade into the backs of the *15th Massachusetts* posted right in front of them. Despite this unfortunate occurrence, the *15th* fought on, the men loading and firing as if "on dress parade," as one member noted.

Sumner soon realized that *Sedgwick's division* could not hold its position in the West Woods much longer in the face of destructive fire coming from front, left and rear, and ordered a complete withdrawal. Some units managed the retreat in order. The *20th Massachusetts* put their rifles to their shoulders, and marched away at an ordinary pace. Other units fled quickly for the cover of the North Woods, even sweeping up some of Hooker's men near the Poffenberger farm in the retreat. Detachments from *Gorman's* and *Dana's brigades* attempted to make a last ditch stand, only to be thrown back by the victorious Rebels of Early's, McLaws' and Anderson's commands. A defensive line was finally organized along the Poffenberger farm consisting of fragments of the *I, II,* and *XII Corps.*

Some 2,100 of Sedgwick's men had fallen in the West Woods in the short span of only fifteen minutes. Many were hit before they were able to fire an angry shot in reply. The *15th Massachusetts* and *42nd New York* lost roughly half of their men, while the *19th Massachusetts* lost all its field officers among its own heavy toll. A total of 12,000 men now lay either dead or wounded on the bloody terrain between the East and West Woods.

Greene's infantry of **XII Corps** *sweeping towards the West Woods and Dunker Church at about 1030.*

Meanwhile, Greene's men, their ammunition replenished, continued to hold their position before the Dunker Church. A heavy attack from Kershaw's South Carolinians, forced the *125th Pennsylvania* back from the West Woods. When Kershaw's tired command was pushed back, another Confederate charge was led by Colonel Van H. Manning, of Walker's division, at 1000. His attack was repulsed when the Federals held their fire until the enemy came into close range. Manning's men bravely attempted to return fire while suffering heavily from the rifle blasts of the Yankees. Major Orrin Greene of the *7th Ohio* reported, "...we poured fire into their advancing columns volley after volley. So terrific was the fire of our men that the enemy fell like grass before the mower; so deadly was the fire that the enemy retired in great disorder, they not being able to rally their retreating forces." Manning himself was wounded in the attack; he left command to Colonel E.D. Hall, who called a retreat.

Greene took advantage of his success, and pursued the Southerners "like hounds after frightened deer," as Major George L. Wood of the *7th Ohio* put it. Greene's men penetrated into the West Woods, providing the Federals with another threatening salient within the Rebel line. If these Yankees received reinforcements in time, the Army of Northern Virginia could be torn in two, ensuring that the sacrifice of the thousands of men lost earlier in the morning would not be in vain. However, the battle was even then shifting away from the Confederate left to the south where a few Rebel brigades lay entrenched in a sunken road.

While *Sedgwick's division* of the *II Corps* was being horribly wrecked in the West Woods, *French's division* was bearing down on the Rebels before the Mumma farmhouse in its attempt to go into support of Greene's men near the Dunker Church. French posted Brigadier General Max *Weber's brigade* on the left, a brigade of green regiments under Colonel Dwight Morris in the center, and Brigadier General Nathan Kimball on the right. His advance took him against the Confederate center, commanded by Harvey Hill. Hill's brigades found protection in a road to the northeast of Sharpsburg that had been carved into the earth by erosion and heavy use. Hill had originally had five fresh brigades, but all but Rodes' and Anderson's had been sent to help Jackson earlier in the fight. After the fighting against the *I* and *XII Corps*, the mangled remnants of Garland's, Anderson's and Colquitt's brigades had returned to the center. They were formed on the left of the main line in the Sunken Road, and were joined by Walker's division and Ripley's brigade, which brought the Confederate numbers to 2,500. To impress upon the soldiers in the center the importance of their position, Lee rode up to tell his men to hold at all costs. Colonel John B. Gordon of the 6th Alabama in Colquitt's brigade replied, "These men are going to stay here, General, till the sun goes down or victory is won!" The colonel was to recall later, "Alas! many of the brave fellows are there now."

French's 5,700 men passed the burning remains of the Mumma house which had been set on fire by Hill's men to preclude its use by Federal sharpshooters. The Yankee line continued on to the Roulette farm, where it came under fire from

Confederate skirmishers. Here, the *132nd Pennsylvania* suffered the cruel misfortune of being near a hive of bees that was struck by a piece of Rebel roundshot; the regiment was thrown into a panic by a swarm of stinging insects. The Federals then advanced over a rise before the Sunken Road.

Weber's brigade held the lead, as the Federals ascended the ridge and came in sight of the Rebel line. Weber dressed his brigade into four ranks and gave an order to advance. Colonel Gordon admired their advance, "It was a thrilling spectacle....Their gleaming bayonets flashed like burnished silver in the sunlight. With the precision of step and perfect alignment of a holiday parade, this magnificent array moved to the charge, every step keeping in time to the tap of the deep sounding drum." Though ready to unleash a volley, Colonel F.M. Parker of the 30th North Carolina restrained his men, telling them not to fire until they could see the belts of the Yankee's cartridge boxes. Gordon himself had his troops wait until they could almost make out the eagles on the buttons of the enemy's uniforms.

At long last a devastating volley ripped into *Weber's brigade* at the close range of 100 yards. Colonel E.A. Osbourne of the 4th North Carolina in G.B. Anderson's brigade remembered, "Instantly the air was filled with the cries of the wounded and dying and the shouts of brave officers, trying to hold their men, who recoiled at the awful and stunning shock so unexpectedly received."

At first the Union line attempted to stand and return fire. Then some fixed bayonets and vainly attempted a charge. Those who were not felled dropped back to the cover of the ridge to continue the fire fight. One soldier recalled, "I fired as fast as I could load, causing the barrel of my rifle to become so hot that it burnt me when I touched it." In their first few moments in combat, *Weber's brigade* had lost a dreadful toll of some 500 men.

To make matters worse, when Morris' rookies came up to support Weber, the *14th Connecticut* panicked and fired into the backs of their comrades. The *14th* then collapsed under the intense pressure, and the *108th New York* and *130th Pennsylvania* managed to get in line before the blaze of musketry from the Sunken Road. Because these Yankees were covered with soot from black powder and smoke, they appeared like apparitions

Confederate dead in the "Bloody Lane" from the 14th North Carolina of G. B. Anderson's brigade.

from the depths of Hades, and caused the Rebels to call out, "Go back there, you black devils."

Anderson saw the Federals falling fast, and attempted to launch a counterattack. It withered to a halt under the tremendous fusillades of the Union troops. On the Confederate left, Rodes also tried to drive the Yankees from the field, only to meet the same fate as Anderson's men. Lieutenant W.W. Bloss of the *108th New York* took up his regimental colors and was wounded when a minie ball crushed the bridge of his nose and almost suffocated him with coagulated blood. He ran to the rear, yelling out to some of his men, "For God's sake...jam a straw up my nose, I am strangling." At first, his compatriots attempted to apply the procedure delicately, only to have the officer grab the straw and shove it fiercely up his nostrils to save his life.

French now received word from Sumner that he was in dire straits and needed French to engage the enemy as vigorously as possible. The division commander responded by sending in his last brigade. Kimball's command soon relieved Weber's and Morris' men and filed out on the crest before the Rebel line. His attempts to storm the Sunken Road met the same terrific musketry as his fellows, and managed to do little more than increase the casualty lists. Eventually the shattered Union units were ordered to lie down in order to protect themselves. Some soldiers fired just over the crest, and then retreated to reload in safety behind the hill before going back up to fire another shot. An incautious Yank ignored such safe tactics, and pluckily sat on a boulder firing away in full view of the Confederate line. Looking back to his compatriots, he yelled, "Come over here, men, you can see 'em better."

Despite the destructive musketry on both sides, some Federals managed to take Lieutenant Colonel J.M. Newton, commander of the 6th Georgia, into Kimball's lines. Newton was mortally wounded and told his captors, "God bless you, boys, you are very kind." He then lamented, "You have killed all my brave boys; they are there in the road." Colonel Gordon noticed a father mortally wounded lying by his son, killed in the fighting. Despite his loss, the parent turned to his commander calling out, "Here we are. My boy is dead, and I shall go soon; but it is all right."

French had lost 1,750 men, a casualty loss of over 30 percent, in his unsuccessful assault on the Confederate center. Fortunately for French, help was on the way in the form of Israel *Richardson's division*. Richardson finally got his 4,000 men across the Antietam at 1030 and advanced with Brigadier General Thomas F. *Meagher's brigade* on the right and John C. *Caldwell's brigade* on the left.

Colonel John R. *Brooke's brigade* followed up in support. The Confederates were reinforced as well, as Richard Anderson's division, containing 3,400 men, moved into Henry Piper's cornfield behind the Sunken Road.

When French's line began to run low on men and ammunition, Richardson sent in his pet unit, Meagher's *Irish Brigade*, to go against the Rebel position. The brave Irishmen passed the crest with emerald banners waving defiantly in the air, and let loose a volley that, in the words of one Irishman, "made the hills ring far and wide." In return they received a galling blast of fire that brigade historian D.P. Conyngham called "the severest and most deadly ever witnessed before." Meagher saw an emerald banner fall to the ground, and called out, "Boys, raise the colors, and follow me!" The *Irish Brigade* drove towards the Confederate line before being forced to a halt by the same deadly blaze of gunfire that had blunted earlier Federal assaults. Though they were taking heavy casualties themselves, Rodes' and Anderson's men refused to budge from their defenses.

Meagher himself had his horse shot out from under him and had to be carried to safety. His Irishmen stayed on the field blazing away until their muskets were so hot that officers reported "the rammers were leaping out of the pipes at every discharge." When ammunition ran low, men were sent to collect cartridges from the dead and wounded lying nearby. The Confederates were inflicting a deadly toll; the *63rd* and *69th New York* lost half of their men, and altogether at least 550 Irishmen had fallen. Meanwhile, *Caldwell's brigade* had managed to threaten the Rebel right flank only to be called back in order to save Meagher's hard pressed Irishmen.

Before leading the *5th New Hampshire* into the battle, Colonel Edward C. Cross gave his men a few terse words of encouragement: "Men, you're about to engage in battle. You have never disgraced your state; I hope you won't this time. If any man runs, I want the file closers to shoot him; if they don't, I shall myself. That's all I have to say." As Caldwell's troops took the crest, Federal shells directed at Rebel guns screamed over their heads. At the same time, Rebel cannoneers responded with vicious blasts of solid shot, that tore up the ground and blasted the Union line. One soldier from New Hampshire fell wounded and called out to Cross, "Oh, God I'm wounded," to which the unsympathetic colonel replied, "It's the fortunes of war, my young man. It's the fortunes of war."

The Confederate defenders of the Sunken Road also suffered heavy losses, particularly among their officers. General Richard H. Anderson fell wounded, while getting his men into position, leaving the command of his division to fall upon the uncertain shoulders of Brigadier General Roger Pryor. Pryor managed to get only one of his brigades into the Sunken Road while Caldwell was coming up. During the fighting Colonel John

John B. Gordon was only a colonel at Antietam. He eventually rose to the rank of Major General, and was a very capable brigade and division commander.

Gordon was hit five times. The final bullet hit the jugular, and the colonel fell face forward into his hat. Had the head piece not been pierced by a bullet, the colonel might have met a gruesome death, drowning in his own blood that poured out from his neck wound.

By 1200 the Confederate line at the Sunken Road was finally beginning to collapse, not only from the heavy toll of casualties, but also from difficulties with the terrain and some severe misunderstandings between the commanders in the field. Colonel Carnot Posey did not like the section of the Sunken Road he was assigned to defend at the right end of the line because there was not enough room to post all his men. He decided to pull his men out, a move that set off calls of retreat and caused Pryor's and Wright's weary men to fall back. Lieutenant Colonel J.N. Lightfoot of the 6th Alabama approached General Rodes and requested permission to fall back to a more defensible position because his men did not have much cover from enemy fire. Rodes granted the request and Lightfoot immediately began

Confederate dead from Starke's Louisiana brigade along the Hager-stown Pike, about 500 yards north of the Dunker Church. The Miller Cornfield is on the road 100 yards on the right.

pulling his men back. When he was asked by his compatriots if the whole brigade was being ordered back, he mistakenly and disastrously answered yes.

As the rest of Rodes' troops retreated from their positions, Colonel Francis Barlow charged into the road with the *61st* and *64th New York*. The New Yorkers secured an enfilading fire on the rest of the Confederate line, and forced back the remaining defenders, with a loss of 300 prisoners. During the retreat, one ornery Rebel lagged behind the rest of his comrades and fired shot after shot until he ran out of ammunition.

The collapse of the Rebel line allowed the Federals to advance and finally take the Sunken Road. Private T.F. DeBugh of French's command recalled, "It seemed like merely a hop, skip, and jump till we were at the lane, and into it, the Confederates breaking away in haste...." Lieutenant Livermore of the *5th New*

Hampshire recalled, "In this road lay so many dead rebels that they formed a line which one might have walked upon as far as I could see, many of whom had been killed by the most horrible wounds of shot and shell, and they just lay there as they had been killed apparently, amid the blood which was soaking in the earth." One Confederate who was lying wounded in the road had ample evidence of the terrible fire his command had been under. He reportedly told his captors, "When I fell, I had one bullet in me, now I have five."

Suddenly, disaster threatened the Confederate center. Rodes attempted to rally his routed troops to create some sort of defense against the advancing Federals, and managed to get only 50 men to join him. Longstreet brought up guns to shell the oncoming enemy and try to bring a halt to the Federal advance. M.D. Miller's battery of the Washington Artillery opened up with a deadly barrage of canister. When the Yankee riflemen began to pick off the gunners, Longstreet ordered his own staff to join the fight; they took a piece, loading and firing it against the enemy, while Longstreet stood holding the reins of their horses, giving direction and advice. Miller loaded his cannons with double shots of canister, the guns recoiling almost a foot after each deadly burst. Their fire "poured into the standing corn stalks such a pelting storm of grape that each explosion seemed like a rushing mighty wing and driving hail. It was sour office now to hold the position gained...the boys protected themselves by hugging the soil. It was not surprising how readily they stuck their noses in the dirt." Unable to take any more, the Yankees fell back from the Piper cornfield to the Sunken Road.

Hill organized a detachment of troops from various regiments, and sent them forward against the Federal line. The Southerners bravely approached to within close quarters of the Federal line in the Sunken Road. Colonel Edward Cross of the *5th New Hampshire* called out to his men, "Put on the war paint!" to which soldiers wiped their faces with the torn ends of cartridge paper. Then the colonel called out, "Give 'em the war whoop!" The effect of this highly unusual exercise bolstered the morale of the New Hampshire soldiers with shouts of "Fire! Fire! Fire faster!" going up and down the line. Lieutenant

Livermore was caught up in the excitement, and grabbed a rifle to fire off a few rounds himself. Cross noticed his subordinate's bravado, and cautioned him, "Mr. Livermore, tend to your company."

When the *81st Pennsylvania* began to enfilade the left flank of the Confederate line, the Southerners could take no more, and fell back through the Piper farm. At this critical point, Hill himself grabbed a musket to personally lead 200 men in a counterattack that had no chance of success. His bravado, though, did succeed at deceiving the Federals about Confederate weakness on this front.

The scene now shifted slightly to the west, where *Greene's division* was still in line near the Dunker Church. Greene's men were waiting reinforcements and believed Sedgwick's command to be in the West Woods. This belief caused a nasty surprise when Ransom's Confederates joined the fray, and surprised Greene's men on the right.

Since his flank was turned, Greene decided to fall back from his advantageous position. It was at this moment that Colonel John R. Cooke launched a bold counterattack with the 3rd Arkansas and 27th North Carolina. During this advance, the color bearer of the 27th North Carolina ran ahead of the rest of the command. When Cooke ordered him to slow down, the soldier replied, "Colonel, I can't let that Arkansas fellow get ahead of me." Cooke saw two guns going to Greene's assistance, and he sent his screaming men in their direction; they shot down almost every horse and half of the men working the battery. Oddly, an unknown Confederate officer, obviously drunk, rode up and called out, "Come on, boys, I'm leading this charge!" Lieutenant Colonel R.W. Singletary was disgusted and shouted at him, "You are a liar, sir! We lead our own charges!"

Cooke's men overtook and captured some of Greene's Yankees, but the Rebels had no time to collect their prisoners' weapons. Instead, the Confederates pressed forward, leaving armed captives in their rear. Cooke moved to the east end of the Sunken Road and *Richardson's division*, and caused considerable mayhem before Kimball threw his brigade in the way. The two forces met at a distance of 200 yards; in one instance a Rebel got close enough to the guns of the *1st Rhode Island Artillery* to have

Another view of confederate dead of Starke's brigade along the Hagerstown Pike, 500 yards north of the Dunker church.

his head bashed in by a Yankee wielding a musket as a club. The blow was so great, that the unfortunate Southerner's brains splattered a nearby gun and "were baked as quickly as if they had been dropped on a hot stove," according to gunner Thomas M. Aldrich. One of the gunners had a morbid sense of curiosity and scraped the mess off the gun to keep as a souvenir.

The Rebels now found themselves increasingly hard pressed, low on ammunition and with no hope of receiving any reinforcements. So they had to retreat. While falling back, they were peppered by fire from the Federals they had left behind earlier as captives. Cooke's depleted and exhausted regiments took up a new position along the Hagerstown Turnpike and awaited the renewal of the battle.

When the Federal advance stalled, Richardson searched desperately for some artillery to support his troops and drive off the Confederate lines. He found some 44 guns belonging to the *I Corps* massed near the Joseph Poffenberger Farm, but McClellan refused to release them to go to his aid. Apparently McClellan feared a Confederate counterattack on this wing, and he wanted to maintain a concentration of artillery that might turn them back. While looking for other guns that might support him, Richardson stopped to take a drink and was struck by a Rebel shell fragment. He was eventually carried to McClellan's headquarters at the Pry house, but the wound proved mortal, and he died on 3 November.

The shattered Confederate center was still very vulnerable to further Union attack. Some 2,500 Southerners had fallen attempting to hold the Sunken Road and repel the Union advance; those who remained standing occupied a thin line, anxiously awaiting the next move on the part of the Federals. General Rodes found that "with the exception of a few men, not more than forty in all, the brigade had completely disappeared." Colonel R.T. Bennet, in command of G.B. Anderson's brigade, recalled, "Masses of Confederate troops in great confusion were seen; portions of Anderson's division broke beyond the power of rallying after five minutes' stay." Any further attack on Lee's center was sure to shatter Lee's army and force it to flee to the banks of the Potomac where it could be captured or cut apart as it tried to cross into Virginia.

Unfortunately for the Union, McClellan and some of his subordinates lacked the nerve to act with the decisiveness that the situation demanded of them. McClellan was not lacking in troops. *Franklin's corps* had arrived in the vicinity of the battle around 0900. It had not been engaged, save one brigade, and had a good 10,000 men on hand. The *V Corps* had likewise seen little action, and offered some 6,600 men to throw into the fray. Thus at 1300, McClellan had at least 16,600 men with whom to renew the contest against the weak and shattered wings of Jackson and Longstreet. Perhaps at no time before or after in the war did the Federals have such an opportunity to crush Lee and his army.

Franklin moved his two fresh divisions to Sumner's support and favored a renewed advance. When he met with Sumner, he was surprised to find the *II Corps* commander "much depressed." Sumner claimed his men were so totally exhausted they could not renew the fight, and urged Franklin to hold his position lest he jeopardize the entire flank. Franklin did not agree, and sent a messenger to McClellan for further instructions. The commander sided with Franklin and directed Sumner "to crowd every man and gun into the ranks, and if he thinks it practicable, he may advance Franklin to carry the woods in front." Sumner in turn disagreed with the orders so much he directed the messenger to report to McClellan that "I have no command. Tell him my command, Bank's command and Hooker's command are all cut up and demoralized. Tell him General Franklin has the only organized command on this part of the field." The reply reached McClellan at his headquarters at 1400, and at last provoked the commander to ride forward and visit the front himself. There he allowed Sumner to persuade him not to launch any further attacks.

McClellan would be offered yet another chance to change his mind. Brigadier General George Sykes of *Porter's division*, which had advanced across the Antietam near the Sunken Road, had learned from one of his soldiers that the Confederate line there was merely a weak shell ripe for a crushing blow. Sykes approached McClellan for permission to make an attack, supported by the rest of the *V Corps*. This bold plan was scrapped when Porter supposedly informed his commander, "Remember, General, I command the last reserve of the last army of the Republic." Such words were enough to dissuade the Young Napoleon from living up to his namesake. So far, McClellan had managed to squander his good fortune. If the battle was to be won, Burnside's troops would have to earn the victory on the army's left flank.

While McClellan refused to commit any of his numerous reserves, Robert E. Lee and Stonewall Jackson were trying to accomplish the impossible: a counterattack against the *Army of the Potomac* with any spare troops that could be collected. To determine the feasibility of an attack, Jackson sent a soldier up a high tree to take a look at the enemy's position. When asked how many troops he saw in the area, the Rebel replied, "Whooee, oceans of them." Shortly after 1230 General John Walker approached Jackson, and learned that Stuart was busy gathering a force of 4,000 to 5,000 troops for a flanking maneuver against the Federal right; Jackson asserted, "We shall drive McClellan into the Potomac." Walker gathered up what troops he could to support the proposed attack. He waited until 1530 for the sound of Stuart's attack, and then went to see Jackson, who informed him the cavalry commander had found the

Confederate dead from Parker's Virginia battery, just east of the Dunker Church.

Federal right anchored on the banks of the Potomac. Saddened by the failure of his operation, Jackson merely mused, "It is a great pity—we should have driven McClellan into the Potomac."

The Fighting Irish of the Army of the Potomac

During the great Irish potato famine of the 1840s, multitudes of the sons and daughters of the Emerald Isle sought to escape the poverty and deprivation of their homeland to seek a better life in America. Many flocked to the cities of the industrial North and then readily joined the Union army when the Civil War broke out in 1861. One whole brigade was comprised solely of Irishmen, consisting of the *63rd, 69th,* and *88th New York,* thus called the *Irish Brigade.* The unit's trademark was its magnificent array of flowing green battle flags endowed with golden harps and shamrocks, proudly confirming the heritage of these soldiers in blue.

The *Irish Brigade* served in almost every major engagement in the Eastern Theatre, and was most famous for its gallant charges at Antietam, Fredericksburg and Gettysburg. At Sharpsburg on 17 September, the Irishmen bravely assaulted the Confederate line in the Sunken Road. They failed to take the position, but inflicted heavy casualties on the enemy. At Fredericksburg, the Brigade lost 545 out of 1,400 men in a desperate charge against the Confederate positions entrenched behind a stone wall at Marye's Heights. By Gettysburg, the Brigade was a mere shadow of itself. The ranks of the *63rd, 69th* and *88th New York* were so depleted that the regiments were consolidated into two companies each. At that time the Brigade also included the *116th Pennsylvania* and *28th Massachusetts.* On the second day of the battle, the Brigade helped brace Sykes' lines by charging Longstreet's Confederates in the wheatfield on Meade's left.

After Gettysburg the *Irish Brigade* was replenished by the large *4th* and *7th New York Heavy Artillery* regiments, and almost totally lost its Irish identity.

At the end of the war, only a few original Irishmen were left, their green banners in tatters, to make the grand march through the capital before being mustered out of the service. The illustrious service of the unit has made it one of the most famous of all brigades in American military history.

Jubal Anderson Early (1816-1894)

A Virginian and West Point graduate, Jubal Anderson Early resigned his commission to take up law. After voting against the secession of his native state in the Virginia Convention, he joined the Confederate military when war broke out and received command of the 24th Virginia. He commanded a brigade at First Bull Run, and fell wounded in an impetuous assault at Williamsburg, Virginia, during the Peninsula campaign. After returning to command in time to participate in the Battle of Malvern Hill, he provided a strong defense at Cedar Mountain, and helped save the battle after the famed Stonewall Brigade broke. His steadiness won him division command and a promotion to major general in January of 1863. In 1864 he became a lieutenant general in command of the Second Corps. He led an audacious invasion of Maryland and won the Battle of Monocacy, only to be turned away from the gates of Washington, D.C., by Major General Horatio Wright's Federals of the *VI Corps*. Early's troops then embarked on a long and unequal duel with the command of Major General Philip Sheridan in the Shenandoah Valley. Early almost recouped his losses with a successful surprise attack at Cedar Creek, but his army was totally wrecked after the Federals rallied. Following the conclusion of the war, Early fled to Canada, and did not return to Virginia until 1869.

Edwin Vose Sumner (1797-1863)

A robust 64 when the Civil War broke out, Edwin V. Sumner was one of the oldest general officers serving in the field operations of the Union Army. Ever since he had received a commission as a second lieutenant in 1819 with the Regular infantry, Sumner remained with the military, serving with the cavalry on the western frontier. He achieved the rank of lieutenant colonel for gallantry in the Mexican American War, and later commanded a campaign against the Cheyenne Indians in the 1850s.

After the War Between the States commenced, the old veteran took command of the *II Corps* of the *Army of the Potomac* and attained the rank of major general after action in McClellan's Peninsula campaign. A tough fighter, Sumner was nicknamed "Bull" or "Bull Head" due to his roaring voice and a soldiers' legend that musket balls bounced off his impregnable skull. Unfortunately, Antietam proved to be Sumner's undoing when he launched an assault by *Sedgwick's division* without protecting his flanks and allowed the Confederates to trap the force in a murderous pocket of fire. Following this failure, the general lost his nerve and refused to allow *Franklin's corps* to launch a counterattack against the depleted Rebel left, a drive that might have won the day for the Federals.

Sumner was stung by criticism of his handling of his troops at Sharpsburg and asked to be removed of field command after the disaster at Fredericksburg. Given the *Department of Missouri*, the old soldier died of pneumonia before he could assume his new position.

John Brown Gordon (1832-1904)

John Gordon was a self made officer with no prior military experience when the War Between the States broke out; by the end of the conflict he rose to command Lee's II Corps, which comprised half of the foot troops of the Army of Northern Virginia. Born in Upson City, Georgia, Walker had an undistinguished academic career, and dropped out of the University of Georgia. Undaunted, he started a career in law, and also attained success by developing mines in his native state. He began the war as a captain in a company known as the Raccoon Roughs, and rose rapidly through the ranks in the Army of Northern Virginia.

At Antietam, he was severely wounded while commanding the 6th Alabama Regiment at the Sunken Road. Though he almost lost an arm to amputation, Gordon recovered from his injuries and returned to the field, where he was promoted to the rank of brigadier general. He served in the Wilderness and accompanied Jubal Early on his assault against Washington in 1864. Following the war, Gordon energetically took to politics, being elected to the U.S. Senate three times. His rather overly romantic *Reminiscences of the Civil War* serves as essential reading for Civil War historians.

CHAPTER XI

Burnside's Bridge

McClellan's original battle plan had called for simultaneous attacks against Lee's left and right flanks in preparation for a final thrust against the Confederate center. As we have seen, the Union attacks against the Cornfield, the East Woods, the West Woods, and the Sunken Road achieved only limited success that McClellan would not exploit with the reserves he had at hand. The main reason Lee had been barely able to hold off all these Federal assaults was the fact that Major General Ambrose E. Burnside, Union commander on the left flank, was late in launching his attack. This threw off McClellan's entire battle plan, and also permitted Lee to shift large numbers of troops to meet the mounting threats farther up the line. By 0900 he had sent Walker's division and G.T. Anderson's brigade of D.R. Jones' division to the left, leaving only 3,000 men of Jones' command to hold the army's right flank. Burnside should have been able to overwhelm this reduced Confederate defense with his 12,000 men, even though he was off to a late start. However, he needed to act before the battle died down completely to the north and released any Confederate troops that might be used to reinforce Jones' line.

Jones was responsible for holding the one and one-half mile line that stretched from the Boonsboro Pike south to the Harpers Ferry Road. Garnett's brigade was on the left, followed by the brigades of Jenkins, Drayton and Kemper. Brigadier General Robert Toombs was ordered to place his brigade in an advanced position to guard the Rohrbach Bridge, the only bridge on this part of the front. His right flank was covered by the 50th Georgia from Drayton's brigade, and a cavalry force under T.T. Munford watched the creek farther downstream. It was not a bad position, if held with enough strength and adequate reserves. The entire line was fronted by Antietam Creek, whose western bank furnished some good defensive positions, particularly at the bluffs overlooking the Rohrbach Bridge. In addition, there was good high ground near Sharpsburg to post artillery and observe enemy movements. However, as we have noted, Jones did not have adequate strength to hold this line, particularly since the creek was fordable at several spots below the bridge, and there were no Confederate reserves available.

The key point in Jones' line was the bluffs above the Rohrbach Bridge, which would be the focus of the Union attack on this flank. The bluff had an abundance of rocks and trees to shelter its defenders, and gave them a clear field of fire into the open fields that approached the Union end of the bridge. Its defenders consisted of about 400 men from the 2nd and 20th Georgia regiments, under the command of Colonel Henry L. Benning.

Unfortunately for Burnside's bluecoats, the Federal left was faced with a plague of severe command crises that hampered any advantages maintained in manpower. This collapse of effective leadership essentially stemmed from the growing differences between McClellan and his subordinate, the bewhiskered Burnside. Though up to now both men had been good friends, affectionately using the nicknames of "Mac" and "Burn," their relationship had recently come under some strain after the battle of South Mountain. McClellan had been annoyed by Burnside's sluggish march in the pursuit of the Confederate army on the 15th, and sent a curt dispatch that criticized his subordinate's actions and demanded a prompt explanation for his failure to follow orders.

Burnside was stung by this condemnation, and was further annoyed by McClellan's organization of the *Army of the Potomac* on the field of battle. Little Mac had dispensed with his use of wing formations after South Mountain and relegated wing commanders Burnside, Sumner, and Franklin to the sole control of their respective corps without really informing them of this action. The latter two generals seemed to acknowledge the move

Major General Ambrose E. Burnside did not like being demoted from left wing commander, and did not handle the IX Corps well. He would lead the Army of the Potomac to defeat at Fredericksburg less than three months later.

without any real concern, but Burnside refused to believe himself to be anything less than a wing commander, wielding the power of two corps, the *I* and *IX*. When McClellan's battle plans removed Hooker from Burnside's control and placed the *I Corps* on the opposite flank of the army, Burnside became incensed, and regarded the act as the equivalent of an embarrassing demotion that he would not accept. Despite having half of his wing taken away from him, the general refused to reduce his rank and still considered himself a wing commander. This situation produced a debilitating effect on the command structure of the *IX Corps*; all orders emanating from McClellan would have to be forwarded through Burnside and then passed along to Jacob Cox for execution.

Of course the greatest obstacle facing the Federal troops was the splendidly crafted triple-arched stone bridge—some 125 feet long and twelve feet wide—that they would have to cross in order to attack the Confederate right. The Federals would have to advance in a close column allowing their flanks to be exposed to a murderous enfilading fire from the well protected Georgians on the bluffs.

Evidently, despite the tremendous disadvantages facing any attempt to advance over the bridge, neither Burnside, nor any serious Federal commander, gave any credence to the possibility of fording the stream itself. A native of the area, Kyd Douglas of Jackson's staff, seemed to think the Antietam was easily passable. He wrote of the bridge, "It was no pass of Thermopylae. Go and look at it and tell me if you don't think Burnside and his corps might have executed a hop, skip, and a jump and landed on the other side. One thing is for certain, they might have waded it that day without getting their waist belts wet in any place."

Burnside was in no way ready to begin his attack when the battle began at dawn on the 17th. He did not have his troops in position, nor did he understand there was any immediate need to advance. The night before, McClellan had written Burnside that he was to remain in waiting until the necessary orders were given to begin the assault across the bridge. As a result, the only action Burnside initially took was to shell Jones' lines with his artillery. One soldier recalled that the noisy guns had little effect but to lull the troops to sleep.

It was not until 0910—just when Sedgwick was marching towards his fatal encounter in the West Woods—that McClellan sent Burnside orders to "carry the bridge, then gain possession of the heights beyond, and to advance along their crest upon Sharpsburg and its rear." A short while later McClellan sent assurances that reinforcements would be available to support the attack. Burnside passed all these commands and messages to acting Corps Commander Cox, who was to supervise the attack.

Cox ordered *Crook's* and *Sturgis' divisions* to take the lead, with the *11th Connecticut*, under Colonel H.W. Kingsbury, thrown out as skirmishers to feel the enemy's position. Once a foothold was gained on the other side of the Antietam, Sam *Sturgis' Second Division* was to plunge over the bridge to exploit the success. Meanwhile, Rodham and the rest of the *Kanawha Division* were to head south in an attempt to cross the Antietam at a ford discovered downstream by Federal engineers, and then move north to link up with the rest of the corps for a drive to Sharpsburg.

The operation did not begin at all smoothly. Crook managed to lose his direction while moving into position and reached the banks of the stream some 440 yards north of the Rohrbach Bridge. His brigade then took cover to engage in a sharp firefight with the enemy on the other side of the creek. Crook reported back to Cox that he was too heavily occupied to be able to advance against the bridge. Meanwhile, the *11th Connecticut* suffered severely from the well-placed shots of the enemy; its commander was hit four times by minie balls. Captain John D. Griswold led a company into the water to wade across to the other side, only to see them cut apart in the attempt. Griswold himself was badly wounded, and managed only enough final strength to drag himself to the western shore, where he collapsed dead. To the south, Rodman found the designated ford, but discovered the bluffs on his side made crossing impossible. He learned from local citizens the location of another possible ford farther to the south and marched his division to find it, so further delaying the flanking maneuver against Toombs' men.

Since Crook had failed to reach the bridge, the task of taking it fell next to *Sturgis' division*. Sturgis sent *Nagle's brigade* to lead the attack, supported by *Ferrero's brigade*. When Sturgis observed the *48th Pennsylvania* having problems getting into position in one of the Rohrbach cornfields, he harshly berated the regiment's commander, "God damn you to hell, sir, don't you understand the English language? I ordered you to advance in line and support the *2nd Maryland*, and what in hell are you doing flanking around this corn...?"

Nagle advanced with the *2nd Maryland* and *6th New Hampshire* in the lead, supported by the *9th New Hampshire* and the *48th Pennsylvania*. His troops fixed their bayonets and charged down the Rohrbach Road in their attempt to reach the bridge. Despite the heavy Union supporting fire, the Southerners leveled blast after blast of minie balls, canister, shot and shell into Nagle's ranks. A private from *48th Pennsylvania* recalled, "Instantly the hills blazed with musketry. There were broad sheets of flame from the wall upon the crest, where the cannon, double shotted, poured streams of canister upon the narrow passage.

*The charge of the **51st New York** and **51st Pennsylvania**, which finally captured Burnside's Bridge.*

The head of the column melted in an instant." When a large piece of railroad iron flew across the stream from a Confederate gun, a German officer exclaimed, "Mein Gott, we shall have a blacksmith's shop to come next." As they bore down on the bridge, the Yankee regiments simply could not bear the cruel fire. Men ran for whatever cover they could find. When he saw his command start to crack, Duryea called out, "What the hell are you doing there? Straighten that line! Forward!" His attempts to keep his men moving were to no avail; the entire attack collapsed; the Federals had suffered heavy casualties, with the *2nd Maryland* losing 44 percent of its numbers, with no real advantages won.

McClellan was by now impatient at Burnside's lack of success; it was already past 1200 and the *IX Corps* still remained on the eastern bank of the Antietam. To speed things up, McClellan dispatched his Inspector General, Colonel Delos B. Sackett, to ensure the bridge was taken. McClellan's complaints only served to agitate Burnside more. He told Sackett, "McClellan appears to think I am not trying my best to carry this bridge; you are the third or fourth one who has been to me this morning with similar orders."

Burnside ordered Cox to make yet another attempt to take the bridge, and Cox entrusted *Ferrero's brigade* with the deadly mission. He directed the *51st Pennsylvania* and *51st New York* to lead the advance, and encouraged his men by crying out, "It is General Burnside's special request that the two 51sts take that bridge. Will you do it?" From the ranks of the Pennsylvanians one soldier inquired, "Will you give us our whiskey, Colonel, if we take it?" Ferrero replied, "Yes, by God you shall all have as much as you want if you take that bridge. I don't mean the whole brigade, but you two regiments shall have as much as you want, if it is in the commissary or I have to send to New York to get it, and pay for it out of my private purse; that is if I live to see you through it. Will you take it?" To this statement the troops let out a harmonious "Yes!"

The 670 men of the twin *51sts* launched their assault at 1230. Instead of charging down the Rohrersville Road under the enemy fire, Ferrero's men formed behind a hill 300 yards above the bridge. When the command to attack was given, they rushed down the slope shouting, "Remember Reno!" Confederate fire was so intense that the two regiments headed for cover instead of rushing the bridge. The New Yorkers sought shelter behind a wood fence to the left of the bridge, while the Pennsylvanians rushed to a stone wall on the right along the creek bank.

Despite their defiant stand against the Yankees, Toombs' soldiers were finding their position untenable. After firing away for three hours, their ammunition was running low, and they were suffering steady casualties from Union infantry and artillery fire. The 2nd Georgia had already lost 50 percent of its men, and most of its field officers were either dead or wounded. Regimental Commander Lieutenant Colonel William R. Holmes fell after being wounded several time by bullets, and more men went out while attempting to recover his body. Despite their fine cover, Rebel sharpshooters were themselves falling casualty to their Federal counterparts. Worse still, Yankees to the north and south of the bridge had finally managed to cross the creek and were bearing down on Toombs' command.

Hooker's division *fording Antietam Creek on the afternoon of 16 September. McClellan telegraphed his first punch by moving* **I Corps** *into position facing Lee's left on the night before the battle began.*

After a few hours of searching, Rodham had finally found Snavely's Ford two miles downstream. He crossed without opposition and was now coming up to assail the right flank of the Georgians. To the north, Crook's men had also managed to find a crossing that brought then to the western bank of the Antietam; they were moving on Benning's left! After successfully delaying the advance of the *IX Corps* for three hours, Toombs found it necessary to retreat to the main Confederate line.

Colonel Robert Porter of the *51st New York* saw the Rebels begin to fall back and threw his men across the bridge followed by the Pennsylvanians. The ranks of the charging columns so jammed the bridge that a halt had to be called. Potter jumped up on the ledge of the bridge, and urged his men on, swearing all the while. Colonel John R. Hartranft of the *51st Pennsylvania,* exhausted from the drive, called out to his troops, "Come on, boys, for I can't haloo anymore." Once across, the Federals sent a few volleys into the ranks of the remaining enemy, and drove the rest of the Confederates away from the bluffs. At about 1300, Cox and Burnside finally claimed the bridge, having lost 550 troops in the costly venture.

The IX Corps for various reasons failed to exploit its success at carrying the bridge. Sturgis saw that his men were exhausted and low on ammunition, so he brought his brigade to a halt on the bluffs across the stream, and waited for reinforcements and the ammunition trains to be brought up. His halt delayed any further Union advance until 1500, as the narrow bridge became jammed with the traffic of soldiers, ammunition wagons, and artillery.

McClellan was now outraged at Burnside's slowness and sent another staff officer, Colonel Thomas M. Key, with a dispatch containing orders to get the attack going again at once. The message also included a secret clause to relieve Burnside with Major General George W. Morell, if an advance was not launched immediately. Nonetheless, the IX Corps did not resume its attack until two hours after the bridge was carried. During the respite, soldiers from both sides engaged in picket fire as the artillery kept up an intermittent fire. At one point, some Federals attempted to light fires to boil coffee, forgetting the resulting smoke would alert Confederate gunners to their position. All of a sudden the unfortunate Yankees came under a heavy shelling. Colonel Ferrero had a close call while sitting on the low wall of the bridge—a shell exploded 15 inches away from him, tearing away at some masonary and blowing a mule to bits.

Meanwhile, the Confederate infantry in Jones' main line patiently waited the Federal attack, preparing for the worst. After climbing a church steeple in Sharpsburg to get a birds eye view of the battlefield, Private Alexander Hunter of the 17th Virginia solemnly reported to his commander, Colonel Montgomery D. Corse, "We are lost, colonel; we haven't a single reserve." "Is it possible?" The colonel replied, only to be told it was a fact as Hunter had not seen a single Rebel to support the present line. Corse "clenched his teeth like a bulldog," and firmly resolved to hold his position. Hunter recalled, "...as the news ran along the line, each man knew we had to stay there and, if needs be, die there."

At 1500, Cox at last gave the command to renew his offensive. *Rodman's division* advanced on the left and *Wilcox's division* on the right, both supported by *Sturgis' division* and the *Kanawha Division*. Colonel Benjamin C. Christ took the right of Rodman's advance and moved up the Rohrersville Road. He was opposed by a strong line of Confederate artillery posted in and near a cemetery perched on a plateau just east of Sharpsburg. In front of the artillery were about 100 men of the 17th Georgia, Holcombe's Legion of South Carolinians, and some sharpshooters.

The *79th New York* drove the first Confederate line back through the farm belonging to John Otto to an apple orchard, where it ran into Garnett's and Jenkins' brigades. When Colonel Christ saw the troops on his left lag behind, he paused to wait for them, and subjected his men to a terrible fire from the Rebel batteries in their front. These Federals did receive some assistance from the *2nd* and *10th U.S. Infantry* under John S. Poland of *Sykes' division*, who drove back the extreme Confederate left under Garnett.

Finally, *Welsh's brigade* fought its way up to the left of Colonel Christ and joined the fight at the orchard. Most of the Confederates were soon driven back, but some retired to a stone house and mill that were converted into forts. They fought off the Yankees until forced to withdraw by hand to hand fighting with bayonets.

Cox now brought up artillery to blast the Confederate guns on the cemetery hill, which had to begin to withdraw. The Federals now ascended the high ground before Sharpsburg only to have their advance halted due to lack of ammunition.

At the same time, *Rodman's division* was closing in on the Rebels from the south. Colonel Harrison C. *Fairchild's brigade* attacked on the right and Colonel Edward *Harland's First Brigade* took the left. During their advance, the Federals were struck by a horrid sight; the charred bodies of wounded Rebels who had been laid on beds of straw only to be burned to death when their resting place caught fire from exploding shells.

Fairchild's brigade was exposed to heavy artillery fire as it moved into position. J.H.E. Whitney of the *9th New York* remem-

Late in the afternoon **Hawkin's Zouaves (9th New York)** *of* IX
Corps *came within sight of Sharpsburg before being turned back.*

bered the enemy missiles falling on the ranks of his comrades:
"...many of the shells striking in front of them and ricocheting
over their heads before exploding; others, more unfortunately,
striking and bursting in the ranks, killing and wounding half a
dozen men at each discharge." A shot exploding in the ranks of
the color guard of the *9th New York* took three men down while
a corporal standing nearby was sent tumbling head over heels
down a hill.

At last General Rodman rode up and ordered what he hoped
would be the climatic charge of the battle. The *9th New York* led
the way, with orders to storm the ridge held by Wise's battery
and Drayton's and Kemper's infantry. It would be one of the
most spectacular infantry charges in the entire war. The Zouave
troops lept up and pressed forward chanting their war cry, "Zoo,
zoo, zoo." One soldier looked back over the trail of their
advance, and observed "As far back as they could see, the track
of the regiment was strewn with the slain who dotted the earth

as so many footsteps of blood to the victory they were striving for." Over 200 men of the unit had already fallen casualty. The troops halted for a while in a ravine to gain a short respite and to reform the already depleted ranks. Their colonel exultantly congratulated his men, shouting out, "Bully Ninth! Bully Ninth! I'm proud of you!"

The *9th* was still under heavy artillery fire. One private recalled,

> The battery...whose shots at first went over our heads had depressed its guns so as to shave the surface of the ground. Its fire was beginning to tell. I remember looking behind and seeing an officer riding diagonally across the field—a most inviting target—instinctively bending his head down over his horse's neck, as though he was riding through the driving rain. While my eye was on him I saw, between me and him, a rolled overcoat with its straps on bound into the air and fall among the furrows. One of the enemy's grapeshot had plowed a groove in the skull of a young fellow and cut his overcoat from his shoulders. He never stirred from his position, but lay there face downward—a dreadful spectacle. A moment after, I heard a man cursing a comrade for lying on him heavily. He was cursing a dying man. As the range grew better, the firing became more rapid, the situation desperate and more exasperating to the last degree. Human nature was on the rack, and there burst from it the most vehement, terrible swearing I ever heard.

When the New Yorkers rose up to resume the charge, the Rebels continued to lay down a most devastating fire; "In a second the air was full of the hiss of bullets and the hurtle of grapeshot. The mental strain was so great that I saw a singular effect mentioned, I think, in the life of Goethe on a similar occasion—the whole landscape turned slightly red." At last, Zouaves reached the Confederate line and took cover behind a stone wall. Orders were given to approach within "whispering distance" of the Rebels and then to give them "a hot fire of 'minis'" followed by a charge with bayonets.

The men of the 14th Virginia tensely awaited the Zouaves final charge. One private wrote,

> Colonel Corse gave but one order—"Don't fire, men until I give the word." As we lay there with our eyes ranging along the musket barrels, our fingers on the triggers, we saw the gilt eagles of the flagpoles emerge above the top of the hill, followed by the

flags drooping on the staffs, then the tops of the blue caps appeared, and next a line of the fiercest eyes ever looked upon. The shouts of their officers were heard, urging their men forward. Less brave, less seasoned troops would have faltered before the array of deadly tubes leveled at them, and at the recumbent line, silent, motionless and terrible, but if there was any giving away we did not see it.

The Federals approached to within 50 yards of the Confederate line but held their fire until one Confederate poked his head up above the corner, providing too inviting a target for the Yankees to pass up. All of a sudden the gaudy lines of the Zouaves let loose a torrential blaze of gunshots, sending thirteen bullets alone into the brain of that unfortunate Southerner whose curiosity has gotten the better of him. The fire of the *9th New York* was so heavy that one defender noted, "there was scarcely a hole in the wall that was not pierced, and a finger could not be raised above it without fear of amputation." Altogether eight color bearers fell while carrying the *9th*'s flag up to the Confederate wall.

The weight of the Union charge at length forced the outnumbered Confederates to flee towards Sharpsburg. Confederate John Dooley of the 1st Virginia wrote of his retreat:

Oh, how I ran or tried to run through the high corn for my heavy belt and cartridge box and musket kept me to half my speed. I was afraid of being struck in the back, and I frequently turned half around in running, so as to avoid if possible so disgraceful a wound.

At this moment, it again appeared that the entire Confederate army was doomed: most of Jones' division was broken and Sharpsburg was already filled with stragglers, men who had enough of battle and were trying to seek some safety in the homes of the town. As Federal shells landed in the vicinity, the troops panicked and sought whatever cover was available to shield themselves from the deadly cannonade.

While one captured Confederate was being taken to the rear, a Federal soldier pointed to the vicinity of the battle and said, "It's all up with you, Johnnie; look there." The prisoner noted "Long lines of blue were coming like the surging billows of the ocean. The bluecoats were wild with excitement, and their measured hurrah, so different from our piercing yell, rose above

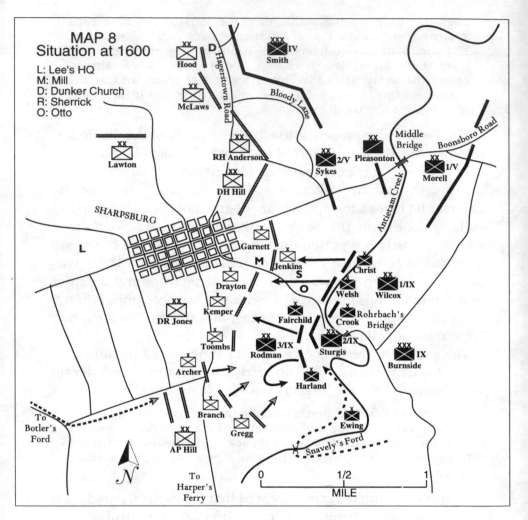

MAP 8
Situation at 1600

L: Lee's HQ
M: Mill
D: Dunker Church
R: Sherrick
O: Otto

the thunder of their batteries beyond the bridge. I thought the guard was right, that it was all up with us, and the whole army would be captured." All that now stood in the way of Burnside and victory was Robert Toombs' tired and depleted brigade. The Georgians were replenished with ammunition and stood defiantly in the face of the advance of *Harland's brigade* on the far left of the Union attack. The *8th New Hampshire* was already taking a lead far in advance of the rest of the brigade.

Lee was sure the battle was over when he saw a column of troops with blue uniforms moving up from the south. These were probably more of Burnside's men, and Lee had no more reserves to block their advance. He sent Lieutenant John Ramsay to look more closely at the column and its intentions, and was astonished to learn that they were flying Confederate banners. He at once realized that these were A.P. Hill's men, rushing to the field after the capture of Harpers Ferry. The blue uniforms were the fresh clothing that some of Hill's men had taken from the stores captured at Harpers Ferry to replace their own threadbare uniforms.

Powell Hill had driven his men at a furious pace after leaving Harpers Ferry early that morning—they covered seventeen miles in eight hours, one of the most notable marches of the war. Hill rode with his column and unmercifully dealt blows with the flat of his sword to speed stragglers on their way. When he neared the field he at once realized the crisis Lee was in, and did not pause to form ordered lines as Burnside had done after taking the bridge. Instead he threw his brigades in piecemeal against Burnside's unprotected flank.

Harland's brigade was totally unaware of Hill's approach, and continued to press its assault against the thin Confederate line that stood between them and victory. Captain D.G. McIntosh's South Carolina battery came up just in time to meet a charge by the *8th Connecticut*. One artilleryman recalled that the Yankees were as thick as "Pharaoh's locusts....Our guns began firing double charges of canister; there was a large U.S. flag just in front of the left gun at which our fire was directed. It was shot down three times when the enemy stopped and laid down. The flag was stuck apparently in the ground and remained flying for a few moments when it was shot down and we saw it no more."

Still, the Connecticut regiment pressed forward, closing in on the battery until the gunners were forced to flee for their lives. But before they abandoned their guns, McIntosh's men poured one last batch of double shotted canister into their ranks. The next day, 48 bluecoats were found in a heap where the cannons had discharged their final deadly shots.

Harland's men were thrilled at their success, but their delight soon turned to dismay when they saw that they were unsupported, and that the enemy troops were bearing down on them from the left. Hill's advance had been seen by Union signalmen, who had flagged the news to Burnside's headquarters, but Burnside had not yet reacted to this new threat. When Brigadier General Isaac Rodman learned of the Rebel attack from his skirmishers, he rode to inform Colonel Lucius Fairchild, only to fall mortally wounded.

Hill's lead brigade under Brigadier General James H. Archer ploughed right into Harland's *8th Connecticut*, which was still preoccupied with a fire fight with Toombs' Georgians in its front. The Connecticut unit had no choice but to fall back in retreat, leaving the left flank of the *16th Connecticut* and the rookie *4th Rhode Island* wide open to an attack by Hill's next unit, Gregg's South Carolina brigade. The Rhode Islanders, who had only been in the service for three weeks, were at first confused by the blue uniforms some of the Confederates wore. Their commander, Colonel William H.P. Steere, felt an advance was in order and requested the commander of the *16th Connecticut* to support him, only to be told, "We must depend on ourselves."

Gregg's attack lost some of its impetus when the general fell from his horse, stunned by a Yankee shell. As he was being carried from the field on a stretcher, one of his bearers exclaimed, "General, you aren't wounded, you are only bruised." Gregg realized the truth of his statement and lept off the stretcher in order to return to the fight.

Gregg's attack now broke the flank of *Harland's brigade*, and sent it sprawling back to the bridge on the double quick. With his left in shambles, Cox ordered his entire command to withdraw. *Ewing's Ohio brigade* made a stand at a stone wall near the Otto cornfield, but held their fire when they saw a body of blue clad troops approach. A few volleys from Gregg's, Archer's and

The Old Lutheran Church on Main Street in Sharpsburg served as a Union hospital after the battle. Burnside's skirmishers reached the base of the hill during their attack late in the battle before being turned back.

Pender's brigades proved their true identity and sent the Northern brigade fleeing off to join the rest of the Federals heading towards the bridge. The Confederate prisoner quoted earlier thoroughly enjoyed this sudden turn of events:

> The air was filled with bursting shells, as if a dozen batteries had opened at once from the direction of Sharpsburg, and while we stood gazing we saw emerging from a cornfield a long line of gray, musket barrels scintillating in the rays of the declining sun and the Southern battle flags gleaming redly against the dark background....From the long line of gray a purplish mist broke, pierced by a bright gleam here and there, and the noise of the volley sounded like the whir of machinery....The triumphant advance, the jubilant shouts, the stirring beat of the drums, the mad, eager rush of the forces in blue were stayed, and back they came without order of formation, and we joined the hurrying throng, not stopping until we reached the valley near the bridge.

Burnside's retreat brought a quick end to the fighting on this flank. His failed drive towards Sharpsburg had cost the Yankees 2,350 men in killed and wounded, while the Confederates lost some 1,000 men; Hill incredibly lost only 63 men. Some of the troops of the *IX Corps*, especially those who had fought on the right with Wilcox, felt cheated of victory, because they were called back when victory was so close. One soldier wrote bitterly, "Triumph was to be limited to results scarcely more gratifying than those of defeat. Those who had lost their limbs and spilled their blood to gain success must lie upon the field still bleeding, hungry, thirsty, and dying by hundreds, because their General was too cowardly to close with the enemy and save them from a terrible fate." Indeed had Burnside or Cox been more aggressive, they might have been able to break the exhausted Confederate line, because they outnumbered the Confederates on the right by at least two to one even after Hill arrived. In addition, part of the *V Corps* lay near the Middle Bridge to support a possible attack. However, neither Burnside, Porter nor McClellan were about to think in terms of pressing forward any more that day. They chose instead to make the best of the small gains they had made.

The last significant action of the day took place on the Piper farm in the center of the battlefield. It seems that a number of Confederate snipers were annoying a battery posted in support of *Smith's division* of the *VI Corps*. The battery's commander complained to Colonel William H. Irwin, who in turn ordered Major Thomas W. Hyde of the *7th Maine* to "Take your regiment and drive the enemy away from those trees and buildings." Hyde saw that his commander was shamefully inebriated, and declared, "Colonel, I have seen a large force of rebel go in there, I should think two brigades." "Are you afraid to go, sir?" chided Irwin who repeated the command. Acquiescing, Hyde said, "Give the order so the regiment can hear it and we are ready, sir." After Irwin did so, the *7th Maine* prepared to launch its attack sometime around 1700.

Before moving off, Hyde had the two young boys who carried the unit's guidons sent to the rear; the lads pretended to do so, but returned to the advance. In the attack one would fall dead from a bullet while the other lost his arm. As the Federals approached the enemy lines, they passed over the Sunken Road, still packed with the dead, dying and wounded. After stopping in the cornfield to redress their lines, the Yankees from Maine surged forward towards the Hagerstown Road. Some regiments of Brigadier General W.T.H. *Brooks' Brigade* wanted to join the charge but their commander responded, "You will never see that regiment again." A battery behind them tried to support their attack by firing over the heads of the advancing line, but accidently dropped a shot into their ranks which knocked out four men. Moving faster now, the Federals came under fire from a Rebel line behind a stone wall along the Hagerstown Road. After driving the Rebels through the Piper farm, Hyde could see that his command was outnumbered by the Southerners, but he pressed on nonetheless. As a sergeant tried to pull down an opening in a fence for the major's horse, an enemy shell caught his haversack, throwing hardtack into the air and bringing a moment of humor to the increasingly grim situation.

As the Maine boys pressed against the Confederates, they found themselves trapped in a horrendous pocket of fire. When a shot pierced the arm of the flag bearer, Corporal Harry Campbell, the dismounted Hyde called out to him, "Take the other hand, Harry." After hearing Campbell give another cry, the major turned to take up the colors, only to find himself ahead of his regiment, which was rapidly retreating. When the Major saw the Rebels approaching close enough for him to be able to read the word "Manassas" on one of their battle flags, he attempted to flee. Hyde was almost surrounded when a cry went up from his men, "Rally, boys, to save the Major." The Yankees surged forth once more to save their commander, and the Rebels were forced back, so allowing Hyde to take his men back to Union ranks. As the Maine troops returned, their comrades raised hats while shouting mighty cheers. Hyde was to recall later, "When we knew our efforts were resultant from no plans or design at headquarters, but were from an inspiration of John Barleycorn in our commander alone, I wished I had been old enough or distinguished enough to disobey orders."

Thus the battle drew to a close shortly before sunset. All told, the *Army of the Potomac* had lost 2,108 men dead, 9,540 wounded and 753 missing, a total of 12,401 casualties. On the other side, Lee had lost 1,546 dead, 7,752 wounded, and 1,018 missing, an aggregate loss of 10,318 men fallen. Altogether, 22,719 Americans fell on the fields of Sharpsburg on that single September

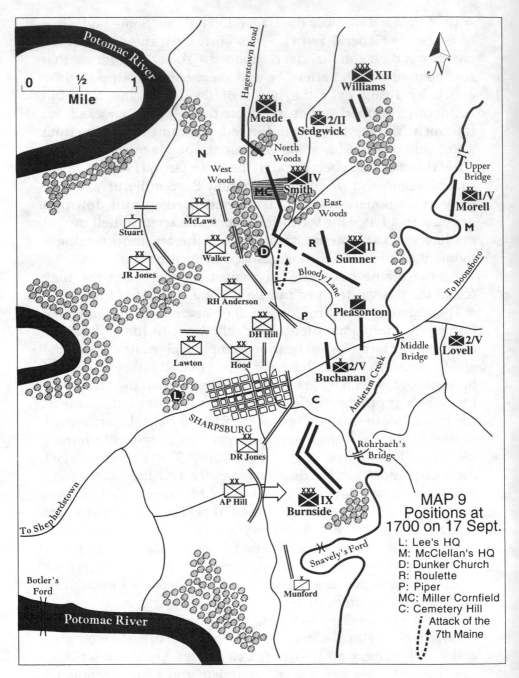

Potomac River

0   ½   1
Mile

Hagerstown Road

XXX XII
Williams

XXX I
Meade

XX 2/II
Sedgwick

North Woods

N

West Woods

XXX IV
Smith

MC

Upper Bridge

XX 1/V
Morell

XX McLaws

East Woods

M

x Stuart

D

R

XXX II
Sumner

To Boonsboro

XX Walker

Bloody Lane

XX JR Jones

XX RH Anderson

P

XX Pleasonton

Middle Bridge

XX 2/V
Lovell

XX DH Hill

XX Lawton

XX Hood

XX 2/V
Buchanan

Antietam Creek

L

SHARPSBURG

C

XX DR Jones

Rohrbach's Bridge

To Shepherdstown

XX AP Hill

XXX IX
Burnside

Snavely's Ford

MAP 9
Positions at
1700 on 17 Sept.

L: Lee's HQ
M: McClellan's HQ
D: Dunker Church
R: Roulette
P: Piper
MC: Miller Cornfield
C: Cemetery Hill
Attack of the
7th Maine

Botler's Ford

Potomac River

x Munford

day, a record that has not been exceeded by any of this nation's battles before or since.

The exhausted troops on both sides were glad to be able to rest where they stood. The historian of Kershaw's brigade recalled:

> It may be easily imagined that both armies were glad enough to fall upon the ground and rest after such a day of blood and carnage, with the smoke, dust, and weltering heat of the day. Before the sound of the last gun had died away in the distance one hundred thousand men were stretched upon the ground fast asleep, while a third of that number were sleeping their last sleep or suffering the effects of fearful wounds.

A Yankee concurred with such sentiments writing, "The men were physically exhausted, hungry, but a few had food, thirsty and with out water, sad at heart—for comrades who had been killed or wounded..." Two Federal soldiers headed for an inviting pile of straw to rest upon. When told there was a dead body lying beneath it, the Federals merely collapsed on the bed, using the body of the corpse as a pillow.

Colonel Francis Palfrey of the *20th Massachusetts* wrote of the awful night that followed that terrible day, "The blessed night came, and brought with it sleep and forgetfulness and refreshment to many; but the murmur of the night wind, breathing over fields of wheat and clover, was mingled with the groans of countless sufferers of both armies. Who can tell, who can even imagine, the horrors of such a night, while the unconscious stars shone above, and the unconscious river went rippling by?"

Ambrose Everett Burnside (1824-1881)

Burnside initially was employed as a tailor before winning an appointment to West Point at age 19. After leaving the army in 1853, Burnside sought a fortune from the patent and production of a breech loading carbine of his own design, only to have the venture fail when the government refused to purchase the weapon. Later, the army purchased 55,000 Burnside carbines for its armies during the Civil War. Fortunately in the meantime, Burnside's good friend and future commander, George B. McClellan, found employment for him with the Illinois Central Railroad until war broke out in 1861. After commanding a brigade at First Bull Run, Burnside waged a successful campaign on the North Carolina coast at a time when the Federals were desperate for military victories. His success brought him to the attention of President Lincoln. He was offered command of the *Army of the Potomac*, but refused, partly because he recognized his own limitations and partly because he preferred to serve under McClellan. However, the old chums had a falling out after the Battle of Antietam, and on 7 November, Burnside accepted Lincoln's request to relieve "Little Mac." Unfortunately, the bewhiskered general's lack of ability was openly evident in a disastrous attack on the Confederate army at Fredericksburg, which caused the loss of 13,000 troops while inflicting less than half as many fatalities on the enemy.

After being relieved of command of the *Army of the Potomac*, Burnside was given command of the *Department of the Ohio*, where he engaged in a forceful effort to stamp out sedition. Among other actions, he arrested the Copperhead politician Clement L. Vallandigham and suppressed the pro-Southern *Chicago Times*. After defeating James Longstreet at Knoxville, Tennessee, Burnside returned to the East and mishandled the *IX Corps* in the attack at the Petersburg Crater. With his military reputation irrevocably tarnished, he finally resigned his commission shortly after the end of the war. He later led a successful career in politics, and was elected governor of Rhode Island as well as U.S. Senator.

Robert Augustus Toombs (1810-1885)

Robert Toombs was a powerful political general from Wilkes County, Georgia. He graduated from New York's Union College in 1828 and entered a career in law. Toombs attained both wealth and eminence in his native state, and almost won the presidency of the Confederate States of America but was defeated by Mississippian Jefferson C. Davis. As Secretary of State in the early days of the Confederacy, he inaugurated a stormy relationship with his fellow government leaders by opposing an attack on Fort Sumter. When his position in Davis' cabinet became uncomfortable, Toombs resigned to take to the battlefield as a brigadier general commanding a brigade of Georgians in Longstreet's division. The cantankerous Georgian was eventually put under arrest for a short period in August of 1862 for neglect of duty. After returning to command a short time later, Toombs confided to his wife he would resign his commission after the next great battle, which turned out to be Antietam.

He was one of the Confederate heroes of the battle when he maintained a stubborn resistance against *IX Corps* at Burnside's Bridge and held up the Federal advance against Lee's right flank for three hours. Toombs stayed with the army until March 1863, when he finally resigned after failing to receive a promotion to major general. He returned to public life, and became the gadfly of the Confederate government, serving as a major critic of Davis' policies. After briefly returning to military service to fight under Johnston, Toombs fled the country after the war, only to return two years later. He once again engaged in Georgia politics but did not take up any real office.

The Youngest Casualty

The youngest Union casualty at Antietam, and perhaps of the entire war, was Charles E. King, a drummer boy in *Company F* of the *49th Pennsylvania*. Young Charley was born in April, 1849, in West Chester, outside of Philadelphia. He was an enthusiastic drummer, and when the war broke out was eager to enlist, a move his father violently objected to. The frustrated lad began spending his free time at a recruiting station, and quickly impressed Captain Benjamin H. Sweeney with his drumming skills. Sweeney interceded with Charles' father, and won permission for the boy to join up by promising that he would personally see that Charles would not be exposed to danger.

After at length gaining his father's approval, young Charles enlisted in *Company F* of the *49th Pennsylvania Volunteers* on September 9, 1861, at the age of 12 years and 5 months. He performed so well that he soon became regimental drum major. He saw his first battle action during the Peninsula campaign and so was a veteran at the time of Antietam.

Charles' regiment fought at Antietam as part of *Hancock's brigade*, *Smith's division, Franklin's VI Corps*. The division did not participate actually in the day's heavy fighting but came on the field late in the action to support Cowan's battery on the Miller farm, near the famous cornfield. The fighting in this sector was all over except for occasional artillery fire. Sometime after 1300 a Confederate shell landed in the ranks of the *49th* and wounded several soldiers, including drummer boy Charles King, who had his abdomen torn open by a piece of shrapnel. The lad lingered on for three days before he died at a hospital on 20 September.

He was 13 years and 5 months old, the battle's youngest casualty.

J.E.B. Stuart's Post Antietam Raid

While McClellan dallied near Sharpsburg, slowly rebuilding his army's strength after the great battle of Antietam, Lee decided to have J.E.B. Stuart lead a strong reconnaissance mission across the river to gather intelligence on the enemy's position. If conditions permitted, the cavalry was then to approach Chambersburg, Pennsylvania, and destroy the Cumberland Valley Railroad bridge there. Lee also advised his subordinate to attempt to capture any individuals maintaining state or Federal offices who could be used as hostages to win the release of Confederate prisoners.

The raid would entail considerable risk because the Potomac had few fords for crossings and the area into which Stuart was to advance was frequented with telegraph lines and railroads that could quickly alert the enemy and speed troops to where they were needed. In warning Stuart of the risks involved, Lee wrote, "Reliance is placed upon your skill and judgment in the successful execution of this plan, and it is not intended or desired that you should jeopardize the safety of your command, or go farther than your good judgment may dictate."

Despite the dangers facing him, Stuart was eager for another opportunity to ride around McClellan as he had back in the Peninsula campaign. Though Lee had ordered him

to take 1,200-1,500 troopers on the mission, the cavalry commander took 1,800 of his men across the Potomac at McCoy's Ford on the morning of 10 October and quickly captured the Yankee picket that had been established there. When they learned of the existence of a large enemy force at Hagerstown, the cavalry moved on to Mercersburg where they purchased the entire stock of shoes of a local merchant. Meanwhile, Captain W.W. Blackford located a local citizen who reportedly owned a map containing all the roads in the immediate area. He approached the home only to be denied access by the women in residence. Undaunted, Blackford forced his way into the house, writing later in his reminiscences, "...I was obliged to dismount and push by the infuriated ladies, rather rough specimens, however, into the sitting room where I found the map hanging on the wall. Angry women do not show to advantage, and the language and looks of these were fearful, as I coolly cut the map out of its rollers and put it in my haversack."

After the Pennsylvania border was reached, Stuart's men plundered the area for anything they needed. They especially rounded up large conestoga horses which would be useful in transporting artillery. Because it was raining the local farmers were threshing wheat in their barns rather than working in the fields where they might have been able to spot and report these movements by the enemy. In fact, the resonant hum of the threshers drew the Confederate troopers to the barns where in some cases, the Confederates posed as Yankees requisitioning food and horses, only to be amused to hear curses against the government and the war.

Towards evening, the cavalry collected their booty and headed for Chambersburg. To their dismay, the railroad bridge there was made out of iron and defied all attempts by the Confederates to do damage to the structure. Before leaving Chambersburg the next day, they set fire to railroad facilities, Federal stores, and an ammunition train captured from Longstreet (originally the booty from Grimes Davis' magnificent escape). Stuart surprised his men as he ordered the command to turn eastward towards Gettysburg instead of heading south. This maneuver took his troops on a long ride around the rear of the *Army of the Potomac* into enemy territory. The cavalry general believed the area around the Potomac's fords downstream was more open terrain and could not be defended, and so offered the Confederates the best opportunity to return to safety in Virginia.

The column turned to the south just before Gettysburg, and headed on a path that took it just ten miles from the flank of McClellan's army. The soldiers rode with only a few halts to rest; their mounts were spared total exhaustion as the riders switched steeds to ride the horses they had captured in Pennsylvania. The weather seemed to favor the Southern raiders as the sun came out and provided a fine day. An early rain kept dust from being kicked that might alert enemy signal stations to spot their movements.

When they arrived near Emmitsburg, Stuart's men were fortunate to capture a Federal courier whose dispatches provided information about the location of Union forces near Frederick and a cavalry force four miles to the east of the Confederates' present position. The troops veered off to the west and south, and headed towards Urbana, where they had been treated to a fine ball over a month before, and reached the Potomac crossing at White's Ford by 12 October. They came upon a Federal force entrenched in a quarry, blocking the Confederate cavalry from reaching safe haven. Since the Federals were alerted to his presence, Stuart decided to forego a battle and bluff the enemy force into submission. When he dispatched a note to the Yankees demanding their surrender, the Federals, perhaps awed by Stuart's reputation, retreated rather than risk a confrontation. A Union detachment of cavalry arrived, as the Confederate troopers were crossing into Virginia, but they also declined to start a fight.

Stuart's three day jaunt had taken him 100 miles around the *Army of the Potomac* with hardly any casualties. Meanwhile, he had caused $250,000 in property damage and captured 1,200 horses. An irate Gideon Welles, Lincoln's Secretary of the Navy, wrote in his diary on 13 October, "We have mortifying intelligence that the Rebel cavalry rode entirely around our great and victorious Army of the Potomac....It is the second time this feat has been performed by J.E.B. Stuart around McClellan's army....It is humiliating and disgraceful. In this raid the Rebels have possessed themselves of a good deal of plunder, reclothed their men from our stores, run off a thousand horses, fat cattle, etc., etc. It is not a pleasant fact to know that we are clothing, mounting, and subsisting not only our troops but the Rebels also."

CHAPTER XII

Lee's Retreat

Despite the massive carnage of the day's hideous bloody battle, both sides prepared to renew the conflict on the morning of 18 September. McClellan seemingly held all the advantages—all he had to do was to renew the attack with his fresh troops, about 20,000 men in the *V* and *VI Corps*. Including the remains of four corps that had carried most of the fighting on the 17th, McClellan had about 60,000 men available, many more than Lee had started the battle with. Even including A.P. Hill's tired but lightly used brigades, Lee had less than 25,000 totally exhausted men to defend his shrunken perimeter.

It is amazing that McClellan did not exploit what was perhaps his most golden opportunity of the campaign. All he had to do was to conduct one last grand charge, and he could have smashed Lee's broken army against the Potomac. Instead, he chose to hold his gains on the right and await the arrival of fresh troops that included *Couch's division* of 6,000 men and another 6,000 being forwarded from Washington. McClellan had been greatly impressed with the ferocity of Lee's defense, and firmly believed that the Confederates had many more troops than they ever did. He was correct in his estimation that many of his units were worn out and needed reorganization, but they were no more disorganized than the troops that fought more than one day at Gettysburg. And they were certainly in better shape than Lee's depleted units, many of which were so shot up that they had no identity left.

Some historians have suggested that McClellan did not want

to win a total victory on the battlefield, and so deliberately let Lee get away. They suggest that McClellan because of his political leanings simply wanted to bring the war to an end and restore the country to its pre-1860 existence. All he needed to do was show Lee that the South could not win a military victory in the field, and that their best future lay in negotiating a settlement to the war. This stance was also why McClellan did not push harder on his drive to Richmond earlier in the year. This theory puts McClellan in much the same awkward pose that the Howe brothers had in 1778—they were charged with leading the British military forces, but were also part of a secret commission that sought to end the war by settlement. This is an interesting interpretation of McClellan's motives in 1862, but one that does not seem to be supported by any statements McClellan made to anyone or by any evidence in his voluminous personal correspondence, particularly the many letters he sent regularly to his wife.

On the opposite side of the field, Lee gathered his field officers to get an overview of the situation that faced him and his men. Upon receiving each commander, he asked, "General, how is it on your part of the line?" Harvey Hill replied his troops had barely held and would not be able to do much against the overwhelming numbers of the Federals on the next day. When Jackson was asked about the condition of his troops, he said that his losses had been excessive with many of his field officers being shot down. When approached for his report, Hood plainly stated that he had no division. Upon hearing this, Lee shouted excitedly, "Great God, General Hood, where is the splendid division you had this morning?" The Kentuckian replied, "They are lying on the field where you sent them, sir; but few have straggled. My division has been almost wiped out." Longstreet arrived at the meeting late because he had stopped in Sharpsburg to help a family put out a fire in their burning home. Lee had feared that Longstreet might have been wounded, and was so relieved to see him that he excitedly placed his hands on the general's shoulders, exclaiming in hearty relief, "Here is my old war horse at last." When asked how his troops were holding up, Longstreet replied that his men had suffered severely and he only had enough strength to throw up a picket line. Most of the officers of the Army of Northern Virginia were of the opinion

Dr. Hurd of the **14th Indiana** *helps care for Confederate wounded after the battle.*

that the command could take no more punishment and would have to be withdrawn across the Potomac.

On this advice Lee merely turned to his commanders and delivered a shocking address, "Gentlemen, we will not cross the Potomac to-night. You will go to your respective commands, strengthen your lines, send two officers from each brigade toward the ford to collect your stragglers, and get them up. Many others have already come up. I have had the proper steps taken to collect all the men who are in the rear. If McClellan wants to fight in the morning, I will give him battle again." With the stragglers collected, the Army of Northern Virginia could only boast some 28,000 men on the field. Out of pride and perhaps a little contempt for his enemy, Lee would wait for McClellan to renew the battle. He had no more reserves.

When the sun rose on Thursday 18 September, except for a smattering of picket fire, neither side made a move. It was as though both sides made an agreement, as one Texan said, "I'll let you alone if you let me alone."

Between both armies lay the somber evidence of the earlier day's battle. In the various accounts of the battle of Antietam, the terrible visage of the aftermath of this nation's bloodiest day seems to have dominated soldiers' views of the fight at Sharpsburg. One of Franklin's Yankees wrote,

The scene of the battle-field was past description. The mangled forms of our own comrades lay stretched upon the ground, side by side with those of the rebels. On almost every rod of ground over one hundred acres, the dead and wounded, some clad in the Union blue and some in Confederate gray, were lying. A ghastly sight, presenting all the horrible features of death which are to be seen on such a field. At one point in our own front, for more than half mile, the rebels lay so thickly as almost to touch one another. On the field where Hooker's men had won and lost the field, the dead and dying were scattered thickly amongst the broken cornstalks, their eyes protruding and their faces blackened by the sun. Wherever the lines of battle had surged to and fro, these vestiges of the terrible work were left. In the edge of the (West) woods, where the Rebels had made a stand against Hooker's advancing divisions, the bodies lay in perfect line, as though they had fallen while on dress parade. Further to the left there was a narrow road, not more than fifteen feet wide, with fences on either side. Here a regiment of rebels was posted; our batteries getting an enfilading fire upon them, and the infantry at the same time opening a murderous fire, the regiment was literally destroyed; not more than twenty of their number escaping. Their bodies filled the narrow road. Some were shot while attempting to get over the fence; and their remains hung on the boards. A more fearful picture than we saw here, could not be conceived.

Frederick L. Hitchcock of the *132nd Pennsylvania* recorded,

The lines of battle of both armies were not only marked by the presence of the dead, but by a vast variety of army equipage, such as blankets, canteens, haversacks, guns, gun-slings, bayonets, ramrods, some whole, others broken—verily a bosom of destruction had done its work faithfully here. Dead horses were everywhere here, and the stench from them and the human dead was terrible. "Uncle" Billy Sherman has said, "War is hell!" yet this definition, with all that imagination can picture, fails to reveal all its bloody horrors.

The positions of some of the dead were very striking. One poor fellow lay face down on a partially fallen stone wall, with one arm and foot extended, as if in the act of crawling over. His position attracted our attention, and we found his body literally riddled with bullets—there must have been hundreds—and most of them shot into him after he was dead, for they showed no marks of blood. Probably the poor fellow had been wounded in trying to reach shelter behind the wall, was spotted in the act by our men, and killed right there, and became thereafter a target for every new man that saw him. Another man lay, still clasping his musket, which he was evidently in the act of loading when a bullet pierced his heart, literally flooding his gun with his life's blood, a ghastly testimonial to his heroic sacrifice.

The Miller cornfield, that had played host to continuous charge after charge, countercharge after countercharge, was now a grotesque charnel house containing the vast numbers of men who had fallen there. A gunner of the *1st Rhode Island* wrote of the scene there:

Over this space the two lines had been putting forth all their energies since light, and the ground was strewn with dead and wounded, horses and men, clothing, knapsacks, canteens, muskets, and side arms broken and twisted in ever imaginable manner. The blue and the gray were indiscriminately mingled, either motionless and lifeless, or dragging their bleeding forms along in search of some less exposed situation. And there were those whose lifeblood was fast or slowly ebbing away, with only strength sufficient to raise a supplicating arm for assistance or relief.

Another soldier wrote of the field around the Cornfield:

The dead were found in all imaginable positions and often horribly mangled. One Confederate had been killed while climbing over a fence, his body remaining in such a position that it might have readily have been taken for that of a live man; another was struck while tearing a cartridge, the charge still remaining between his stiffened fingers; the head of another was taken off by a cannon ball; while a manly-looking Union soldier apparently had no wound anywhere, but closer inspection showed that a ball had entered one ear coming out the other. It was simply horrible to look upon these heaps and windrows of festering bodies that once contained the spirits of the best soldiers of the two armies. The cornfield near which the *88th (Pennsylvania)* stood was a veritable field of blood, being almost

Union burial party after the battle. Frassanito identified the location as a field next to the Hagerstown Pike just west of the Miller Cornfield.

covered with gore, shreds of hair, bones, and brain...the men soon sickened at these repulsive sights, few going more than once over the field.

The historian of the *60th New York* wrote of the forms of the dead after being struck by rigor mortus,

> I noticed one rebel with five shots in his head. He was kneeling on one knee, his gun lying on his left hand as though he had been in the act of taking aim. When I saw him he had probably been dead some 12 hours, but other dead lay against him so he had not fallen from the position he was in when shot. Others were in a sitting posture; some were lying on their backs, with their arm outstretched, and fingers spread, as if they were clutching or keeping off a foe. Where the artillery had swept them with grape and canister, their line of battle could be traced by the dead bodies that lay on it—sometimes as far as the eye could see.

Lying out in the heat of the day, the bodies became swollen, bloated and turned sickeningly black. A Federal on the field of battle said of the spectacle, "Nearly all (the dead) lay with their faces up and eyes wide open presenting a spectacle to make one shudder....Their limbs and bodies were so enlarged that their clothing seemed ready to burst." Throughout the previous night and even during the day, individuals with little moral qualms scoured the dead for trophies and booty. Many bodies could be seen with their shoes removed and their pockets turned inside out, robbed of items they would no longer have a use for. One Yankee brought in a piece of paper found on the body of a Confederate. It contained the tracing of the hand of an infant, a child born while the new father was away at war. Below the tracing were the words from his wife, "If you want to kiss the baby you must kiss this hand." For some of the rookie troops, the fields of Sharpsburg presented their first introduction to the grim realities of war, as Alfred S. Roe of the *10th Massachusetts* noted: "...what an introduction to the embryo soldier that terrible field of Antietam must have been! Had he cherished any delusive fancy as to the romance of the war, the rapidly swelling corpses of lately active thinking men must have reduced him to the hard pan with sickening haste."

As Thursday passed away, enemy troops sniped at one another, setting up crude breastworks of dead bodies for protection. In front of the Federal lines near the Sunken Road, Yankees were forced to listen to the never ending cries of the dying and wounded of both sides before them. Determined to assist the wounded, one Federal attempted to ease the suffering of one of the enemy's fallen, and braved the picket fire to crawl out between the lines to give a Southerner a drink of water. In other parts of the field, an informal truce existed for troops to collect bodies, care for the wounded, and even discuss recent events with the enemy. While one Federal was scouring the field for wounded friends needing assistance, he chanced upon a lieutenant from the Louisiana Tigers, who was searching the field for his dead brother. With tears in his eyes, the Southerner pointed to the bodies of his deceased comrades to say, "Most of my men lie there." After carrying on a short conversation, both men parted company, expressing the hope they would not be forced to meet on the battlefields the next day.

Fortunately for the troops of both sides there would be no renewal of the fight on the 19th either. Lee realized that

McClellan was bound to receive more reinforcements, so he finally decided to pull his troops across the Potomac on the night of the 18th. They crossed safely at Boteler's Ford and moved on to Martinsburg, Virginia, in the Shenandoah Valley. During the movement, a band struck up the tune of "Maryland, My Maryland" only to meet the protests and catcalls of their comrades, openly displaying their bitterness over their adventures and treatment in the Free State. While the survivors of the 1st Texas passed by the 6th North Carolina, a soldier of the Lone Star State called out good naturedly "Hallou, fellers! Have you a good supply of tar on your heels this morning?" Evidently the North Carolinians were not in the mood for such jokes. "Yes," came a sour reply, "and it's a real pity you'uns didn't come over and borrow a little the other day; it mout have saved that flag o'your'n." Other troops paraphrased the song and sang "Damn My Maryland."

In the early morning hours of the 19th, Walker reported to Lee that only a few ambulances and a battery lay upon the Maryland side of the Potomac, whereupon Lee let out a great sigh of relief: "Thank God!" Undaunted by the setbacks of his campaign in Maryland, Lee was still pondering the possibility of returning to the offensive by crossing back over the Potomac at Williamsport up to the west. However, he had only to look at his army to see that his men were all worn out by the almost continuous fighting and marching since Cedar Mountain.

Characteristically, McClellan took his time in launching a pursuit. As usual, he claimed that his army was too worn out and his supplies were too depleted to make an advance. Thus, most of his troops sat idle while others went about burying the dead and collecting wounded who remained on the field.

While most of the army remained at Sharpsburg to attend to the remnants of the battle on the 19th, Fitz-John Porter made a weak attempt at a crossing on the Potomac. He sent the *1st U. S. Sharpshooters* supported by the *4th Michigan* into Virginia. The Federals encountered fire from two Confederate batteries and took four of their guns as trophies. After the fight, Porter recalled his force that night and prepared for a stronger attack the next day. Upon seeing the captured guns, Brigadier General Charles Griffin, whose battery had been cut up at the first great battle of the war, exclaimed, "I've recaptured one of my old guns that was lost at Bull Run."

When he reported to Lee, Pendleton made out the situation to be much worse than it actually was, and claimed that he had lost all the guns of the Reserve Artillery to the enemy. Lee also feared that McClellan might be crossing in force in an attempt to attack his army while it was on the move. To meet this threat, Lee dispatched A.P. Hill with his Light Division to force the Federals back into Maryland.

The next morning the Confederates slammed into three Federal brigades sent across the river by Porter. One South Carolinian described the attack:

> Our whole first line of three brigades moved as one man, as steadily, coolly, deliberately as if on the drill ground....What a spectacle it must have been to the enemy!...the same men who had marched nearly five hundred miles in Virginia and Maryland, in rags, on insufficient food, and many of them without a shoe to their feet; the same men, who had, but the day before, been withdrawn before the treble number of Federals; these same men turned upon them, unconfused by moral appearances, unterrified by the formidable array of artillery and infantry, and sternly moved through thunder and slaughter to the last ditch-clinch!

As the increasingly hard pressed Yankees fell back, the *118th Pennsylvania* was cut apart when it lost its commander and did not receive orders to retreat. The Pennsylvanians found themselves alone against an enemy division and had no choice but to flee in panic when their defective Belgian muskets would not work properly. They made inviting targets as they waded across the ford, and the Confederate soldiers poured a deadly fire into the retreating mass. Porter's artillery on the Maryland side of the Potomac attempted to cover the retreat: "The roar of the pieces, and howl and explosion of the shells, was awful. Sometimes a shell burst right in the ranks tearing and mangling all around it." One Rebel was literally thrown into the air by one almighty explosion. The sharp fight at Shepherdstown lost Porter 363 men killed, wounded, and missing, of which 269 were from the *118th Pennsylvania*. The Federals had found that the Rebels still had a formidable bite. After learning their lesson, they would not cross the Potomac in force for some time.

As the final days of September passed McClellan still refused to budge from Antietam, as he gathered supplies and reinforcements to strengthen his army before engaging in any attempt to return to Virginia to engage Lee. His hesitancy made Lincoln and Halleck so annoyed that the President himself came to visit the army on 1 October. Though he thought he had won assurances that McClellan would move sometime soon, the army continued to stay on the Maryland side of the Potomac. Almost a week after Lincoln's visit, Halleck sent a dispatch to McClellan, ordering him to take to the offensive, while promising 30,000 reinforcements to ease the general's crippling fears that he could do nothing substantial while outnumbered by the enemy. Still, as on the Peninsula, the general continued to call for more supplies, and more troops.

McClellan's failure to move allowed Lee to bring his army back up to strength by taking in most of the stragglers he had lost going into Maryland, as well as new recruits. By 10 October, his army was rejuvenated to a total strength of over 64,000 men. McClellan's inactivity also allowed Stuart to launch one of his most famous raids, his "second ride around McClellan" of 9-12 October, that succeeded in destroying a great amount of property in Chambersburg, Pennsylvania. (see sidebar)

Lincoln's growing impatience can be seen in his response to McClellan's complaint that the horses of his cavalry were fatigued. "Will you pardon me for asking what the horses of your army have done since the battle of Antietam that fatigues anything."

Finally, over a full month after the battle, McClellan declared his intention to return to Virginia on 26 October. He even stalled long enough for Lee to be able to dispatch Longstreet to Culpeper to impede the Federal advance. Lincoln decided enough was enough. On 5 November he sent orders for McClellan to step down and turn the army over to Burnside. Many leaders in Washington felt that this was a risky move. McClellan might refuse to step down, and so cause a major crisis. There was also no certainty as to how the army might receive the action. Further, Lincoln's choice to head the army, Burnside, had already rejected the offer to command the army twice before and might do so again. Fortunately for the Republic, the transition went smoothly. Burnside, perhaps still smarting from his treat-

The **118th Pennsylvania (Corn Exchange Regiment)** *crossed the Potomac at Shepherdstown only to be decimated by a sharp Confederate counterattack on 20 September.*

ment by his old friend during Antietam, accepted the position. Thus ended the great struggle that was the Antietam campaign.

While the battle between Lee and McClellan at Antietam was effectively a draw, both sides had reasons to claim victory. Although the final culmination of the campaign was not the triumph the Confederacy needed to end the war, Southerners had some reason to be satisfied with the outcome. The greatest success of September of 1862, the capture of the Federal garrison at Harpers Ferry, came with only a slight loss of life. No doubt, Lee might have accomplished a great deal more had not a copy of Special Orders 191 been found. Once he had found out McClellan was on the move, Lee moved with the necessary speed to save his army from destruction. Assisted by Harvey

Hill's stalwart defense at Turner's Gap, and Jackson's and A.P. Hill's speed, as well as Federal sluggishness, he managed to have enough of his army up on the field for the fight near the banks of the Antietam. In supervising the battle, Lee and his lieutenants once again demonstrated their outstanding brilliance, shifting troops where needed to blunt the thrusts of his adversary. In the cases where they did not have organized reinforcements available, lines were improvised and thrown into the fray. Though hard pressed throughout the battle, the generals and men had refused to quit and retreat. However, they had reached the limits of their endurance and without reinforcements they could do no more but retreat.

In falling back to Virginia, Lee lost the influence his movements might have had if a victory had been won on 17 September. Though supposedly loyal to the South, Maryland had not risen to join the Confederate cause or even provide Lee with much in the way of manpower and supplies. Worse still, the campaign did little to weaken the resolve of the war effort of the North. Perhaps the most important result the battle was to have for the South was to force the political powers in Great Britain to reconsider the possibility of granting Confederate recognition. After learning of the outcome of Antietam, Prime Minister Palmerston wrote to Russell that the matter of recognition "is full of difficulty, and can only be cleared up by some more decided events between the contending armies." On 28 October the British cabinet voted against Russell and Gladstone and refused to offer recognition to the Confederacy. Shortly afterwards the cabinet also declined a French plan to suggest a six month armistice and a suspension of the Union blockade.

Despite the inconclusiveness of the battle of Antietam, McClellan perceived the campaign and battle as a great victory won through his own skill, the bravery of his men and the grace of God. Indeed, he had some reason to be jubilant. He pulled the army together after months of disappointing and humiliating defeats, reorganized it, fought Lee to a standstill and forced the Confederates back into Virginia. While the general could be content with that, he had betrayed his men and himself by failing to take advantage of the tremendous opportunities given to him. After the dismal Peninsula campaign, he was granted a gift which

Not everyone in the North supported Lincoln's Emancipation, which was issued after the battle of Antietam. One New Jersey soldier said he would not have enlisted if he knew Lincoln was going to free the Negroes.

few military leaders ever attain after great defeats—a second chance. When he took the field against Lee in Maryland, his fortunes were increased when fate bestowed on him Special Orders 191. Despite such incredible luck, the general squandered all the breaks given to him. He failed to get his troops on the road on the evening of 13 September immediately after receiving orders, and he failed to attack on the 15th and the 16th. Still, there were many chances for McClellan to redeem himself. Despite his sloppy coordination of the battle of Antietam, had he committed the full strength of his army, he might have been able to bring the battle to a decisive conclusion had he used Franklin and Porter on either the 17th or 18th. However, his fear of the enemy's strength and an inability to bring himself to commit his army decisively brought his downfall. McClellan had often proven himself an able general. He had created the *Army of the Potomac*, he had organized great campaigns, his plans of battle were sound; the will behind them was too weak to achieve a real victory.

Blackford's (Soteler's) Ford, where Lee's army crossed back into Virginia on the night of 18-19 September.

While the Antietam campaign was not decisive militarily, Lincoln managed to salvage a victory out of the inconclusive battle. The President desired to infuse a revolutionary sentiment to reinvigorate the Federal war effort, and decided emancipation of slavery was just the element needed; it would undercut the basis of the South's economic and social structure, would give the North a semblance of moral superiority over its adversary by taking up the cause of human freedom, and would force European nations to seriously consider the unpopularity of allying with a faction that supported slavery. On 2 July, Lincoln had read a preliminary proclamation before his cabinet and asked for the opinions of his advisors. Secretary of State Seward gave the most sagacious advice, urging the President to wait until the Union forces won a real victory before issuing the decree; if issued in a moment of defeat, it would waste the political capital of the gesture, and seem as though the Federal government was making the move in desperation rather than strength. Antietam was not much of a victory, but after the failures of the Peninsula and Second Bull Run, Lincoln would take what he could get. He issued the Emancipation Proclamation on 22 September, promising to free all slaves in those states still in rebellion against the Union after 1 January 1863. Thus the Antietam campaign served to make emancipation a primary war issue, one on which the Republic would live or die. However, for the Emancipation to succeed, the South would have to be subdued, and that would take two and one-half more years of gruelling warfare and tens of thousands of lives.

The Emancipation Proclamation

The announcement of the Emancipation Proclamation on 22 September 1862 is popularly believed to be a key turning point of the war because it made the end of all slavery a Northern war goal. However, this is not what Lincoln originally intended, as the terms of the Proclamation reveal.

The Emancipation Proclamation did not free all the slaves in the South, just the slaves in those areas that were still in insurrection as of 1 January 1863. It said nothing of the slaves held in districts of the Confederacy under northern control at the time—which included New Orleans (the South's largest city by far), much of Tennessee, and chunks of the Atlantic coast, not to mention the slaves held in the border states of Maryland, Kentucky and Missouri. The Emancipation was actually an offer permitting the South to stop fighting and return to the Union by 1 January and still keep its slaves. If it did not do so, slavery would be eliminated in any future Confederate territory to be conquered. Thus the Proclamation should best be viewed as a war measure designed to undercut the South's economic and social fabric in order to reduce the Confederacy to submission. The Proclamation also had the positive effect of making the European powers, particularly Britain, more hesitant to support the Confederacy now that the partial elimination of slavery was an avowed Northern war aim. It also pleased the many Northern abolitionists who had been lobbying for years for the end of slavery. (It did not, though, please all Northern soldiers; some said that they would not have enlisted if they had known that their President was going to free the "niggers.") However, Lincoln did not announce what he planned to do about the slaves held in the border states and areas of the South under Union control on 1 January 1863. These were not freed by the Emancipation Proclamation, and the issue of slavery ("involuntary servitude") would not be addressed in its entirety until the 15th Amendment would be passed in early 1865.

Burying the Dead

For many days after the battle, the carnage of this nation's bloodiest day lay in evidence of the awful battle on the fields near Sharpsburg. Captain John P. Reynolds was combing the field when he spotted this horrible scene,

Under a fence by the way-side I was attracted by the soles of some shoes, too small for men's feet, sticking straight up into the air, six in a row. As I got nearer I noticed that they were Confederate bodies, placed side by side for burial but evidently left behind. Their bare ankles, dirty and sallow, showed below their blanket which covered their heads and curiosity prompted me to lift. Three young bearded faces, ghastly in death, with three pairs of glassy eyes, caused a shudder and I was glad enough to re-place it.

A good deal of those killed at Antietam were fortunate to receive as proper a burial as the circumstances would permit. In these cases the body would be wrapped in a sheet and lowered into a shallow hole, the grave marked thusly,

Jesse Tyson
Co I. 88. Regt. Penna. Vols.
Killed Sept. 17, 1862
A brave soldier and a kind comrade
Rest in peace

Most of the Confederate dead were not treated with such ceremony by the Federals. Hitchcock, after witnessing the burial details on duty, wrote,

The work was rough and heartless, but only comporting with the character of war. The natural reverence for the dead was wholly absent. The poor bodies, all of them heroes in their death, even though in a mistaken cause, were "planted" with as little feeling as though they were so many logs. A trench was dug where the digging was easiest, about seven feet wide and long enough to accommodate all the bodies in a certain radius; these were then placed to one side, cross-wise of the trench, and buried without anything to keep the earth from them. In the case of the Union dead the trenches were usually two or three feet deep, and the bodies were wrapped in blankets before be-ing covered, but with the rebels no blankets were used and the trenches were so shallow as to leave toes exposed after a shower.

No ceremony whatsoever attended this gruesome service but it was generally accompanied by ribald jokes, at the expense of the poor "Johnny" they were "planting." This was not the fruit of debased natures or degenerate hearts on the part of the boys, who well knew it might be their turn next, under the fortunes of war, to be buried in a like manner but it was the recklessness and thoughtlessness, born of the hardening influences of war.

Soon after the battle, citizens from the North arrived to scour the battlefield for relatives lost or killed during the battle. Despite the sickening visages of rotting corpses, these individuals often opened several graves in the course of their grim search.

After the war, 4,776 bodies of the Federal soldiers who died at the battle of Antietam were interred at the Antietam National Cemetery on the field where the fight took place. Some 1,836 of those buried there were never identified. Almost all of the Confederate dead were buried in trenches and unmarked graves. As many of them as could be found later were transferred to a cemetery in Hagerstown.

Photographing the Battlefield

The art of military photography was still in its infancy at the start of the Civil War. The science of photography itself was scarcely 20 years old, and only a few military scenes had been attempted in the late 1840s in Mexico and India. The first battlefield scenes dated to the Crimean War of 1854-55, and these were only static shots of officers, siege works, and rear areas. Limitations of the primitive camera process itself proscribed the taking of actual combat scenes, nor was anyone ever close enough to the front to take pictures of battlefield casualties. The first actual pictures of combat losses apparently were made in Northern Italy in 1859 and China in 1860, during the Second Opium War. None of these photographs, however, received widespread publication.

The American Civil War, then, was the first conflict to be widely photographed. James Gibson made a number of good pictures of the siege works and other features at Yorktown in the spring of 1862, but none showed troops or casualties. A further step was taken at Fair Oaks at the end of May, when the public for the first time saw photographs of graves of recent casualties. One of the most significant early photographs was taken by Gibson on 28 June 1862 of casualties being treated at a field hospital at Savage's Station.

By the end of the Peninsula campaign there were several teams of photographers in the field, all vying to be the first to photograph troops in action, or at least to photograph casualties lying on the battlefield. The prize in this quest fell to Alexander Gardner and James Gibson, who headed north from Washington DC in mid September in hopes of catching up with McClellan's army before it engaged Lee. By sheer luck they reached the Union army at Antietam late on 17 September, the day of the battle, or on the next day. Their timely arrival enabled them to photograph the battlefield while the scars of combat were still fresh, and a number of bodies of slain soldiers were still unburied.

Gardner and Gibson took at least 70 photographs of the battlefield in the four days from 19-22 September. They spent much of their time at McClellan's headquarters and each of the Antietam bridges, but also photographed groups of unburied dead wherever they could. Many of their photos are now quite famous, including scenes of Confederate dead along the Hagerstown Pike and heaps of bodies in the Sunken Lane. Three weeks after the battle they returned to take 25 shots during Lincoln's visit with McClellan in early October.

By the end of October, Gardner's and Gibson's macabre photographs were being displayed in studios in Washington and New York, and the shocked American public for the first time saw dead, twisted bodies on actual battlefields. These were certainly a far cry from the stylized patriotic scenes in *Harpers Weekly* and other periodicals. Long lines of viewers formed to gaze and ponder silently at the photos, and purchase copies of the prints to take home and display in their parlors. Ironically, Matthew Brady got credit for the photographs because Gardner and Gibson were working for him when they took the pictures, and he issued the souvenir prints.

Within a few months after Antietam, Gardner and Gibson left Brady to work on their own. They and other photographers proceeded to take famous scenes at Second Fredericksburg, Gettysburg, Atlanta, Petersburg, and Richmond, all of which contribute to our present day understanding of the war as much as still life photographs can.

The photographs taken at Antietam, Gettysburg, and Petersburg/Richmond have all been studied in detail by photographic historian William Frassanito, who has taken great pains to attempt to identify the actual location of each picture. His book *Antietam, the Photographic Legacy of America's Bloodiest Day* (1978) is highly recommended.

Note: Photographs at the time of the war were done in three primitive formats, none of which is in common use today. The daguerreotype had its image made on silver-coated copper, the ambrotype was imprinted on glass, and the tintype had its image made on a thin piece of iron. None used negatives, and each image was unique. During the 1850s a process was developed to make multiple images off wet glass plates, and soon carte de vistes (calling card shaped portraits) and three dimensional steropic views became popular, both styles printed on thick paper or card stock. It was these two mediums that Brady used to display and sell the Antietam views taken by Gardner and Gibson.

The Bloodiest Battles

Antietam was not the war's bloodiest battle (a distinction held by Gettysburg, see list), but was the bloodiest single day of the war. Stat-

THE TEN BLOODIEST BATTLES OF THE CIVIL WAR	
Battle	**Total # of Casualties**
Gettysburg	40,638
Chickamauga	28,399
Seven Days	27,535
Antietam	23,381
Wilderness	22,033
Chancellorville	21,862
Shiloh	19,897
Atlanta	19,715
Second Manassas	19,204
Stones River	18,459
Source: The Civil War Book of Lists	

istician Thomas C. Livermore in his famous study *Numbers and Losses in the Civil War* computed that each side gave as much damage as it received, which rarely happened in battles of that era—the Union army lost 155 men per 1,000, while each 1,000 caused 156 enemy casualties; the Confederates lost 226 men per 1,000, while each 1,000 caused 225 Union casualties. On the following page is a list of significant regimental casualty rates as computed by William F. Fox in his 1898 study *Regimental Losses in the American Civil War*.

SIGNIFICANT UNION REGIMENTAL LOSSES AT ANTIETAM				
Unit	Division	Present	Losses	Percentage
12th Mass.	Ricketts' I	334	224	67.0
9th NY	Rodman's IX	373	235	63.0
69th NY	Richardson's II	317	196	61.8
63rd NY	Richardson's II	341	202	59.2
3rd Wis.	Williams' XII	340	200	58.8
59th NY	Sedgwick's II	381	224	58.7
15th Mass.	Sedgwick's II	606	344	56.7
14th Ind.	French's II	320	180	56.2

SIGNIFICANT CONFEDERATE REGIMENTAL LOSSES AT ANTIETAM				
Unit	Division	Present	Losses	Percentage
1st Texas	Hood's	226	189	82.3
16th Miss.	Anderson's	228	114	63.1
27th NC	Walker's	325	199	61.2
15th Va.	McLaws'	128	75	58.5
18th Ga.	Hood's	176	101	57.3
10th Ga.	McLaws'	148	84	56.7
17th Va.	Rickett's	55	31	56.3
4th Texas	Hood's	200	107	53.5
7th SC	McLaws'	268	140	52.2

Note: This list is incomplete because engaged strengths and loss figures are not known for all Confederate units at the time of the battle.

Army Strengths at Antietam

Most authorities agree that Lee had about 40,000 men on the field during the battle of Antietam. The exact number is impossible to tell because the Confederates did not report daily head counts. They did compile regular bimonthly pay musters, but the August 31 report had not been properly done because it fell during the immediate aftermath of the battle of Second Manassas. Few of the units paused regularly to count noses during the strain of the Antietam campaign, and the degree of heavy straggling makes its difficult to compute the army's strength by adding known post-battle strengths to conflict losses at the battle.

McClellan had about 87,000 men on the field at the time of the battle.

Of these, about 15,000 in the *V* and *VI Corps* were not engaged in the fight. An additional 12,000 under Couch and Humphreys reached the field on the morning of 18 September, after the battle was over.

Studies show that the average union regimental strength at Antietam was 346, while the Confederate average was 166. Due to recent heavy battle losses and much straggling, there were numerous Confederate regiments with less than 100 men— for example, the 8th Virginia had 34 men, the 8th South Carolina 45, and the 56th Virginia had 80. Not all Confederate regiments were that miniscule, however. Some recently beefed up North Carolina commands had over 500 men in their ranks.

ARMY OF NORTHERN VIRGINIA		
General Robert E. Lee		
Unit	Commander	Strength Engaged
Longstreet's command	Maj. Gen. James Longstreet	—
McLaw's division	Maj. Gen. Lafayette McLaws	2,961
Anderson's division	Maj. Gen. Richard H. Anderson	4,000
Jones' division	Brig. Gen. David R. Jones	3,392
Walker's division	Brig. Gen. John G. Walker	3,994
Hood's division	Brig. Gen. John Hood	2,304
Evan's Independent Brig.	Brig. Gen. Nathan G. Evans	399
Corps Artillery	—	596
Total		17,646

Jackson's command	Maj. Gen. Thos. J. Jackson	—
Ewell's division	Brig. Gen. A.R. Lawton; Brig. Gen. Jubal A. Early	4,127
Light division	Maj. Gen. A.P. Hill	2,568
Jackson's division	Brig. Gen. John R. Jones	—
	Brig. Gen. William E. Starke, Col. A.G. Grisby	2,094
Hill's division	Maj. Gen. Daniel H. Hill	5,795
Total		14,584
Reserve Artillery		621
Cavalry	Maj. Gen. J.E.B. Stuart	4,500
	Aggregate, Army of Northern Virginia	37,351

ARMY OF THE POTOMAC		
Major General George B. McClellan		
Unit	**Commander**	**Strength Engaged**
I Corps	Maj. Gen. Joseph Hooker; Brig. Gen. Geo. G. Meade	—
1st Division	Brig. Gen. John P. Hatch; Brig. Gen. Abner Doubleday	3,425
2nd Division	Brig. Gen. Jas. B. Ricketts	3,158
3d Division	Brig. Gen. Geo G. Meade; Brig. Gen. Truman Seymour	2,855
Total		9,438
II Corps	Maj. Gen. Edwin V. Sumner	—
1st Division	Maj. Gen. Israel B. Richardson; Brig. Gen. John C. Caldwell; Brig. Gen. Winfield S. Hancock	4,029
2d Division	Maj. Gen. John Sedgwick	5,437
3d Division	Brig. Gen. William French	5,740
Total		15,206

IV Corps		
1st Division	Maj. Gen. Darius N. Couch	—
V Corps	Maj. Gen. Fitz John Porter	—
1st Division	Maj. Gen. Geo. W. Morell	NE
2d Division	Brig. Gen. George Sykes (5 bns only)	2,274
3d Division	Brig. Gen. Andrew A. Humphreys	NE
Res Artillery		950
Total		3,224
VI Corps	Maj. Gen. William B. Franklin	—
1st Division	Maj. Gen. Henry W. Slocum	NE
2nd Division	Maj. Gen. William F. Smith (Irwin's Brigade only)	2,585
Total		2,585
IX Corps	Maj. Gen. Ambrose E. Burnside: Brig. Gen. Jacob D. Cox	—
1st Division	Brig. Gen. Orlando B. Willcox	3,248
2d Division	Brig. Gen. Samuel D. Sturgis	3,254
3d Division	Brig. Gen. Isaac P. Rodman	2,914
Kanawha Division	Brig. Gen. Jacob D. Cox	3,154
Total		12,693
XII Corps	Maj. Gen. Joseph K. F. Mansfield; Brig. Gen. Alpheus S. Williams	—
1st Division	Brig. Gen. Williams	4,735
	Brig. Gen. S. W. Crawford; Brig. Gen. Geo. H. Gordon	—
2d Division	Brig. Gen. Geo. S. Greene	2,504
Corps Artillery		392
Total		7,631
Calvary Division	Brig. Gen Alfred Pleasonton	4,320
Aggregate, Army of the Potomac		55,956
NE = not engaged		

Bibliography

There is a fair sized body of good literature about Antietam, more than most battles, though certainly not as much as there is about Gettysburg. The most thorough account of the battle is *Landscape Turned Red* by Stephen W. Sears (New York, 1983). James V. Murfin's *The Gleam of Bayonets* (New York, 1965) is not as clearly written, while Edward J. Stackpole's *From Cedar Mountain to Antietam* (Harrisburg, 1959) is only a summary of the action. *Antietam: The Soldier's Battle* by John M. Priest (Shippensburg, PA, 1989) has excellent anecdotal material and fine tactical maps, but focuses too much on detail at the cost of synthesizing an account of the battle. The best older account of the campaign is *The Antietam and Fredericksburg* by F. W. Palfrey (New York, 1882). Some of the best and freshest interpretations of the battle and campaign can be found in *Antietam: Essays on the 1862 Maryland Campaign*, edited by Gary W. Gallagher (1989).

There is at present no good monograph on the Harpers Ferry operation. The general story of that post is told in Manly Wade Wellman's *Harpers Ferry: Prize of War* (Charlotte, 1960). John M. Priest has written a good detailed analysis of the battle of South Mountain in *Before Antietam: The Battle of South Mountain* (Shippensburg, PA, 1992). Reverend John W. Schildt has written a number of interesting and useful monographs on various aspects of the battle and campaign. This includes *Drums Along the Antietam* (1972), *Roads to Antietam* (1985), *Connecticut at Antietam* (1988), *The Ninth Corps at Antietam* (1988), and *Four Days in October* (1978).

A good analytical account of the campaign from the Southern point of view can be found in Vol. 2 of *Lee's Lieutenants: A Study in Command* by Douglas Stouthall Freeman (New York, 1942). Freeman gives an especially good analysis of Confederate command structure, and the causes of all the straggling in Lee's army. Freeman also wrote a top notch biography of the Confederate commander in chief, the four volume *R.E. Lee*. More good reading on the great Confederate general can be found in *Gray Fox* by Burke Davis (New York, 1956), and *Lee* by Clifford Dowdey (New York, 1965). Lee's image as a Confederate hero is thoughtfully if controversially explored by Thomas L. Connelly in *The Marble Man* (New York, 1977). Many fewer studies have been attempted of the North's enigmatic commander during the campaign. The best are *George S. McClellan, Shield of the Union* by Warren W. Hassler (Baton Rouge, 1957), and *George B. McClellan, the Young Napoleon* by Stephen W. Sears (New York, 1988).

The following biographies of other leading generals in the campaign will be of interest. On the Confederate side: *Mighty Stonewall* by Frank Vandiver (New York, 1957); *Lee's Maverick General, Daniel Harvey Hill* by Hal Bridges (New York, 1961); *General A. P. Hill, The Story of a Confederate Warrior* by James Robertson (New York, 1987); and *General James Longstreet, The Confederacy's Most Controversial Soldier* by Jeffrey Wert (New York, 1993). Unfortunately, there are few good biographies of McClellan's leading generals, most of whom fell into disfavor soon after the campaign. Two about his key corps commanders were *Fighting Joe Hooker* by Walter H. Herbert (New York, 1941) and *Burnside* by William Marvel (Chapel Hill, 1991). Also recommended is *General John Sedgwick* by Richard Winslow III (1982).

The best way to study the campaign may well be to read the actual words of the participants themselves. Battle reports for all the officers of both armies from regimental to army level can be found in Volume XIX of the monumental series *War of the Rebellion: A Compilation of the Official Records of the Union and Confederate Armies* (Washington, 1890-1901). The most interesting of the numerous memoirs written later by the campaign's leading participants is *McClellan's Own Story* (New York, 1886), which is as significant for what it says as for what it does not.

Recommended autobiographies by leading Confederate officers in the campaign include: *From Manassas to Appomattox* by James Longstreet (Philadelphia, 1896); and *Advance and Retreat* by John B. Hood (Philadelphia, 1880).

A number of leading officers on both sides wrote important essays on the campaign for *Century Magazine* in the 1880s. These were reprinted in volume 2 of *Battles and Leaders of the Civil War* (New York, 1884-1888; reprinted 1956 and later). Notable articles include features by D.H. Hill, Jacob Cox and William Franklin on South Mountain, John G. Walker on Harpers Ferry, and Cox, Walker, James Longstreet and Kyd Douglas on Antietam.

The following unit histories give lively and detailed accounts of the battles and marches of the campaign: *The 88th Pennsylvania Regiment in the War of the Union* by John Vautier (New York, 1984), *History of the Pennsylvania Reserve Corps* by J.R. Sypher (Lancaster, 1865), *The Iron Brigade* by Alan T. Nolan (1983); *The Irish Brigade* by Paul Jones (New York, 1900). Also: *The History of a Brigade of South Carolinians* by J.F.J. Caldwell (Philadelphia, 1866); *John Dooley, Confederate Soldier* (Georgetown, 1945); *Hood's Texas Brigade* by J.B. Polley (New York, 1910); and *Up Came Hill, The Story of the Light Division and Its Commanders* by Nathan Schenck (Harrisburg, 1958). The role of the artillery in the battle can be studied in *The Long Arm of Lee* by Jennings C. Wise (Lynchburg, 1915) and, on the Union side, in *Grape and Canister* by L. Van Loan Naisawald (New York, 1960).

The Battlefield

The Antietam National Battlefield comprises 810 acres of the original 12 square miles of the battlefield. Though the area has changed somewhat since the battle was fought so many years ago (the East and West Woods have been cut away considerably since the war), the remnants of the Sunken Road and the site of Burnside's Bridge allow one to gain a good impression about how the battle was fought.

The easiest way to reach the field is by car, but the more energetic Civil War buff might choose to bike or hike the towpath of the Chesapeake and Ohio Canal leading from Georgetown through southern Maryland, following the majestic Potomac River. There are campsites every five miles along the route which leads right to Harpers Ferry and an area rich in the history of the Antietam Campaign and of this nation. From Harpers Ferry, reaching the battlefield is not difficult, but requires both time and effort. Maps are available from American Youth Hostels. An indispensable companion to any tour of the battlefield is Dr. Jay Luvaas' and Colonel Harold W. Nelson's *U.S. Army War College Guide to the Battle of Antietam* (Carlisle, PA, 1987), which was also instrumental in the preparation of this work.

Fictional Literature

Numerous lyrics have been written about the Antietam Campaign by soldiers and romantic poets, but none have gained the prominence of John Greenleaf Whittier's dubious "Barbara Frietchie." Some fictional accounts of the battle itself are *Old Fusee, or The Cannoneers Last Shot* published in 1883 and Donald J. Sobol's *The Last Dispatch; A Story of Antietam.*

Simulation Games

Two games dealing with the Battle of Antietam are *A Gleam of Bayonets* published by TRS and the newer *In Their Quiet Fields*, published by The Gamers. An outstanding rendition of the fight at Turner's Gap is *South Mountain*, published by West End Games.

ORDER OF BATTLE

ANTIETAM

Army of the Potomac
Maj. Gen. George Brinton McClellan

I Corps
Maj. Gen. Joseph Hooker(w)
Brig. Gen. George Gordon Meade

First Division
Brig. Gen. John P. Hatch(w)
Brig. Gen. Abner Doubleday

First Brigade
Col. Walter Phelps, Jr.
22nd New York
24th New York
30th New York
84th New York
2nd U.S. Sharpshooters

Second Brigade
Brig. Gen. Abner Doubleday
Col. William P. Wainwright(w)
Lt. Col. J. William Hoffman
7th Indiana
76th New York
95th New York
56th Pennsylvania

Third Brigade
Brig. Gen. Marsena R. Patrick.
21st New York
23rd New York
35th New York
80th New York (20th Militia)

Fourth Brigade
Brig. Gen. John Gibbon
19th Indiana
2nd Wisconsin
6th Wisconsin
7th Wisconsin

Artillery
Capt J. Albert Monroe.
New Hampshire Light, First
Battery
1st Rhode Island Light,
Battery D
1st New York Light, Battery
L
4th U.S., Battery B

Second Division
Brig. Gen. James B. Ricketts

First Brigade
Brig. Gen. Abram Duryeé
97th New York
104th New York
105th New York
107th New York

Second Brigade
Col. William A. Christian
Col. Peter Lyle(w).
26th New York
94th New York
88th Pennsylvania
90th Pennsylvania

Third Brigade
Brig. Gen. George L. Hartsuff(w)
Col. Richard Coulter
12th Massachusetts
13th Massachusetts
83rd New York (9th Militia)
11th Pennsylvania

Artillery
1st Pennsylvania Light,
Battery F
Pennsylvania Light, Battery C

Third Division
Brig. Gen. George G. Meade
Brig. Gen. Truman Seymour.

First Brigade
Brig. Gen. Truman Seymour
Col. R. Biddle Roberts
1st Pennsylvania Reserves
2nd Pennsylvania Reserves
3rd Pennsylvania Reserves
5th Pennsylvania Reserves
6th Pennsylvania Reserves
13th Pennsylvania Reserves

Second Brigade
Col. Robert Magilton
3rd Pennsylvania Reserves
4th Pennsylvania Reserves
7th Pennsylvania Reserves

8th Pennsylvania Reserves

Third Brigade
Col. Thomas F. Gallagher(w)
Lt. Col. Robert Anderson
  9th Pennsylvania Reserves
  10th Pennsylvania Reserves
  11th Pennsylvania Reserves
  12th Pennsylvania Reserves
Artillery
  1st Pennsylvania Light,
    Battery A
  1st Pennsylvania Light,
    Battery B
  5th U.S., Battery C

II Corps
Maj. Gen. Edwin V. Sumner

First Division
Maj. Gen. Israel B. Richardson(mw)
Brig. Gen. John C. Caldwell
Brig. Gen. Winfield Scott Hancock
  First Brigade
  Brig. Gen. John C. Caldwell
    5th New Hampshire
    7th New York
    61st New York
    64th New York
    81st Pennsylvania
  Second Brigade
  Brig. Gen. Thomas F. Meagher
    29th Massachusetts
    63rd New York
    69th New York
    88th New York
  Third Brigade
  Col. John R. Brooke
    2nd Delaware
    52nd New York
    57th New York
    66th New York
    53rd Pennsylvania
  Artillery
    1st New York Light, Battery B
    4th U.S., Batteries A and C
Second Division
Maj. Gen. John Sedgwick(w)
Brig. Gen. Oliver O. Howard
  First Brigade
  Brig. Gen. Willis A. Gorman
    15th Massachusetts

1st Minnesota
34th New York
82nd New York (2nd Militia)
Massachusetts
  Sharpshooters, First
  Company
Minnesota Sharpshooters,
  Second Company
Second Brigade
Brig. Gen. Oliver O. Howard
Col. Joshua T. Owen
Col. De Witt C. Baxter
  69th Pennsylvania
  71st Pennsylvania
  72nd Pennsylvania
  106th Pennsylvania
Third Brigade
Brig. Gen. Napoleon J. T. Turner
  Dana(w)
Col. Norman J. Hall
  19th Massachusetts
  20th Massachusetts
  7th Michigan
  42nd New York
  59th New York
Artillery
  1st Rhode Island Light,
    Battery A
  1st U.S., Battery I
Third Division
Brig. Gen. William H. French
  First Brigade
  Brig. Gen. Nathan Kimball
    14th Indiana
    8th Ohio
    132nd Pennsylvania
    7th West Virginia
  Second Brigade
  Col. Dwight Morris
    14th Connecticut
    108th New York
    130th Pennsylvania
  Third Brigade
  Brig. Gen. Max Weber(w)
  Col. John W. Andrews
    1st Delaware
    5th Maryland
    4th New York

Unattached Artillery
1st New York Light, Battery G
1st Rhode Island Light,
Battery B
1st Rhode Island Light,
Battery G

V Corps
Maj. Gen. Fitz John Porter
First Division
Maj. Gen. George W. Morell
First Brigade
Col. James Barnes
2nd Maine
18th Massachusetts
1st Michigan
13th New York
25th New York
118th Pennsylvania
Massachusetts
Sharpshooters, Second
Company
Second Brigade
Brig. Gen. Charles Griffin
2nd District of Columbia
9th Massachusetts
32nd Massachusetts
4th Michigan
14th New York
62nd Pennsylvania
Third Brigade
Col. T.B.W. Stockton
20th Maine
16th Michigan
12th New York
17th New York
44th New York
83rd Pennsylvania
Michigan Sharpshooters,
Brady's Company
1st U.S. Sharpshooters
Artillery
Massachusetts Light,
Battery C
1st Rhode Island Light,
Battery C
5th U.S., Battery D
Second Division
Brig. Gen. George Sykes

First Brigade
Lt. Col. Robert C. Buchanan
3rd U.S.
4th U.S.
12th U.S., First Battalion
12th U.S., Second Battalion
14th U.S., First Battalion
14th U.S., Second Battalion
Second Brigade
Maj. Charles S. Lovell
1st U.S.
2nd U.S.
6th U.S.
10th U.S.
11th U.S.
17th U.S.
Third Brigade
Col. Gouverneur K. Warren
5th New York
10th New York
Artillery
1st U.S., Battery E
1st U.S., Battery G
5th U.S., Battery I
5th U.S., Battery K
Artillery Reserve
Lt. Col. William Hays
1st Battalion New York
Light, Battery A
1st Battalion New York
Light, Battery B
1st Battalion New York
Light, Battery C
1st Battalion New York
Light, Battery D
New York Light, 5th Battery
1st U.S., Battery K
4th U.S., Battery G

VI Corps
Maj. Gen. William B. Franklin
First Division
Maj. Gen. Henry W. Slocum
First Brigade
Col. Alfred T.A. Torbert
1st New Jersey
2nd New Jersey
3rd New Jersey
4th New Jersey

Second Brigade
Col. Joseph J. Bartlett
  5th Maine
  16th New York
  27th New York
  96th Pennsylvania
Third Brigade
Brig. Gen. John Newton
  18th New York
  31st New York
  32nd New York
  95th Pennsylvania
Artillery
Captain Emory Upton
  Maryland Light, Battery A
  Massachusetts Light,
    Battery A
  New Jersey Light, Battery A
  2nd U.S., Battery D
Second Division
Maj. Gen. William F. Smith
  First Brigade
Brig. Gen. Winfield Scott Hancock
Col. Amasa Cobb
  6th Maine
  43rd New York
  49th New York
  137th Pennsylvania
  5th Wisconsin
Second Brigade
Brig. Gen. W.T.H. Brooks
  2nd Vermont
  3rd Vermont
  4th Vermont
  5th Vermont
  6th Vermont
Third Brigade
Col. William H. Irwin
  7th Maine
  20th New York
  33rd New York
  49th New York
  77th New York
Artillery
Capt. Romeyn B. Ayres
  Maryland Light, Battery B
  New York Light, 1st Battery
  5th New York, Battery F

IV Corps (main body remained in the Peninsula)
First Division (attached to VI
  Corps)
Maj. Gen. Darius N. Couch
  First Brigade
Brig. Gen. Charles Devens, Jr
  7th Massachusetts
  10th Massachusetts
  36th New York
  2nd Rhode Island
Second Brigade
Brig. Gen. Albion P. Howe
  62nd New York
  93rd Pennsylvania
  98th Pennsylvania
  102nd Pennsylvania
  139th Pennsylvania
Third Brigade
Brig. Gen. John Cochrane
  65th New York
  67th New York
  122nd New York
  23rd Pennsylvania
  61st Pennsylvania
  82nd Pennsylvania
Artillery
  New York Light, Third
    Battery
  1st Pennsylvania Light,
    Battery C
  1st Pennsylvania Light,
    Battery D
  2nd U.S., Battery G

IX Corps
Maj. Gen. Ambrose E. Burnside
Maj. Gen. Jesse L. Reno(k)
Brig. Gen. Jacob D. Cox
  First Division
Brig. Gen. Orlando B. Willcox
  First Brigade
Col. Benjamin C. Christ
  28th Massachusetts
  17th Michigan
  79th New York
  50th Pennsylvania
Second Brigade
Col. Thomas Welsh

8th Michigan (transferred
from First Brigade)
46th New York
45th Pennsylvania
100th Pennsylvania
Artillery
Massachusetts Light, 8th
Battery
2nd U.S., Battery E
Second Division
Brig. Gen. Samuel D. Sturgis
First Brigade
Brig. Gen. James Nagle
2nd Maryland
6th New Hampshire
9th New Hampshire
48th Pennsylvania
Second Brigade
Brig. Gen. Edward J. Ferrero
21st Massachusetts
35th Massachusetts
51st New York
51st Pennsylvania
Artillery
Pennsylvania Light, Battery D
4th U.S., Battery E
Third Division
Brig. Gen. Isaac P. Rodman(mw)
First Brigade
Col. Harrison S. Fairchild
9th New York
89th New York
103rd New York
Second Brigade
Col. Edward Harland
8th Connecticut
11th Connecticut
16th Connecticut
4th Rhode Island
Artillery
5th U.S, Battery A
Kanawha Division
Brig. Gen. Jacob D. Cox
Col. Eliakim P. Scammon
First Brigade
Col. Eliakim P. Scammon
Col. Hugh Ewing
12th Ohio
23rd Ohio

30th Ohio
Ohio Light Artillery, 1st
Battery
West Virginia Cavalry,
Gilmore's Company
West Virginia Cavalry,
Harrison's Company
Second Brigade
Col. George Crook
11th Ohio
28th Ohio
36th Ohio
Chicago Dragoons,
Schambeck's Company
Kentucky Light Artillery,
Simmond's Battery
Unattached Troops
6th New York Cavalry
Ohio Cavalry, 3rd
Independent Company
2nd New York, Battery L
3rd U.S. Artillery, Battery L
3rd U.S. Artillery, Battery M

XII Corps
Maj. Gen. Joseph K. Mansfield(k)
Brig Gen. Alpheus S. Williams
First Division
Brig. Gen. Alpheus S. Williams
Brig Gen. Samuel W. Crawford(w)
Brig. Gen. George H. Gordon
First Brigade
Brig. Gen. Samuel W. Crawford
Col. Joseph Knipe
10th Maine
28th New York
46th Pennsylvania
124th Pennsylvania
125th Pennsylvania
128th Pennsylvania
Third Brigade
Brig. Gen George H. Gordon
Col. Thomas H. Ruger(w)
27th Indiana
2nd Massachusetts
13th New Jersey
107th New York
Pennsylvania Zouaves
d'Afrique
3rd Wisconsin

Second Division
Brig. Gen. George S. Greene
  First Brigade
  Lt. Col. Hector Tyndale(w)
  Maj. Orrin J. Crane
    5th Ohio
    7th Ohio
    66th Ohio
    28th Pennsylvania
  Second Brigade
  Col. Henry J. Stainrook
    3rd Maryland
    102nd New York
    111th Pennsylvania
  Third Brigade
  Col. William B. Goodrich(k)
  Lt. Col Jonathan Austin
    3rd Delaware
    Prunell Legion (Maryland)
    60th New York
    78th New York
  Artillery
  Capt. Clermont L. Best
    Maine Light, 4th Battery
    Maine Light, 6th Battery
    1st New York Light, Battery M
    New York Light, 10th
      Battery
    Pennsylvania Light, Battery E
    Pennsylvania Light, Battery F
    4th U.S., Battery F
Cavalry Division
Brig. Gen. Alfred J. Pleasonton

First Brigade
Major Charles J. Whiting
  5th U.S.
  6th U.S.
Second Brigade
Col. John F. Farnsworth
  8th Illinois
  3rd Indiana
  1st Massachusetts
  8th Pennsylvania
Third Brigade
Col. Richard H. Rush
  4th Pennsylvania
  6th Pennsylvania
Fourth Brigade
Col. Andrew T. McReynolds
  1st New York
  12th Pennsylvania
Fifth Brigade
Col. Benjamin F. Davis
  8th New York
  3rd Pennsylvania
Artillery
  2nd U.S., Battery A
  2nd U.S., Battery B
  2nd U.S., Battery L
  2nd U.S., Battery M
  3rd U.S., Battery C
  3rd U.S., Battery G
Unattached
  15th Pennsylvania Cavalry

The Army of Northern Virginia
Gen. Robert E. Lee

Longstreet's Command
Maj. Gen. James Longstreet
  McLaws' Division
  Maj. Gen. Lafayette McLaws
    Kershaw's Brigade
    Brig. Gen. Joseph B. Kershaw
      2nd South Carolina
      3rd South Carolina
      7th South Carolina
      8th South Carolina
    Cobb's Brigade
    Brig. Gen Howell Cobb
    Lt. Col. C.C. Sanders
    Lt. Col. William MacRae

      16th Georgia
      24th Georgia
      Cobb's (Georgia) Legion
      15th North Carolina
    Semmes' Brigade
    Brig. Gen. Paul J. Semmes
      10th Georgia
      53rd Georgia
      15th Virginia
      32nd Virginia
    Barkesdale's Brigade
    Brig. Gen. William Barkesdale
      13th Mississippi

17th Mississippi
18th Mississippi
21st Mississippi
Artillery
Maj. S.P. Hamilton
Col. H.C. Cabell
  Manly's (North Carolina)
    Battery
  Pulaski (Georgia) Artillery
  Richmond (Fayette) Artillery
  Richmond Howitzers (1st
    Company)
  Troup (Georgia) Artillery
Anderson's Division
Maj. Gen. Richard H. Anderson(w)
Brig. Gen. Roger Pryor
  Wilcox's Brigade
  Col. Alfred Cumming
    8th Alabama
    9th Alabama
    10th Alabama
    11th Alabama
  Mahone's Brigade
  Col. William A. Parham
    6th Virginia
    12th Virginia
    16th Virginia
    41st Virginia
    61st Virginia
  Featherston's Brigade
  Col. Carnot Posey
    12th Mississippi
    16th Mississippi
    19th Mississippi
    2nd Mississippi Battalion
  Armistead's Brigade
  Brig. Gen. Lewis A. Armistead(w)
  Col. J.G. Hodges
    9th Virginia
    14th Virginia
    38th Virginia
    53rd Virginia
    57th Virginia
  Pryor's Brigade
  Brig. Gen. Roger Pryor
    14th Alabama
    2nd Florida
    8th Florida
    3rd Virginia

Wright's Brigade
Brig. Gen. Ambrose R. Wright
  44th Alabama
  3rd Georgia
  22nd Georgia
  48th Georgia
Artillery
Maj. John S. Saunders
  Donaldsonville (Louisiana)
    Artillery (Maurin's
    Battery)
  Huger's (Virginia) Battery
  Moorman's (Virginia)
    Battery
  Thompson's (Grimes')
    (Virginia) Battery
Jones Division
Brig. Gen. David R. Jones
  Toombs Brigade
  Brig. Gen. Robert Toombs,
  Col. Henry L. Benning
    2nd Georgia
    15th Georgia
    17th Georgia
    20th Georgia
  Drayton's Brigade
  Brig. Gen. Thomas F. Drayton
    50th Georgia
    51st Georgia
    15th South Carolina
  Pickett's Brigade
  Brig. Gen Richard Garnett
    8th Virginia
    18th Virginia
    19th Virginia
    28th Virginia
    56th Virginia
  Kemper's Brigade
  Brig. Gen. James L. Kemper
    1st Virginia
    7th Virginia
    11th Virginia
    17th Virginia
    24th Virginia
  Jenkins' Brigade
    1st South Carolina
    2nd South Carolina Rifles
    5th South Carolina
    6th South Carolina

4th South Carolina Battalion
Palmetto (South Carolina)
Sharpshooters
Anderson's Brigade
George T. Anderson
1st Georgia
7th Georgia
8th Georgia
9th Georgia
11th Georgia
Artillery
Wise (Virginia) Artillery
(J.S. Brown's Battery)
Walker's Division
Brig. Gen. John G. Walker
Walker's Brigade
Col. Van H. Manning(w)
Col. E.D. Hall
3rd Arkansas
27th North Carolina
46th North Carolina
48th North Carolina
30th Virginia
French's (Virginia) battery
Ransom's Brigade
Brig. Gen. Robert Ransom Jr.
24th North Carolina
25th North Carolina
35th North Carolina
Branch's Field Artillery
(Virginia)
Hood's Division
Brig Gen. John B. Hood
Hood's Brigade
Col. W.T. Wofford
18th Georgia
Hampton (South Carolina)
Legion
1st Texas
4th Texas
5th Texas
Law's Brigade
Col. E. McIver Law
4th Alabama
2nd Mississippi
11th Mississippi
6th North Carolina
Artillery
Maj. B. W. Frobel

German Artillery (South
Carolina)
Palmetto Artillery (South
Carolina)
Rowan Artillery (North
Carolina)
Evans' Brigade (Independent)
Brig. Gen. Nathan Evans
Col. P.F. Stevens
17th South Carolina
18th South Carolina
22nd South Carolina
23rd South Carolina
Holcombe (South Carolina)
Legion
Macbeth (South Carolina)
Legion
Artillery
Washington (Louisiana) Artillery
1st Company
2nd Company
3rd Company
4th Company
Lee's Battalion
Col. Stephen D. Lee
Ashland (Virginia) Artillery
Bedford (Virginia) Artillery
Brooks (South Carolina)
Artillery
Eubank's (Virginia) battery
Madison (Louisiana) Light
Artillery
Parker's (Virginia) battery

Jackson's Command
Maj. Gen. Thomas J. Jackson
Ewell's Division
Brig. Gen. A.R. Lawton(w)
Brig. Gen. Jubal A. Early
Lawton's Brigade
Col. Marcellus Douglass(k)
Maj. J.H. Lowe
Col. John H. Lamar
13th Georgia
26th Georgia
31st Georgia
38th Georgia
60th Georgia
61st Georgia

Early's Brigade
Brig. Gen. Jubal A. Early
Col. William Smith(w)
   13th Virginia
   25th Virginia
   31st Virginia
   44th Virginia
   49th Virginia
   52nd Virginia
   58th Virginia
Trimble's Brigade
Col. James A. Walker(w)
   15th Alabama
   12th Georgia
   21st Georgia
   21st North Carolina
   1st North Carolina Battalion
Hays' Brigade
Brig. Gen. Harry T. Hays
   5th Louisiana
   6th Louisiana
   7th Louisiana
   8th Louisiana
   14th Louisiana
Artillery
   Chesapeake (Maryland)
      Artillery (Brown's Battery)
   Courtney (Virginia)
      Artillery (Latimer's
      battery)
   Johnson's (Virginia) battery
   Louisiana Guard Artillery
      (D'Aquin's Battery)
   First Maryland Battery
      (Dement's battery)
   Staunton (Virginia)
      Artillery (Balthis'
      battery)
Hill's Light Division
Maj. Gen. Ambrose P. Hill
   Branch's Brigade
   Brig. Gen. L. O'B. Branch(k)
   Col. James H. Lane
      7th North Carolina
      18th North Carolina
      28th North Carolina
      33rd North Carolina
      37th North Carolina

Gregg's Brigade
Brig. Gen. Maxcy Gregg(w)
   1st South Carolina
      (Provisional Army)
   1st South Carolina Rifles
   12th South Carolina
   13th South Carolina
   14th South Carolina
Field's Brigade
Col. J.M. Brockenbrough
   40th Virginia
   47th Virginia
   55th Virginia
   22nd Virginia Battalion
Archer's Brigade
Brig. Gen. James J. Archer
Col. Peter Turney
   5th Alabama
   19th Georgia
   1st Tennessee (Provisional
      Army)
   7th Tennessee
   14th Tennessee
Pender's Brigade
Brig. Gen. William D. Pender
   16th North Carolina
   22nd North Carolina
   34th North Carolina
   38th North Carolina
Thomas' Brigade
Col. Edward L. Thomas
   14th Georgia
   35th Georgia
   45th Georgia
   49th Georgia
Artillery
   Crenshaw's (Virginia)
      battery
   Fredericksburg (Virginia)
      Artillery
   Letcher (Virginia) Artillery
   Pee Dee (South Carolina)
      Artillery
   Purcell (Virginia) Artillery
Jackson's Division
Brig. Gen. John R. Jones(w)
Brig. Gen. William E. Starke(k)
Col. A.J. Grigsby

Winder's Brigade
Col A.J. Grigsby
Lt. Col. R.D. Gardner
Maj. H.J. William
  2nd Virginia
  4th Virginia
  5th Virginia
  27th Virginia
  33rd Virginia
Taliaferro's Brigade
Col. E.T.H. Warren
Col. James W. Jackson
Col. James L. Sheffield
  47th Alabama
  48th Alabama
  10th Virginia
  23rd Virginia
  37th Virginia
Jones' Brigade
Col. Bradley T. Johnson
Capt. John E. Penn(w)
Capt. A.C. Page(w)
Capt. R.W. Withers
  21st Virginia
  42nd Virginia
  48th Virginia
  1st Virginia Battalion
Starke's Brigade
Brig. Gen. William E. Starke
Col. Leroy A. Stafford(w)
Col. Edmund Pendleton
  1st Louisiana
  2nd Louisiana
  9th Louisiana
  10th Louisiana
  15th Louisiana
  Coppens' (Louisiana)
    battalion
Artillery
Maj. L.M. Shumaker
  Allegheny (Virginia)
    Artillery (Carpenter's
    battery)
  Brockenbrough's
    (Maryland) battery
  Danville (Virginia) Artillery
    (Wooding's battery)
  Hampden (Virginia)
    Artillery (Caskie's battery)

Lee (Virginia) Battery
  (Raine's battery)
Rockbridge (Virginia)
  Artillery (Poague's battery)
Hill's Division
Maj. Gen. Daniel H. Hill
  Ripley's brigade
  Brig. Gen. Roswell S. Ripley(w)
  Col. George Doles
    4th Georgia
    44th Georgia
    1st North Carolina
    3rd North Carolina
  Rodes' Brigade
  Brig. Gen. R.E. Rodes(w)
    3rd Alabama
    5th Alabama
    6th Alabama
    12th Alabama
    26th Alabama
  Garland's Brigade
  Brig. Gen. Samuel Garland Jr.(k)
  Col. D.K. McRae(w)
    5th North Carolina
    12th North Carolina
    13th North Carolina
    20th North Carolina
    23rd North Carolina
  Anderson's Brigade
  Brig. Gen. George B.
    Anderson(mw)
  Col. R.T. Bennet
    2nd North Carolina
    4th North Carolina
    14th North Carolina
    30th North Carolina
  Colquitt's Brigade
  Col. A.H. Colquitt
    13th Alabama
    6th Georgia
    23rd Georgia
    27th Georgia
    28th Georgia
  Artillery
    Hardaway's (Alabama)
      battery
    Jeff Davis (Alabama)
      Artillery
    Jones (Virginia) battery

King William (Virginia)
Artillery
Reserve Artillery
Brig. Gen. William N. Pendleton
Brown's Battalion
Col J. Thompson Brown
Powhatten Artillery
(Dance's battery)
Richmond Howitzers, 2nd
company (Watson's
battery)
Richmond Howitzers, 3rd
Company (Smith's
battery)
Salem Artillery (Hupp's
battery)
Williamsburg Artillery
(Coke's battery)
Cutts Battalion
Lt. Col. A.S. Cutts
Blackshears' (Georgia)
battery
Irwin (Georgia) Artillery
(Lane's battery)
Lloyd's (North Carolina)
battery
Patterson's (Georgia) battery
Ross' (Georgia) battery
Jones' Battalion
Maj. H.P. Jones
Morris (Virginia) Artillery
(R.C.M. Page's battery)
Orange (Virginia) Artillery
(Peyton's battery)
Turner's (Virginia) battery.
Wimbish's (Virginia) battery
Nelson's Battalion
Maj. William Nelson

Amherst (Virginia) Artillery
(Kirkpatrick's battery)
Fluvanna (Virginia)
Artillery (Ancell's battery)
Huckstep's (Virginia)
battery
Johnson's (Virginia) battery
Milledge (Georgia) Artillery
(Milledge's battery)
Cavalry
Maj. Gen. J.E.B. Stuart
Hampton's Brigade
Brig. Gen. Wade Hampton
1st North Carolina
2nd South Carolina
10th Virginia
Cobb's (Georgia) Legion
Jeff Davis Legion
Lee's Brigade
Brig. Gen. Fitzhugh Lee
1st Virginia
3rd Virginia
4th Virginia
5th Virginia
9th Virginia
Robertson's Brigade
Col. Thomas T. Munford
2nd Virginia
6th Virginia
7th Virginia
12th Virginia
17th Virginia Battalion
Horse Artillery
Maj. John Pelham
Chew's Virginia battery
Hart's (South Carolina)
battery
Pelham's (Virginia) battery

Union Generals and Brigade Commanders Killed During the Antietam Campaign

Harpers Ferry

Col. Dixon S. Miles (MW)

South Mountain

Maj. Gen. Jesse L. Reno (KIA) (IX Corps)

Antietam

Major Gen. Joseph K. Mansfield (KIA) (XII Corps)

Major Gen. Israel B. Richardson (MW) (1st Div, II Corps)

Brig. Gen. Isaac P. Rodman (MW) (3rd Div, IX Corps)

Col. William B. Goodrich (KIA) (1st Brig, 2nd Div, XII)

Confederate Generals and Brigade Commanders Killed During the AntietamCampaign

South Mountain

Brig. Gen. Samuel Garland, Jr. (KIA) (D.H. Hill's Division)

Antietam

Brig. Gen. George B. Anderson (MW) (D.H. Hill's Division)

Brig. Gen. L.O.B.Branck (KIA) (A.P. Hill's Division)

Brig. Gen. William Stance (KIA) (Jackson's Division)

Col. Marcellus Douglass (KIA) (Ewell's Division)

Index